Copyright Acknowledgments

Grateful acknowledgment is made to the following sources for permission to reprint material copyrighted or controlled by them:

Excerpt from *Desert Challenge: An Interpretation of Nevada*, by Richard G. Lillard (1942), Alfred A. Knopf, a division of Random House, Inc.

"Nevada: Beautiful Desert of Buried Hopes," by Anne Martin, reprinted from *The Nation*, July 26, 1922.

"Mining Illusions: The Case of Rawhide, Nevada," by Peter Goin and C. Elizabeth Raymond, reprinted from *Changing Mines in America* (2004), by permission of the Center for American Places.

"Twentieth Century Marvel," by Joseph E. Stevens, reprinted from *Hoover Dam: An American Adventure* (1988), by permission of the University of Oklahoma Press.

Excerpts from *Reno's Big Gamble: Image and Reputation in the Biggest Little City*, by Alicia Barber (2008), by permission of University Press of Kansas.

Excerpt from *Yes I Can: The Story of Sammy Davis Junior*, by Sammy Davis Junior and Jane and Burt Boyar (1965), Farrar, Straus & Giroux.

Excerpt from *Fighting Back: A Life in the Struggle for Civil Rights*, by James McMillan (1997), reprinted by permission of the University of Nevada Oral History Program.

"States' Rights Enterprise," by Gilman M. Ostrander, reprinted from *Nevada: The Great Rotten Borough, 1859-1964* (1966), Alfred A. Knopf, a division of Random House, Inc.

"Musings of a Native Son," by William Douglass, reprinted from *East of Eden, West of Zion: Essays on Nevada*, edited by Wilbur S. Shepperson (1989), the University of Nevada Press. Copyright © 1989 by Wilbur S. Shepperson.

"A-Bombs in the Backyard: Southern Nevada Adapts to the Nuclear Age, 1951-1963," by A. Constandina Titus, reprinted from the *Nevada Historical Society Quarterly* (winter 1983).

"Nevada Red Blues," by Adrian C. Louis, reprinted from *Among the Dog Eaters* (1992), West End Press.

"Nevada No Longer" and "Hawthorne," by Shaun T. Griffen, reprinted from *Bathing in the Ashes: Poems* (1999), the University of Nevada Press.

"Tidings," by Gary Short, reprinted from *Flying Over Sonny Liston: Poems* (1996), the University of Nevada Press.

Excerpt from *Earthtones: A Nevada Album*, by Ann Roland (1995), the University of Nevada Press. Copyright © 1995 by the University of Nevada Press.

Table of Contents

Introduction

This Curious Place Called Nevada

There has been nothing ordinary about the history of the State of Nevada. Throughout its existence Nevada has been home to unconventional life styles that were often at odds with mainstream America. Established on the turbulent western mining frontier of the mid-nineteenth century, Nevada attracted an unusually high level of moral criticism over the years for its lenient divorce laws, tolerance of legal prostitution, and pervasive gambling culture. For three-quarters of a century after admission to the Union in 1864, Nevada failed to develop an economy capable of sustaining even modest economic growth, but during the Great Depression it finally found its economic salvation in the form of legalized casino gambling. Scrutiny from beyond its borders greatly intensified as a result.

Nevada, everyone agrees, has pursued a different path. One historian has recently described the state as having a "maverick spirit," while another has characterized Nevada as a "cultural wilderness" where short-term economic and environmental exploitation prevailed while the public weal, defined as quality education and human services, received short shrift. One prominent scholar, examining the state's colorful history from the perspective of the University of California, Berkeley, concluded that there was much to criticize and little to praise, dismissing Nevada as "a great rotten borough." That condemnation seemed much too harsh to one of the state's most acclaimed historians, Wilbur Shepperson. After spending a lifetime contemplating Nevada's uniqueness, he took a more tolerant and subtly nuanced position. Yet

Shepperson conceded the existence of an overriding moral and cultural ambivalence that he attributed to the state's location between the conservative Mormon outpost of Utah and dynamic and diverse California. Nevada, Shepperson explained, was suspended, if not torn, between these two extremes, trapped somewhere "East of Eden and West of Zion."

Early Perceptions of the Great Basin State

For much of its first century, the state of Nevada attracted few new residents, its desert environment incapable of sustaining economic vitality and a growing population. As late as 1940, the state's population stood at just 110,247, most of whom survived along the economic margins with no better prospects in sight. That condition changed quickly when a massive infusion of federal defense dollars during the Second World War (1941-1945) produced an unprecedented prosperity and set the stage for a flourishing postwar gambling-based tourist economy. The economic and social transformation was stunning. By the eve of the new millennium, the state's population had increased twenty-fold, its economy had become one of the nation's fastest growing, and its dominant city of Las Vegas had become one of the world's most famous, most visited, most intriguing, most studied metropolises.

Such had not always been the case. The first white visitors to explore the territory during the mid-nineteenth century encountered a barren, forbidding landscape. A famous early visitor, New York City newspaper publisher Horace Greeley, traversed Nevada Territory in 1859 in a rickety horse-drawn wagon and later described his adventure as tantamount to surviving in a land where "famine sits enthroned." Two years later a young Missourian, Samuel Clemens (soon to take the pen name of Mark Twain), made the same overland trek by stagecoach, heading toward Virginia City and the gold and silver bonanza of the Comstock: "On the nineteenth day we crossed the Great American Desert—forty memorable miles of bottomless sand, into which the coach wheels sunk from six inches to a foot . . . .. The road was white with the bones of oxen and horses . . . [and] the long-chains, wagon tires, and rotting wrecks of vehicles . . . . The desert," he said somberly, "was a prodigious graveyard. Do not these relics suggest something of the idea of the fearful suffering and privation the early emigrants to California suffered?"

Nevada, this famous-writer-to-be suggested, was a place to get through as rapidly as possible, not any place a rational person would want to establish permanent residency. Its environment was a study in contrasts: lush mountain forests and pristine lakes surrounded by vast expanses of sagebrush-dotted desert, assaulted by broiling summer temperatures and cold winter snowstorms. From the earliest days of white settlement, residents and visitors alike objected to the searing heat of the summer months and the sharp winds and freezing temperatures that visited much of the state during the winter. During his time in Virginia City and Carson City, Twain was especially impressed by a phenomenon locals called the "Washoe Zephyr," a powerful windstorm of swirling dust that he identified as "a peculiarly Scriptural wind . . . . It blows over flimsy houses, lifts single roofs occasionally, rolls up tin ones like sheet music, and now and then blows a stagecoach over and spills the passengers." Greeley and Twain were among the first of many visitors to the Great Basin who were stunned by the harsh physical environment and the unrelenting extremes of climate.

Not until well into the twentieth century did visitors begin to take a more tolerant view of the uniqueness and surprising variety that Nevada's outdoors offered. During the 1930s, novelist and essayist Wallace Stegner, one of the leading nature writers of his generation, described Nevada as a land of many contrasts, "both hard and simple," but a place where a determined person could make "a beautiful life." Mining engineer and essayist Mark Requa, writing in 1933, extolled the unusual beauty of the raw Nevada desert when he observed, "The heat of the day had given way to the inexplicably pleasing coolness of a desert night in summer. Overhead the Milky Way shone with a brilliance unknown to dwellers in eastern States," while "the distant mountains seemed to be surrounded with an indefinable something that attracted and held the attention of the onlooker." Requa had developed a "fascination for the desert, which, once experienced, can never be entirely forgotten."

Nevada's forbidding environment attracted new residents with diverse cultural backgrounds. The mining frontier of the nineteenth century became a laboratory for racial and ethnic diversity, but the results were often less than harmonious. Outbursts of racial conflict and occasional violence were not unusual, while sharp discriminatory policies and practices were a daily fact of life. From the beginning Native Americans felt the hard hand of white settlement. As early as 1859, the territory's first federal Indian agent began a process of restricting the nomadic tribes—Western Shoshone, Northern Paiute, Southern Paiute, Washo—to reservations. That process was essentially completed by 1875. For centuries Nevada tribes had lived off the land as hunters and gatherers, moving from one place to another with the seasons. All efforts to confine them to reservations and convert them to farming proved spectacularly unsuccessful.

Statehood Based Upon a Precarious Economic Foundation

The Comstock attracted a large and diverse number of immigrants. By the mid-1860s, German Lutherans, German Catholics, Welsh, and French held church services and published newspapers in their native languages. Various nationalities established distinctive welfare and cultural societies such as the Turnverein, the Caledonian, and the Italian Benevolent. A smattering of Basques also made their way to the Comstock. These were a hardy people whose home lay in the mountain country along the border of France and Spain; they arrived in California during the initial gold rush, and hundreds came to Nevada after 1860, often working in towns as butchers or herding sheep on the open land and selling meat to mining communities. Between 1920 and 1950 another small wave of Basques emigrated to Nevada and the American West, attracted by opportunities in agriculture, ranching, and small business, often relocating at the behest of relatives already firmly established across the northern tier of the state.

Social and economic scales on the Comstock and in other Nevada communities placed blacks, Indians, Mexicans, and Chinese at the bottom, and each group struggled to survive. Thousands of Chinese came to the United States to work as laborers constructing western railroad lines; when the Central Pacific line across Nevada was completed in 1869, they were thrust onto the state's tight labor market, producing an outcry for their deportation. Anti-Chinese sentiment remained high for years, with acts of violence against them not unusual. In 1879, the legislature passed several laws aimed at reducing their political participation and restricting their employment opportunities, and the next year Nevadans voted by a resounding 17,442 to 183 in favor of a resolution urging Congress to halt all Chinese immigration into the United States. This stunning prejudicial sentiment placed Nevadans directly in the American mainstream because in 1882, Congress passed the Chinese Exclusion Act, the first time any ethnic group was denied entry into the United States.

If its racial practices were consistent with those to be found throughout the United States, Nevada's strong strain of social liberalism set it apart. Throughout much of its history, Nevada was the target of criticism for its unapologetic embrace of social conventions not accepted elsewhere. On the mining frontier, gambling was an integral part of daily life. Unlike all other states, Nevada's legislature never got around to making prostitution illegal, permitting individual counties to make that decision. At a time when most states required a one- or two-year waiting period for the granting of a divorce, a Nevada law passed in 1861 by the territorial legislature permitted a seemingly overly lenient six-month waiting period. By the early twentieth century, Nevada tolerated various levels of gambling, permitted prizefighting, allowed brothels to operate legally and became known for "quickie" divorces. Such behavior gave Nevada a reputation as the "Sin State." That reputation was intensified in 1931 with the legalization of casino gambling. In 1955, two years after leaving the presidency, Harry S. Truman flew across Nevada heading for San Francisco. As he looked down upon a vast panorama of sagebrush and snow-capped mountains, he envisioned much more than a desert landscape:

> Then we came to the great gambling and marriage destruction hell, known as Nevada. To look at it from the air it is just that—hell on earth. There are tiny green specks on the landscape where dice, roulette, light-of-loves, crooked poker and gambling thugs thrive. Such places should be abolished and so should Nevada. It should never have been made a State. A county in the great State of California would be too much of a civil existence for that dead and sinful Territory. Think of that awful, sinful place having two Senators and a Congressman in Washington, and Alaska and Hawaii not represented. It is a travesty on our system and a disgrace to free government.

Truman softened his tone as California came into view, noting that as his aircraft left "the hell hole of iniquity" it passed over Lake Tahoe, "one of the most beautiful spots in the whole world." As he wrote in his diary, Truman may have been giving vent to a longstanding enmity he held for Nevada Senator Patrick McCarran, a relentless critic of his presidential leadership. Or he may have simply been repeating an old refrain, that Nevada benefited excessively from the ability of its small congressional delegation to secure more than its share of federal funds.

Most likely, however, Truman, a keen student of American history, knew that a thinly populated Nevada entered the Union in 1864 because Abraham Lincoln and the Republican party anticipated a very close presidential election and wanted to secure three additional electoral votes from the strongly pro-Union residents of Nevada; even more important, Lincoln believed that he would need those votes in Congress to secure passage of the Thirteenth Amendment that would abolish slavery. Subsequent Nevada mythmakers sought to put a patriotic spin on things by arguing that the Union needed the rich silver lode of the Comstock to help finance the Civil War, but such was not the case. The federal government already had such access because of Nevada's territorial status. Nonetheless, Nevada was "Battle Born," as the state motto proudly proclaims. Except for the extraordinary political conditions of the Civil War, Nevada would likely not have gained statehood until well into the twentieth century.

When the newly created state cast its electoral votes for Lincoln, it contained but 45,000 residents; many would abandon the state when the boom on the Comstock subsided. Nevada lacked a solid economic base, and the speculative, boom-and-bust nature of mining could not provide one. Although the population stood at 62,266 in 1880, a deep and protracted depression reduced that number to just 42,335 in 1900, and threats to rescind statehood floated through the corridors of Congress. That drastic fate did not become reality, but economic conditions did not improve much during the first four decades of the twentieth century. It was not that enterprising Nevadans did not encourage growth. Tourism seemed a likely solution, but promotions by railroad companies and construction of a modest highway system during the 1920s produced few tangible benefits. The economic bonanza anticipated from the nation's first federal reclamation project that created the Truckee-Carson Irrigation District in 1903 failed to materialize. Ardent irrigation enthusiasts, such as Nevada's lone congressman (and later Senator) Francis Newlands, had raised overly optimistic expectations that vast portions of Nevada desert would be transformed into a bountiful agricultural oasis.

The quest for economic stability remained unrequited. Cattle and sheep ranching expanded slowly, but the state's aridity determined that ranching could not sustain a statewide economic renaissance. Discovery of rich deposits of silver and gold in central Nevada early in the twentieth century attracted thousands of miners. Tonopah and Goldfield temporarily boomed, but by 1920 the bonanza had run its course. Tonopah survived as the seat of Nye County, but Goldfield, at one point the state's largest city with a self-proclaimed 30,000 residents (probably a substantial exaggeration), was reduced to a miniscule population approaching that of a ghost town. Subsequent development of large open-pit copper mines near Ely and Yerington became part of the state's minerals economy, as did several gold mining operations near Elko during the late twentieth century.

Nevada Becomes the "Sin State"

With mining, agriculture, tourism, and ranching unable to sustain a viable economy, Nevadans seized eagerly upon what few options presented themselves. It seemed as if state business and political leaders were desperately grasping at elusive straws. After the legislature legalized "glove contests" in 1897, Nevada hosted a steady procession of highly publicized championship prizefights that attracted national attention. Between 1897 and 1910, bouts were promoted in Carson City, Reno, Goldfield, Tonopah, and Las Vegas that attracted thousands of out-of-state sports fans at a time when boxing was illegal elsewhere and widely condemned for its negative social influences. Prizefights could, at best, provide a modest and short-lived boost to the state's economy, but a historical tradition was born that has continued to the present day with the staging of championship prizefights in Las Vegas to attract "high roller" gamblers to the city's casinos.

When several other states legalized boxing during the 1920s, Nevada had to find another gambit. It did so by promoting its lax divorce laws. When the wife of the president of U. S. Steel spent six months in Reno in 1905 to meet the state's residency requirement, a much-publicized economic boomlet ensued. Several motion picture stars and other prominent individuals obtained highly publicized divorces in the state. While traditionalists vigorously condemned the short residency requirement as an assault upon the institution of marriage, a phalanx of Reno lawyers developed thriving practices by devoting themselves almost exclusively to providing legal services for thousands of divorce seekers each year, while hotels, restaurants, and shops catered to the residential "divorce colony." By the 1920s, up-scale dude ranches outside of Reno offered a pseudo-western experience to help would-be divorcees wile away their time before they appeared before a judge for a brief hearing in the Washoe County Court House to end their marriage.

After other western states sought to cut themselves in on the action by reducing their residency requirement, in 1927 the Nevada Legislature reduced the waiting time to three months. For more than two decades, the arrival of transcontinental passenger trains was greeted by a gaggle of attorneys handing out business cards. In 1931, Reno District Court Judge George A. Bartlett published an extended essay based on many years presiding over divorce cases. Bartlett provided candid advice to young couples on the realities of marriage, even touching upon such social taboos as infidelity and birth control. The judge also expounded upon his opinion that sometimes divorce was the best way of dealing with a dysfunctional marriage. His well-intentioned book, however, merely hammered home the fact that Nevada—with Reno now tarred as "divorce capital of America"—stood far outside the national consensus. Close observers did not miss the irony of the situation: Nevada not only mined the process of dissolving marriages, but it simultaneously encouraged their creation with for-profit marriage chapels in Reno and Las Vegas.

When several other states, likewise suffering from the Great Depression, lowered their residency requirements for a divorce to three months, in 1931 the resolute Nevada Legislature reduced the requirement to just six weeks. And so the divorce mill continued to grind. In that year, 4,745 divorces were granted in Reno, a number that reached 5,884 in 1945. Although scarcely mentioned in the national media, Las Vegas also established a thriving divorce industry, with the number of divorces granted in Clark County actually exceeding Washoe County (Reno) by the 1950s. By the 1960s, however, most other states had liberalized their divorce laws, and with the national divorce rate soaring, the issue faded from public view. Until that time, a steady stream of articles appeared in newspapers and magazines that focused attention upon Nevada's unconventional approach to traditional values. Many of these articles also linked divorce to the tolerance of prostitution, especially Reno's flourishing "Stockade"—a large-scale brothel located near the business district along the Truckee River. Many of these accusatory articles highlighted the flippant comment made during the height of national Prohibition by flamboyant mayor E. E. Roberts, a lawyer by profession, who stunned the congregation at the Reno Methodist Church in 1927 during the Prohibition Era with the observation that he saw nothing wrong with Reno's casual approach to the frailties of human nature, even suggesting that further improvements could be made: "I should like to see Reno with a whiskey barrel and a tin cup on every corner." Roberts took a pragmatic view of human nature, suggesting in another statement that Reno's tolerance of behaviors that were illegal elsewhere merely was "tearing off the mask of hypocrisy and doing in the open what we know is going on all over our nation today behind closed doors."

Nevada's Big Bet

Despite its well-established reputation for social unconventionality, the Nevada Legislature nonetheless stunned the rest of the country when it legalized wide-open casino gambling in 1931. Many Nevadans interpreted the law as merely recognizing reality: gambling—a legacy of the state's mining frontier—was both widespread and popular across the state, and legalization would make it possible for locals to enjoy their games of chance without having to resort to deception and legal charade. If the hard-pressed county treasuries—originally designated as the recipient of the small gaming fees—could pick up a few dollars of new revenue, so much the better. Opposition did emerge, primarily from the Women's Christian Temperance Union, the Nevada Federation of Women's Clubs, and the Mormon and Methodist churches, but the powerful Reno-based banker and political boss, George Wingfield, had a firm grip on a sufficient number of legislators, and Governor Fred Balzar signed the bill into law on March 19, 1931. Nevadans ruefully noted that in a state where gambling had long been a popular social convention, the only change created by the legislation was that the green felt tables and slot machines were moved from the backrooms of bars and hotels and put out front for all to see—and use. Because the ominous pall of the Great Depression hovered over Nevada, the immediate impact of legalized gambling was relatively limited. Local residents constituted the majority of players, the clubs were small with plain, unimaginative decor, and the table stakes were usually low. Tourism, reflecting the national economic malaise, did not pick up as some business leaders had hoped until the late 1930s, but the operators of the small gambling establishments in Reno and Las Vegas lacked imagination and vision.

This parochial atmosphere began to change rapidly during the Second World War. Massive expenditures of federal defense dollars in Nevada attracted an influx of construction and industrial workers, and the opening of several military bases brought tens of thousands of military personnel. The state's economy suddenly was more vibrant than at any time in history, and the small casinos were immediate beneficiaries. Nevada had stumbled upon a unique solution to its long search for an economic miracle. The impact was seen most vividly in southern Nevada. By 1950, the once small railroad town of Las Vegas had entered a period of economic expansion that has not yet slowed. With a population of just 8,400 residents in 1940, Clark County grew to more than 48,000 residents just ten years later. When the notorious New York City mobster Benjamin "Bugsy" Siegel opened the Flamingo Hotel-Casino the day after Christmas in 1946 along the two-lane highway heading south out of town toward Los Angeles, he set in motion the development of the world-famous Las Vegas Strip. Within a few years, increasingly larger and more opulent gambling and entertainment emporiums opened—the Thunderbird (1948), Desert Inn (1950), Sands and Sahara (1952), and the Dunes, Stardust, Riviera, and New Frontier (1955). The much-celebrated opening of lavish Caesars Palace in 1966 capped the initial era of frenetic growth along the Strip, one that was also accompanied by substantial development in downtown Las Vegas where such popular clubs as Benny Binion's Horseshoe Club, the Fremont, and the Golden Nugget catered to a loyal clientele.

In postwar Reno a similar transformation, albeit much smaller, reshaped the "Biggest Little City in the World." During the 1930s several small gambling clubs had operated along Center Street, the most prominent being the Bank Club (owned and operated by two prominent bootleggers) that could accommodate 300 patrons at one time. The arrival of two California transplants during the mid-1930s set the stage for Reno's transformation. Determined to democratize gambling as a legitimate leisure activity for middle- and working-class Americans, Raymond Smith opened Harolds Club on Virginia Street and benefited from a nationwide billboard advertising campaign for his western-themed casino that featured a comical covered wagon and the famous words "Harolds Club or Bust." A few doors away, William Harrah opened a small bingo club in 1937 that he transformed during the 1940s into a full-service casino designed to attract an upscale clientele, emphasizing gourmet restaurants and performances by famous entertainers in the showroom, all packaged with an air of exclusivity. Harrah not only advertised nationally (while simultaneously benefiting from his competitor's ubiquitous "Harolds Club or Bust" campaign), but he also offered free bus rides over the Sierra for northern California patrons.

As the gaming industry expanded, a small state government that had no experience controlling gambling seemed content to continue its laissez-faire policies. County government initially had primary responsibility for oversight and collection of taxes. Very quickly, operatives dispatched by organized-crime families from east coast and midwestern cities moved in and became firmly entrenched. Several government officials supposedly responsible for supervising casino operations and collecting taxes were known to be part owners of mob-operated casinos. That unsavory situation invited close examination by the federal government. In November 1950, Senator Estes Kefauver brought his U.S. Senate Select Committee on Organized Crime in Interstate Commerce to Las Vegas and conducted what proved to be an embarrassing several days of public testimony for Nevadans. When Kefauver departed, no one could doubt that some of the most prominent of Nevada's new business elite had close connections to major crime syndicates. Further, the Kefauver Committee made it clear that state officials knew this and had done little, if anything, about it. Even worse, the lack of stringent state oversight had not only permitted "underworld characters" to establish themselves in the gaming industry, but had given them "a seeming cloak of respectability."

In the long run, the blistering Kefauver report actually worked to the benefit of the gaming industry. Its recommendation to establish a high federal tax on gaming operations, coupled with the prospect of federal intervention as an outside regulator, forced Nevada's political and economic elite to protect their state's new economy with a series of important reforms. Senator Patrick McCarran effectively derailed Kefauver's tax proposals in Congress, but even he confessed, "It isn't a very laudable position for one to have to defend gambling. One doesn't feel very lofty when his feet are resting on the argument that gambling must prevail in the State that he represents." From the days of the Kefauver hearings forward, the *sine qua non* of state politicians of either party was to defend and promote vigorously the state's gaming industry.

Consequently, protecting Nevada's new basic industry became the major objective of both political parties. In 1955, Republican Governor Charles Russell persuaded the legislature to establish a Gaming Control Board vested with substantial powers of investigation and control over the granting of future gambling licenses; nonetheless, those individuals already licensed were permitted to remain, a major concession that invited future federal investigations. Democratic Governor Grant Sawyer (1959-1966) continued Russell's effort to establish a viable control over gaming. At one crucial point he publicly encouraged his regulators to "hang tough" in the face of criticism and opposition, bluntly stating that "a gambling license is a privilege—it is not a right." In his successful 1966 campaign for governor, Republican Paul Laxalt emphasized the necessity of maintaining Nevada's regulation while finding a way to exclude undesirable operators. In particular, the state had been stung by damaging articles in the *New York Times*, the *Washington Post*, and several national magazines, all of which detailed the influence of organized crime in Nevada's casinos. In 1969, Laxalt convinced the legislature to pass the Corporate Gaming Act, which made it feasible for major American corporations to invest in Nevada gaming properties. These developments, coupled with the continued strengthening of the Gaming Control Board, meant that the mobsters were on the way out. By the 1980s, control of Nevada's major properties had largely devolved to *Fortune* 500 corporations, who viewed their investments in Nevada as prudent, respectable, and certainly profitable.

Despite the reform effort, casino growth slowed and gaming revenues flattened out during the late 1970s. By 1985, state leaders openly expressed concerns for the state's economic future. At that juncture, however, the industry underwent an unprecedented period of expansion and revival, driven by the emergence of a new generation of entrepreneurs in Las Vegas such as the visionary Steve Wynn. Along the Strip arose such luxurious mega-resorts as the Mirage, Bellagio, Luxor, Mandalay Bay, Excalibur, New York New York, MGM, Paris Las Vegas, Treasure Island, Venetian, and Wynn Las Vegas. Many other substantial properties also took their place on and off the Strip, making Las Vegas and Clark County the most rapidly growing urban area in the United States. By 2006, the population of Clark County had reached 1,800,000, with many new large suburban and ex-urban developments still in the planning stages.

The transformation of Las Vegas into a major entertainment-gaming destination dominated the history of Nevada from the Second World War until the present. In the process, "the city that never sleeps" became one of the world's most famous cities, its unique lifestyle the subject of intensive examination by scholars, journalists, and cultural commentators. When *Look* magazine called Las Vegas "Wild, Wooly, and Wide-Open" in a widely read 1940 article that focused attention upon 24-hour gambling and substantial evidence of prostitution, local citizens were aghast. They took particular offense at the sentence proclaiming that in Las Vegas, "Sin is [considered] a civic virtue." As the years passed, however, Las Vegans came to recognize that its unique racy image helped attract millions of visitors each year. Moral condemnations by outsiders no longer mattered and were generally considered to be positive advertisement. In 2004, the local convention authority created a stir across the United States when it launched a suggestive promotional theme: "What Happens in Vegas Stays in Vegas."

America's Playground and More

By 1960, Las Vegas had overtaken once-dominant Reno in population and political and economic influence. Since the late nineteenth century, Reno had dominated the economic and political life of the State, but that changed quickly after the Second World War. Unlike the leadership of Las Vegas, Reno's elite did not embrace gaming enthusiastically, but instead attempted to hold it at arm's length, for decades effectively containing it within a small unofficial "red-lined" area in the center of town. Reno's leaders tended to emphasize its churches, public schools, and state university, all of which contributed to an environment where traditional family life could flourish. Such an outlook, however, did not enable Reno to compete with its rambunctious rival to the South. By 2000, Clark County contained 70 percent of the state's population and wielded much of the state's political power.

Although gaming provided an impetus for the amazing Las Vegas story, the city and surrounding Clark County, as well as the entire state, also benefited from an enormous infusion of federal dollars. Federal largesse made it possible for Nevada to avoid taxing incomes and inheritances. In 1935, President Franklin Roosevelt dedicated the engineering marvel of Boulder Dam (renamed in 1947 after the engineer/politician who had championed its construction, former President Herbert Hoover), which created Lake Mead, a source of water sufficient to support the spectacular growth of Clark County. The dam's enormous hydroelectric generators provided electricity for southern Nevada and parts of southern California as well. During the Second World War, the establishment of Nellis Air Base and the construction of the Basic Magnesium plant in Henderson contributed substantially to the city's economic diversification. By 1943, the plant employed 10,000 workers—more than employed in all the state's mines at the time—as it produced an alloy crucial to the manufacture of lightweight military electronic equipment and of explosives. The military also built air bases in Fallon, Stead, Tonopah and Wendover, each contributing to the state's economic expansion.

During the early 1950s, the uninhabited fragile desert north of Las Vegas became the primary testing ground for American nuclear weapons. Pentagon decision-makers apparently assumed that Nevada's desert had no other useful purpose, and with the winds of the Cold War swirling furiously, patriotic Nevadans welcomed the establishment of the Nevada Test Site. The substantial, although supersecret, amount of federal money that followed was also enthusiastically welcomed. As the first aboveground tests were detonated, Las Vegans cheered even as the ground shook and windows shattered (and in a few widely reported instances, the bounce of dice at Las Vegas craps tables was affected). Residents watched mushroom-shaped clouds rise high into the desert sky eighty miles north of town while they sipped early morning cocktails at celebratory parties. When federal officials assured Nevadans that the tests posed no health hazards from radiation exposure, few asked questions. Decades later, however, medical scientists attributed the relatively high rates of cancer among residents east of the test site to a decade of nuclear explosions, which had spewed vast quantities of radioactive material into the air. In the early 1980s, when the Department of Defense proposed building the technically complex, multibillion-dollar MX nuclear missile launch system in the Nevada and Utah deserts, political leaders of both parties mounted staunch opposition until the project was shelved. Anti-nuclear sentiment grew even more intense in the 1990s when the

Department of Energy announced its intention to place an enormous repository deep underground at Yucca Mountain to store for centuries the toxic and radioactive waste produced by nuclear power plants, none of which were located in Nevada. In 2012, the issue remained unresolved, with federal energy officials pushing for the establishment of a permanent repository and Nevada politicians of all persuasions resolutely lined up in opposition.

Nevada's defenders have long decried what they consider to be a distorted image of the state fostered by the national media. A small army of Nevada novelists, poets, artists, photographers, anthropologists, environmentalists, and historians have sought to present a softer, sophisticated, more diverse and (in their view) more accurate image of the state. Their efforts have produced an impressive array of books and cultural artifacts, but their audience has often been restricted largely to their fellow Nevadans, most of whom already appreciate the many rich and diverse dimensions of Nevada that exist beyond the Las Vegas Strip. Several historians, most notably such pioneering scholars as Wilbur Shepperson, Russell Elliott and Eugene Moehring, focused attention upon the complexity of the state's history, and novelists Walter Van Tilburg Clark and Robert Laxalt established themselves as prominent American novelists of national stature. Environmental writers, from the pioneering John Muir to John McPhee and Ann Ronald, have written eloquently and persuasively about the power and grandeur of remote Nevada landscapes that have eluded casual visitors unable to see beyond the bright lights of the casino districts or the vast stretches of sand and sagebrush along the highway. The hidden Nevada contains a trove of cultural and natural treasures that the serious student must not overlook.

The Great Recession

Given its early history of economic struggle, it is ironic that Nevada's major problems in recent decades resulted from an extended period of growth. No longer were a declining population and economic stagnation on the public agenda, but rather population growth, social problems, education, delivery of medical services, suburban sprawl, and environmental protection. During the nineteenth century, railroad companies brought immigrants from China into the state to supplement the labor force, and ethnic and racial diversification has continued to the present. During the recent past, the lure of employment in the casinos and burgeoning construction projects attracted large numbers of immigrants from Latin America and Southeast Asia, whose labor has become essential to support the estimated fifty million tourists who visited the state each year. Also contributing significantly to Nevada's rapid increase in population has been a heavy influx of relatively affluent Americans who have found in Nevada a place in which to live out their retirements. Nevada became a major retirement magnet due to the combination of warm weather, outdoor recreation opportunities, and steadfast refusal to tax inheritances or incomes.

As Nevada moved into the twenty-first century, it seemed that the future was exceedingly bright. Year after year, various rankings of states had placed Nevada near the top in population and economic growth, although near the bottom in such categories as funding for public schools, higher education, and social services. Both Las Vegas and Reno grew rapidly in the midst of an enormous boom in housing and commercial development. Once-small communities like Henderson and Sparks became large cities in their own right. Substantial numbers of businesses and corporations with no connection to gaming were relocating to the state, helping to create a more-diversified economic base. And, in Las Vegas, billions of dollars in major resort construction were underway or on the drawing boards.

These positive economic trends proved illusory. In fact, the state's economy was in the midst of an unsustainable bubble—highlighted by overdevelopment of new housing and a subsequent upsurge in mortgage foreclosures—that placed Nevada in great peril. That bubble burst in the autumn of 2008 when a frightening financial meltdown engulfed the nation's financial markets in what future historians will likely call The Great Recession. The tremors, first felt along Wall Street and Pennsylvania Avenue, soon rippled across Nevada with devastating impact. In the weeks prior to the pivotal elections of 2008, the very real possibility of a collapse of major banks and investment companies produced a national crisis reminiscent of the Great Depression. Within months the unemployment rate had jumped to 10 percent nationally, and in Nevada it reached 14 percent. In 2012, Nevada had the highest unemployment rate in the United States, its recovery severely hampered by a devastated construction market. At the heart of the crisis was an artificial boom in housing and commercial construction that resulted from irresponsible lending practices by mortgage lenders and federal housing policies that encouraged millions of Americans to purchase homes they could not afford. By 2010, half of all mortgaged Nevada homes were "underwater," meaning that the owner owed more to the bank or mortgage company than the house was worth on a severely depressed market. Within three years the average value of a Nevada home had fallen by 50 percent.

Prior to the Great Recession, the major issues confronting Nevada politicians and voters were protecting the state's fragile desert environment, securing adequate water supplies, diversifying a growing economy, and expanding public services and education to serve a growing population. Those priorities were shelved as the realities of the economic crisis were driven home by rising unemployment, the virtual halt of housing and commercial construction, a sobering drop in tourism, and a corresponding precipitous decline in tax revenues. Nevada's tourist-dependent economy was hit hard as discretionary spending by Americans was squeezed; by 2010, gaming revenues had plummeted by 20 percent. Nevadans had always subscribed to a minimalist view of government, and the economic crisis greatly intensified that outlook. Highlighting the angry and frightened mood of voters, the insurgent national Tea Party movement resonated strongly in Nevada. An amorphous uprising difficult to define with precision, the Nevada Tea Party argued that government had become too costly and that budgets had to be reduced. The anti-federal government undertones of the Tea Party uprising seemed to resurrect similar attitudes that had been a staple of the Sagebrush Rebellion that had roiled the political waters of rural Nevada during the 1970s and 1980s. The rallying cry of "No New Taxes" became a familiar refrain that extended beyond Tea Party activists to include most Republican and Democratic candidates for state and local office.

The economic collapse placed Nevada at the top of national rankings in unemployment and housing mortgage foreclosures. The Great Recession had an immediate and powerful impact upon state politics and policies. Massive budget cuts to public schools, universities, and social services placed the state at or near the bottom of rankings of the fifty states in these important categories. Many thoughtful observers of all political persuasions were left to ponder whether or not Nevada, with a long history of overcoming previous economic challenges, was up to the task once more.

"First Meeting of Piutes and Whites"
(1883)

Sarah Winnemucca

The daughter of a leader of the Northern Piute Tribe that had lived for centuries in north-central Nevada, Sarah Winnemucca was born in 1844 near the Humboldt Sink. She grew up at a time when the arrival of white settlers threatened the existence of her people. Her grandfather Chief Truckee and her father Winnemucca had viewed white settlement as inevitable and had advocated cooperation and co-existence as the only viable alternative. Sarah learned English and Spanish as a child and spent several years living in Genoa, Nevada, and California with white families. Her entire life was spent torn between the two cultures, and she was never completely comfortable with either. Between 1866 and 1875 she served the U. S. Army as an interpreter at Fort McDermitt, and in 1878 she assisted General Oliver Howard's forces as a scout and interpreter when they put down an uprising of the Bannock tribe from the Oregon Territory. During the 1880s she visited several East Coast cities in an attempt to inform the American public about the disastrous impact of white settlement upon Native Americans. In 1883, Winnemucca published Life Among the Piutes, *which included both a brief autobiography and an overview of the history of her people. Shortly after relocating to Idaho in 1891 to live with a sister, she died suddenly at the age of 47.* Life Among the Piutes *is believed to be the first book ever published by a Native American woman. In 2005, a statue of Sarah Winnemucca by sculptor, Benjamin Victor, was permanently placed in the United States Statuary Hall in Washington, D. C., with a replica located in a place of honor in the Nevada State Capitol in Carson City.*

I was born somewhere near 1844, but am not sure of the precise time. I was a very small child when the first white people came into our country. They came like a lion, yes, like a roaring lion, and have continued so ever since, and I have never forgotten their first coming. My people were scattered at that time over nearly all the territory now known as Nevada. My grandfather was chief of the entire Piute nation, and was camped near Humboldt Lake, with a small portion of his tribe, when a party traveling eastward from California was seen coming. When the news was brought to my grandfather, he asked what they looked like? When told that they had hair on their faces, and were white, he jumped up and clasped his hands together, and cried aloud, —

"My white brothers—my long-looked for white brothers have come at last!"

He immediately gathered some of his leading men, and went to the place where the party had gone into camp. Arriving near them, he was commanded to halt in a manner that was readily understood without an interpreter. Grandpa at once made signs of friendship by throwing down his robe and throwing up his arms to show them he had no weapons; but in vain,—they kept him at a distance. He knew not what to do. He had expected so much pleasure in welcoming his white brothers to the best in the land, that after looking at them sorrowfully for a little while, he came away quite unhappy. But he would not give them up so easily. He took some of his most trustworthy men and followed them day after day, camping near them at night, and traveling in sight of them by day, hoping in this way to gain their confidence. But he was disappointed, poor dear old soul!

I can imagine his feelings, for I have drank deeply from the same cup. When I think of my past life, and the bitter trials I have endured, I can scarcely believe I live, and yet I do; and, with the help of Him who notes the sparrow's fall, I mean to fight for my down-trodden race while life lasts.

Seeing they would not trust him, my grandfather left them, saying, "Perhaps they will come again next year." Then he summoned his whole people, and told them this tradition:—

"In the beginning of the world there were only four, two girls and two boys. Our forefather and mother were only two, and we are their children. You all know that a great while ago there was a happy family in this world. One girl and one boy were dark and the others were white. For a time they got along together without quarreling, but soon they disagreed, and there was trouble. They were cross to one another and fought, and our parents were very much grieved. They prayed that their children might learn better, but it did not do any good; and afterwards the whole household was made so unhappy that the father and mother saw that they must separate their children; and then our father took the dark boy and girl, and the white boy and girl, and asked them, 'Why are you so cruel to each other?' They hung down their heads, and would not speak. They were ashamed. He said to them, 'Have I not been kind to you all, and given you everything your hearts wished for? You do not have to hunt and kill your own game to live upon. You see, my dear children, I have power to call whatsoever kind of game we want to eat; and I also have the power to separate my dear children, if they are not good to each other.' So he separated his children by a word. He said, 'Depart from each other, you cruel children— go across the mighty ocean and do not seek each other's lives.'

"So the light girl and boy disappeared by that one word, and their parents saw them no more, and they were grieved, although they knew their children were happy. And by-and-by the dark children grew into a large nation; and we believe it is the one we belong to, and that the nation that sprung from the white children will some time send some one to meet us and heal all the old trouble. Now, the white people we saw a few days ago must certainly be our white brothers, and I want to welcome them. I want to love them as I love all of you. But they would not let me; they were afraid. But they will come again, and I want you one and all to promise that, should I not live to welcome them myself, you will not hurt a hair on their heads, but welcome them as I tried to do."

How good of him to try and heal the wound, and how vain were his efforts! My people had never seen a white man, and yet they existed, and were a strong race. The people promised as he wished, and they all went back to their work.

The next year came a great emigration, and camped near Humboldt Lake. The name of the man in charge of the trains was Captain Johnson, and they stayed three days to rest their horses, as they had a long journey before them without water. During their stay my grandfather and some of his people called upon them, and they all shook hands, and when our white brothers were going away they gave my grandfather a white tin plate. Oh, what a time they had over that beautiful gift,—it was so bright! They say that after they left my grandfather called for all his people to come together, and he then showed them the beautiful gift which he had received from his white brothers. Everybody was so pleased; nothing like it was ever seen in our country before. My grandfather thought so much of it that he bored holes in it and fastened it on his head, and wore it as his hat. He held it in as much admiration as my white sisters hold their diamond rings or a sealskin jacket. So that winter they talked of nothing but their white brothers. The following spring there came great news down the Humboldt River, saying that there were some more of the white brothers coming, and there was something among them that was burning all in a blaze. My grandfather asked them what it was like. They told him it looked like a man; it had legs and hands and a head, but the head had quit burning, and it was left quite black. There was the greatest excitement among my people everywhere about the men in a blazing fire. They were excited because they did not know there were any people in the world but the two,—that is, the Indians and the whites; they thought that was all of us in the beginning of the world, and, of course, we did not know where the others had come from, and we don't know yet. Ha! Ha! oh, what a laughable thing that was! It was two negroes wearing red shirts!

The third year more emigrants came, and that summer Captain Fremont, who is now General Fremont.

My grandfather met him, and they were soon friends. They met just where the railroad crosses Truckee River, now called Wadsworth, Nevada. Captain Fremont gave my grandfather the name of Captain Truckee, and he also called the river after him. Truckee is an Indian word, it means *all right*, or *very well*. A party of twelve of my people went to California with Captain Fremont. I do not know just how long they were gone.

During the time my grandfather was away in California, where he staid till after the Mexican war, there was a girl-baby born in our family. I can just remember it. It must have been in spring, because everything was green. I was away playing with some other children when my mother called me to come to her. So I ran to her. She then asked me to sit down, which I did. She then handed me some beautiful beads, and asked me if I would like to buy something with them. I said:—

"Yes, mother, —some pine nuts."

My mother said:—

"Would you like something else you can love and play with? Would you like to have a little sister?" I said,—

"Yes, dear mother, a little, little sister; not like my sister Mary, for she won't let me play with her. She leaves me and goes with big girls to play;" and then my mother wanted to know if I would give my pretty beads for the little sister.

Just then the baby let out such a cry it frightened me; and I jumped up and cried so that my mother took me in her arms and said it was a little sister for me, and not to be afraid. This is all I can remember about it.

When my grandfather went to California he helped Captain Fremont fight the Mexicans. When he came back he told the people what a beautiful country California was. Only eleven returned home, one having died on the way back.

They spoke to their people in the English language, which was very strange to them all.

Captain Truckee, my grandfather, was very proud of it, indeed. They all brought guns with them. My grandfather would sit down with us for hours, and would say over and over again, "Goodee gun, goodee, goodee gun, heap shoot." They also brought some of the soldiers' clothes with all their brass buttons, and my people were very much astonished to see the clothes, and all that time they were peaceable toward their white brothers. They had learned to love them, and they hoped more of them would come. Then my people were less barbarous than they are nowadays.

That same fall, after my grandfather came home, he told my father to take charge of his people and hold the tribe, as he was going back to California with as many of his people as he could get to go with him. So my father took his place as Chief of the Piutes, and had it as long as he lived. Then my grandfather started back to California again with about thirty families. That same fall, very late, the emigrants kept coming. It was this time that our white brothers first came amongst us. They could not get over the mountains, so they had to live with us. It was on Carson River, where the great Carson City stands now. You call my people bloodseeking. My people did not seek to kill them, nor did they steal their horses,—no, no, far from it. During the winter my people helped them. They gave them such as they had to eat. They did not hold out their hands and say:—

"You can't have anything to eat unless you pay me." No, —no such word was used by us savages at that time; and the persons I am speaking of are living yet; they could speak for us if they choose to do so.

The following spring, before my grandfather returned home, there was a great excitement among my people on account of fearful news coming from different tribes, that the people whom they called their white brothers were killing everybody that came in their way, and all the Indian tribes had gone into the mountains to save their lives. So my father told all his people to go into the mountains and hunt and lay up food for the coming winter. Then we all went into the mountains. There was a fearful story they told us children. Our mothers told us that the whites were killing everybody and eating them. So we were all afraid of them. Every dust that we could see blowing in the valleys we would say it was the white people. In the late fall my father told his people to go to the rivers and fish, and we all went to Humboldt River, and the women went to work gathering wild seed, which they grind between the rocks. The stones are round, big enough to hold in the hands. The women did this when they got back, and when they had gathered all they could they put it in one place and covered it with grass, and then over the grass mud. After it is covered it looks like an Indian wigwam.

Oh, what a fright we all got one morning to hear some white people were coming. Each one ran as best they could. My poor mother was left with my little sister and me. Oh, I never can forget it. My poor mother was carrying my little sister on her back, and trying to make me run; but I was so frightened I could not move my feet, and while my poor mother was trying to get me along my aunt overtook us, and she said to my mother: "Let us bury our girls, or we shall all be killed and eaten up." So they went to work and buried us, and told us if we heard any noise not to cry out, for if we did they would surely kill us and eat us. So our mothers buried me and my cousin, planted sage bushes over our faces to keep the sun from burning them, and there we were left all day.

Oh, can any one imagine my feelings *buried alive*, thinking every minute that I was to be unburied and eaten up by the people that my grandfather loved so much? With my heart throbbing, and not daring to breathe, we lay there all day. It seemed that the night would never come. Thanks be to God! The night came at last. Oh, how I cried and said: "Oh, father, have you forgotten me? Are you never coming for me?" I cried so I thought my very heartstrings would break.

At last we heard some whispering. We did not dare to whisper to each other, so we lay still. I could hear their footsteps coming nearer and nearer. I thought my heart was coming right out of my mouth. Then I heard my mother say, "'T is right here!" Oh, can any one in this world ever imagine what were my feelings when I was dug up by my poor mother and father? My cousin and I were once more happy in our mothers' and fathers' care, and we were taken to where all the rest were.

I was once buried alive; but my second burial shall be for ever, where no father or mother will come and dig me up. It shall not be with throbbing heart that I shall listen for coming footsteps. I shall be in the sweet rest of peace,—I, the chieftain's weary daughter.

Well, while we were in the mountains hiding, the people that my grandfather called our white brothers came along to where our winter supplies were. They set everything we had left on fire. It was a fearful sight. It was all we had for the winter, and it was all burnt during that night. My father took some of his men during the night to try and save some of it, but they could not; it had burnt down before they got there.

These were the last white men that came along that fall. My people talked fearfully that winter about those they called our white brothers. My people said they had something like awful thunder and lightning, and with that they killed everything that came in their way.

This whole band of white people perished in the mountains, for it was too late to cross them. We could have saved them, only my people were afraid of them. We never knew who they were, or where they came from. So, poor things, they must have suffered fearfully, for they all starved there. The snow was too deep.

Early in the following spring, my father told all his people to go to the mountains, for there would be a great emigration that summer. He told them he had had a wonderful dream, and wanted to tell them all about it.

He said, "Within ten days come together at the sink of Carson, and I will tell you my dream."

The sub-chiefs went everywhere to tell their people what my father had told them to say; and when the time came we all went to the sink of Carson.

Just about noon, while we were on the way, a great many of our men came to meet us, all on their horses. Oh, what a beautiful song they sang for my father as they came near us! We passed them, and they followed us, and as we came near to the encampment, every man, woman, and child were out looking for us. They had a place all ready for us. Oh, how happy everybody was! One could hear laughter everywhere, and songs were sung by happy women and children.

My father stood up and told his people to be merry and happy for five days. It is a rule among our people always to have five days to settle anything. My father told them to dance at night, and that the men should hunt rabbits and fish, and some were to have games of football, or any kind of sport or playthings they wished, and the women could do the same, as they had nothing else to do. My people were so happy during the five days,—the women ran races, and the men ran races on foot and on horses.

My father got up very early one morning, and told his people the time had come,—that we could no longer be happy as of old, as the white people we called our brothers had brought a great trouble and sorrow among us already. He went on and said,—

"These white people must be a great nation, as they have houses that move. It is wonderful to see them move along. I fear we will suffer greatly by their coming to our country; they come for no good to us, although my father said they were our brothers, but they do not seem to think we are like them. What do you all think about it? Maybe I am wrong. My dear children, there is something telling me that I am not wrong, because I am sure they have minds like us, and think as we do; and I know that they were doing wrong when they set fire to our winter supplies. They surely knew it was our food."

And this was the first wrong done to us by our white brothers.

Now comes the end of our merrymaking.

Then my father told his people his fearful dream, as he called it. He said,—

"I dreamt this same thing three nights,—the very same. I saw the greatest emigration that has yet been through our country. I looked North and South and East and West, and saw nothing but dust, and I heard a great weeping. I saw women crying, and I also saw my men shot down by the white people. They were killing my people with something that made a great noise like thunder and lightning, and I saw the blood streaming from the mouths of my men that lay all around me. I saw it as if it was real. Oh, my dear children! You may all think it is only a dream,—nevertheless, I feel that it will come to pass. And to avoid bloodshed, we must all go to the mountains during the summer, or till my father comes back from California. He will then tell us what to do. Let us keep away from the emigrant roads and stay in the mountains all summer. There are to be a great many pine-nuts this summer, and we can lay up great supplies for the coming winter, and if the emigrants don't come too early, we can take a run down and fish for a month, and lay up dried fish. I know we can dry a great many in a month, and young men can go into the valleys on hunting excursions, and kill as many rabbits as they can. In that way we can live in the mountains all summer and all winter too."

So ended my father's dream. During that day one could see old women getting together talking over what they had heard my father say. "They said,—

"It is true what our great chief has said, for it was shown to him by a higher power. It is not a dream. Oh, it surely will come to pass. We shall no longer be a happy people, as we now are; we shall no longer go here and there as of old; we shall no longer build our big fires as a signal to our friends, for we shall always be afraid of being seen by those bad people."

"Surely they don't eat people?"

"Yes, they do eat people, because they ate each other up in the mountains last winter."

This was the talk among the old women during the day.

"Oh, how grieved we are! Oh, where will it end?"

That evening one of our doctors called for a council, and all the men gathered together in the council-tent to hear what their medicine man had to say, for we all believe our doctor is greater than any human being living. We do not call him a medicine man because he gives medicine to the sick, as your doctors do. Our medicine man cures the sick by the laying on of hands, and we have doctresses as well as doctors. We believe that our doctors can communicate with holy spirits from heaven. We call heaven the Spirit Land.

Well, when all the men get together, of course there must be smoking the first thing. After the pipe has passed round five times to the right, it stops, and then he tells them to sing five songs. He is the leader in the song-singing. He sings heavenly songs, and he says he is singing with the angels. It is hard to describe these songs. They are all different, and he says the angels sing them to him.

Our doctors never sing war-songs, except at a war dance, as they never go themselves on the warpath. While they were singing the last song, he said,—

"Now I am going into a trance. While I am in the trance you must smoke just as you did before; not a word must be spoken while I am in the trance."

About fifteen minutes after the smoking was over, he began to make a noise as if he was crying a great way off. The noise came nearer and nearer, until he breathed, and after he came to, he kept on crying. And then he prophesied, and told the people that my father's dream was true in one sense of the word,—that is, "Our people will not all die at the hands of our white brothers. They will kill a great many with their guns, but they will bring among us a fearful disease that will cause us to die by hundreds."

We all wept, for we believed this word came from heaven.

So ended our feast, and every family went to its own home in the pine-nut mountains, and remained there till the pine-nuts were ripe. They ripen about the last of June.

Late in that fall, there came news that my grandfather was on his way home. Then my father took a great many of his men and went to meet his father, and there came back a runner, saying, that all our people must come together. It was said that my grandfather was bringing bad news. All our people came to receive their chieftain; all the old and young men and their wives went to meet him. One evening there came a man, saying that all the women who had little children should go to a high mountain. They wanted them to go because they brought white men's guns, and they made such a fearful noise, it might even kill some of the little children. My grandfather had lost one of his men while he was away.

So all the women that had little children went. My mother was among the rest; and every time the guns were heard by us, the children would scream. I thought, for one that my heart would surely break. So some of the women went down from the mountain and told them not to shoot any more, or their children would die with fright. When our mothers brought us down to our homes the nearer we came to the camp, the more I cried,—

"Oh, mother, mother, don't take us there!" I fought my mother,—I bit her. Then my father came, and took me in his arms and carried me to the camp. I put my head in his bosom, and would not look up for a long time. I heard my grandfather say,—

"So the young lady is ashamed because her sweetheart has come to see her. Come, dearest, that won't do after I have had such a hard time to come to see my sweetheart, that she should be ashamed to look at me."

Then he called my two brothers to him, and said to them, "Are you glad to see me?" And my brothers both told him that they were glad to see him. Then my grandfather said to them,—

"See that young lady; she does not love her sweetheart any more, does she? Well, I shall not live if she does not come and tell me she loves me. I shall take that gun, and I shall kill myself."

That made me worse than ever, and I screamed and cried so hard that my mother had to take me away. So they kept weeping for the little one three or four days. I did not make up with my grandfather for a long time. He sat day after day, and night after night, telling his people about his white brothers. He told them that the whites were really their brothers, that they were very kind to everybody, especially to children; that they were always ready to give something to children. He told them what beautiful things their white brothers had,—what beautiful clothes they wore, and about the big houses that go on the mighty ocean, and travel faster than any horse in the world. His people asked him how big they were. "Well, as big as that hill you see there, and as high as the mountain over us."

"Oh, that is not possible,—it would sink, surely."

"It is every word truth, and that is nothing to what I am going to tell you. Our white brothers are a mighty nation, and have more wonderful things than that. They have a gun that can shoot a ball bigger than my head, that can go as far off as that mountain you see over there."

The mountain he spoke of at that time was about twenty miles across from where we were. People opened their eyes when my grandfather told of the many battles they had with the Mexicans, and about their killing so many of the Mexicans, and taking their big city away from them, and how mighty they were. These wonderful things were talked about all winter long. The funniest thing was that he would sing some of the soldier's roll-calls, and the air to the Star-spangled Banner, which everybody learned during the winter.

He then showed us a more wonderful thing than all the others that he had brought. It was a paper, which he said could talk to him. He took it out and he would talk to it, and talk with it. He said, "This can talk to all our white brothers, and our white sisters, and their children. Our white brothers are beautiful, and our white sisters are beautiful, and their children are beautiful! He also said the paper can travel like the wind, and it can go and talk with their fathers and brothers and sisters, and come back to tell what they are doing, and whether they are well or sick."

After my grandfather told us this, our doctors and doctresses said,—

"If they can do this wonderful thing, they are not truly human, but pure spirits. None but heavenly spirits can do such wonderful things. We can communicate with the spirits, yet we cannot do wonderful things like them. Oh, our great chieftain, we are afraid your white brothers will yet make your people's hearts bleed. You see if they don't; for we can see it. Their blood is all around us, and the dead are lying all about us, and we cannot escape it. It will come. Then you will say our doctors and doctresses did not know. Dance, sing, play, it will do no good; we cannot drive it away. They have already done the mischief, while you were away."

But this did not go far with my grandfather. He kept talking to his people about the good white people, and told them all to get ready to go with him to California the following spring.

Very late that fall, my grandfather and my father and a great many more went down to the Humboldt River to fish. They brought back a great many fish, which we were very glad to get; for none of our people had been down to fish the whole summer.

When they came back, they brought us more news. They said there were some white people living at the Humboldt sink. They were the first ones my father had seen face to face. He said they were not like "humans." They were more like owls than any thing else. They had hair on their faces, and had white eyes, and looked beautiful.

I tell you we children had to be very good, indeed, during the winter; for we were told that if we were not good they would come and eat us up. We remained there all winter; the next spring the emigrants came as usual, and my father and grandfather and uncles, and many more went down on the Humboldt River on fishing excursions. While they were thus fishing, their white brothers came upon them and fired on them, and killed one of my uncles, and wounded another. Nine more were wounded, and five died afterwards. My other uncle got well again, and is living yet. Oh, that was a fearful thing, indeed!

After all these things had happened, my grandfather still stood up for his white brothers.

Our people had council after council, to get my grandfather to give his consent that they should go and kill those white men who were at the sink of Humboldt. No; they could do nothing of the kind while he lived. He told his people that his word was more to him than his son's life, or any one else's life either.

"Dear children," he said, "think of your own words to me;—you promised. You want me to say to you, Go and kill those that are at the sink of Humboldt. After your promise, how dare you to ask me to let your hearts be stained with the blood of those who are innocent of the deed that has been done to us by others? Is not my dear beloved son laid alongside of your dead, and you say I stand up for their lives. Yes, it is very hard, indeed; but, nevertheless, I know and you know that those men who live at the sink are not the ones that killed our men."

While my grandfather was talking, he wept, and men, women, and children, were all weeping. One could hardly hear him talking.

After he was through talking, came the saddest part. The widow of my uncle who was killed, and my mother and father all had long hair. They cut off their hair, and also cut long gashes in their arms and legs, and they were all bleeding as if they would die with the loss of blood. This continued for several days, for this is the way we mourn for our dead. When the woman's husband dies, she is first to cut off her hair, and then she braids it and puts it across his breast; then his mother and sisters, his father and brothers and all his kinsfolk cut their hair. The widow is to remain unmarried until her hair is the same length as before, and her face is not to be washed all that time, and she is to use no kind of paint, or to make any merriment with other women until the day is set for her to do so by her father-in-law, or if she has no father-in-law, by her mother-in-law, and then she is at liberty to go where she pleases. The widower is at liberty when his wife dies; but he mourns for her in the same way, by cutting his hair off.

It was late that fall when my grandfather prevailed with his people to go with him to California. It was this time that my mother accompanied him. Everything had been got ready to start on our journey. My dear father was to be left behind. How my poor mother begged to stay with her husband! But my grandfather told her that she could come back in the spring to see her husband; so we started for California, leaving my poor papa behind. All my kinsfolk went with us but one aunt and her children.

The first night found us camped at the sink of Carson, and the second night we camped on Carson River. The third day, as we were traveling along the river, some of our men who were ahead, came back and said there were some of our white brothers' houses ahead of us. So my grandfather told us all to stop where we were while he went to see them. He was not gone long, and when he came back he brought some hard bread which they gave him. He told us that was their food, and he gave us all some to taste. That was the first I ever tasted.

Then my grandfather once more told his people that his paper talked for him, and he said,—

"Just as long as I live and have that paper which my white brothers' great chieftain has given me, I shall stand by them, come what will." He held the paper up towards heaven and kissed it, as if it was really a person. "Oh, if I should lose this," he said, "we shall all be lost. So, children, get your horses ready, and we will go on, and we will camp with them tonight, or by them, for I have a sweetheart along who is dying for fear of my white brothers." He meant me; for I was always crying and hiding under somebody's robes, for we had no blankets then.

Well, we went on; but we did not camp with them, because my poor mother and brothers and sisters told my grandfather that I was sick with crying for fright, and for him not to camp too close to them. The women were speaking two words for themselves and one for me, for they were just as afraid as I was. I had seen my brother Natchez crying when the men came back, and said there were white men ahead of us. So my grandfather did as my mother wished him to do, and we went on by them; but I did not know it, as I had my head covered while we were passing their camp. I was riding behind my older brother, and we went on and camped quite a long way from them that night.

So we traveled on to California, but did not see any more of our white brothers till we got to the head of Carson River, about fifteen miles above where great Carson City now stands.

"Now give me the baby." It was my baby-sister that grandpa took from my mother, and I peeped from under my mother's fur, and I saw some one take my little sister. Then I cried out,—

"Oh, my sister! Don't let them take her away."

And once more my poor grandfather told his people that his white brothers and sisters were very kind to children. I stopped crying, and looked at them again. Then I saw them give my brother and sister something white. My mother asked her father what it was, and he said it was *Pe-har-be*, which means sugar. Just then one of the women came to my mother with some in her hand, and grandpa said:—

"Take it, my child."

Then I held out my hand without looking. That was the first gift I ever got from a white person, which made my heart very glad.

When they went away, my grandfather called me to him, and said I must not be afraid of the white people, for they are very good. I told him that they looked so very bad I could not help it. . . .

from *Roughing It*
(1871)

Mark Twain
(Samuel Clemens)

When his older brother Orion was named secretary to the territorial governor of Nevada, 26-year-old Samuel Clemens made the long journey from Missouri to Carson City by stagecoach in 1861. His three years in Nevada proved to be a marvelous adventure. Shortly after his arrival, he caught gold fever and invested heavily in several claims in the isolated Esmeralda District where, as biographer Ron Powers writes, Clemens endured "five miserable months of shabby quarters, leaking roofs, bad food, too much whiskey, hard work, [and] dashed hopes." He walked 120 miles to Virginia City where his brother had arranged a position as a cub reporter for the Daily Territorial Enterprise *at the munificent pay of $20 a week. The raw town at the foot of Mt. Davidson was in a boom period in the autumn of 1862, and Clemens reported on the stabbings, shootings, duels, and bloody fights that punctuated daily life, while spending his nights carousing with the boys. Early in 1863, Clemens began using the pseudonym "Mark Twain." Many of his newspaper stories were laced with irony, subtle humor, and broad exaggerations. Much to his delight, gullible readers frequently swallowed his elaborate fabrications. At one point, however, that skill got him in hot water. Under the influence of too much whiskey, he dashed off a "news item" that he intended only as an in-house joke for his editor. Somehow it was picked up by the printing foreman and appeared in May of 1864 as a news story, fortunately for him without a byline. A charity ball in Carson City had raised funds to send medical supplies, foodstuffs, and blankets to Union* *troops on the front lines, but his "report" indicated that a plan was afoot to divert the monies to "a Miscegenation Society somewhere in the East," a society with the goal of encouraging inter-racial marriage. The Emancipation Proclamation was but eighteen months old, and few Union supporters anywhere were enamored of such a social prospect, certainly not in frontier Nevada. Twain never issued a public retraction, but privately blamed his miscalculation upon "a drunken jest." In the process he learned much about American racial attitudes that would appear in such novels as* Huckleberry Finn. *By the time Mark Twain headed back east in 1867 (after sojourns in San Francisco and Hawaii), he had established himself as a writer with considerable future promise, a career whose roots lay firmly embedded in the early mining frontier of Nevada.*

My brother had just been appointed Secretary of Nevada Territory—an office of such majesty that it concentrated in itself the duties and dignities of Treasurer, Comptroller, Secretary of State, and Acting Governor in the Governor's absence. A salary of eighteen hundred dollars a year and the title of "Mr. Secretary," gave to the great position an air of wild and imposing grandeur. I was young and ignorant, and I envied my brother. I coveted his distinction and his financial splendor, but particularly and especially the long, strange journey he was going to make, and the curious new world he was going to explore. He was going to travel! I never had been away from home, and that word "travel" had a seductive charm for me. Pretty soon he would be hundreds and hundreds of miles away on the great plains and deserts, and among the mountains of the Far West, and would see buffaloes and Indians, and prairie-dogs, and antelopes, and have all kinds of adventures, and maybe get hanged or scalped, and have ever such a fine time, and write home and tell us all about it, and be a hero. And he would see the gold-mines and the silver-mines, and maybe go about of an afternoon when his work was done, and pick up two or three pailfuls of shining slugs and nuggets of gold and silver on the hillside. And by and by he would become very rich, and return home by sea, and be able to talk as calmly about San Francisco and the ocean and "the isthmus" as if it was nothing of any consequence to have seen those marvels face to face. What I suffered in contemplating his happiness, pen cannot describe. And so, when he offered me, in cold blood, the sublime position of private secretary under him, it appeared to me that the heavens and the earth passed away, and the firmament was rolled together as a scroll! I had nothing more to desire. My contentment was complete. At the end of an hour or two I was ready for the journey. Not much packing up was necessary, because we were going in the overland stage from the Missouri frontier to Nevada, and passengers were only allowed a small quantity of baggage apiece. There was no Pacific railroad in those fine times of ten or twelve years ago—not a single rail of it.

I only proposed to stay in Nevada three months—I had no thought of staying longer than that. I meant to see all I could that was new and strange, and then hurry home to business. I little thought that I would not see the end of that three-month pleasure excursion for six or seven uncommonly long years!

I dreamed all night about Indians, deserts, and silver bars, and in due time, next day, we took shipping at the St. Louis wharf on board a steamboat bound up the Missouri River. . . .

We were approaching the end of our long journey. It was the morning of the twentieth day. At noon we would reach Carson City, the capital of Nevada Territory. We were not glad, but sorry. It had been a fine pleasure trip; we had fed fat on wonders every day; we were now well accustomed to stage life, and very fond of it; so the idea of coming to a standstill and settling down to a hum-drum existence in a village was not agreeable, but on the contrary depressing.

Visibly our new home was a desert, walled in by barren, snow-clad mountains. There was not a tree in sight. There was no vegetation but the endless sagebrush and greasewood. All nature was gray with it. We were plowing through great deeps of powdery alkali dust that rose in thick clouds and floated across the plain like smoke from a burning house. We were coated with it like millers; so were the coach, the mules, the mail-bags, the driver—we and the sagebrush and the other scenery were all one monotonous color. Long trains of freight-wagons in the distance enveloped in ascending masses of dust suggested pictures of prairies on fire. These teams and their masters were the only life we saw. Otherwise we moved in the midst of solitude, silence, and desolation. Every twenty steps we passed the skeleton of some dead beast of burden, with its dust-coated skin stretched tightly over its empty ribs. Frequently a solemn raven sat upon the skull or the hips and contemplated the passing coach with meditative serenity.

By and by Carson City was pointed out to us. It nestled in the edge of a great plain and was a sufficient number of miles away to look like an assemblage of mere white spots in the shadow of a grim range of mountains overlooking it, whose summits seemed lifted clear out of companionship and consciousness of earthly things.

We arrived, disembarked, and the stage went on. It was a "wooden" town; its population two thousand souls. The main street consisted of four or five blocks of little white frame stores which were too high to sit down on, but not too high for various other purposes; in fact, hardly high enough. They were packed close together, side by side, as if room were scarce in that mighty plain. The sidewalk was of boards that were more or less loose and inclined to rattle when walked upon. In the middle of the town, opposite the stores, was the "plaza," which is native to all towns beyond the Rocky Mountains—a large, unfenced, level vacancy, with a liberty pole in it, and very useful as a place for public auctions, horse trades, and mass-meetings, and likewise for teamsters to camp in. Two other sides of the plaza were faced by stores, offices, and stables. The rest of Carson City was pretty scattering.

We were introduced to several citizens, at the stage-office and on the way up to the Governor's from the hotel—among others, to a Mr. Harris, who was on horseback; he began to say something, but interrupted himself with the remark:

"I'll have to get you to excuse me a minute; yonder is the witness that swore I helped to rob the California coach—a piece of impertinent intermeddling, sir, for I am not even acquainted with the man."

Then he rode over and began to rebuke the stranger with a six-shooter, and the stranger began to explain with another. When the pistols were emptied, the stranger resumed his work (mending a whiplash), and Mr. Harris rode by with a polite nod, homeward bound, with a bullet through one of his lungs, and several through his hips; and from them issued little rivulets of blood that coursed down the horse's sides and made the animal look quite picturesque. I never saw Harris shoot a man after that but it recalled to mind that first day in Carson.

This was all we saw that day, for it was two o'clock, now, and according to custom the daily "Washoe Zephyr" set in; a soaring dust-drift about the size of the United States set up edgewise came with it, and the capital of Nevada Territory disappeared from view. Still, there were sights to be seen which were not wholly uninteresting to new-comers; for the vast dust-cloud was thickly freckled with things strange to the upper air—things living and dead, that flitted hither and thither, going and coming, appearing and disappearing among the rolling billows of dust—hats, chickens, and parasols sailing in the remote heavens; blankets, tin signs, sage-brush, and shingles a shade lower; door-mats and buffalo-robes lower still; shovels and coal-scuttles on the next grade; glass doors, cats, and little children on the next; disrupted lumber yards, light buggies, and wheelbarrows on the next; and down only thirty or forty feet above ground was a scurrying storm of emigrating roofs and vacant lots.

It was something to see that much. I could have seen more, if I could have kept the dust out of my eyes.

But, seriously, a Washoe wind is by no means a trifling matter. It blows flimsy houses down, lifts shingle roofs occasionally, rolls up tin ones like sheet music, now and then blows a stage-coach over and spills the passengers; and tradition says the reason there are so many bald people there is, that the wind blows the hair off their heads while they are looking skyward after their hats. Carson streets seldom look inactive on summer afternoons, because there are so many citizens skipping around their escaping hats, like chambermaids trying to head off a spider.

The "Washoe Zephyr" (Washoe is a pet nickname for Nevada) is a peculiarly Scriptural wind, in that no man knoweth "whence it cometh." That is to say, where it *originates*. It comes right over the mountains from the West, but when one crosses the ridge he does not find any of it on the other side! It probably is manufactured on the mountaintop for the occasion, and starts from there. It is a pretty regular wind, in the summertime. Its office-hours are from two in the afternoon till two the next morning; and anybody venturing abroad during those twelve hours needs to allow for the wind or he will bring up a mile or two to leeward of the point he is aiming at. And yet the first complaint a Washoe visitor to San Francisco makes, is that the sea-winds blow so, there! There is a good deal of human nature in that.

We found the state palace of the Governor of Nevada Territory to consist of a white frame one story house with two small rooms in it and a stanchion-supported shed in front—for grandeur—it compelled the respect of the citizen and inspired the Indians with awe. The newly arrived Chief and Associate Justices of the territory, and other machinery of the government, were domiciled with less splendor. They were boarding around privately, and had their offices in their bedrooms. . . .

By and by I was smitten with the silver fever. "Prospecting parties" were leaving for the mountains every day, and discovering and taking possession of rich silver-bearing lodes and ledges of quartz. Plainly this was the road to fortune. The great "Gould and Curry" mine was held at three or four hundred dollars a foot when we arrived; but in two months it had sprung up to eight hundred. The "Ophir" had been worth only a mere trifle, a year gone by, and now it was selling at nearly *four thousand dollars a foot!* Not a mine could be named that had not experienced an astonishing advance in value within a short time. Everybody was talking about these marvels. Go where you would, you heard nothing else, from morning till far into the night. Tom So-and-So had sold out of the "Amanda Smith" for $40,000—hadn't a cent when he "took up" the ledge six months ago. John Jones had sold half his interest in the "Bald Eagle and Mary Ann" for $65,000, gold coin, and gone to the States for his family. The widow Brewster had "struck it rich" in the "Golden Fleece" and sold ten feet for $18,000—hadn't money enough to buy a crepe bonnet when Sing-Sing Tommy killed her husband at Baldy Johnson's wake last spring. The "Last Chance" had found a "clay casing" and knew they were "right on the ledge"— consequence, "feet" that went begging yesterday were worth a brick house apiece today, and seedy owners who could not get trusted for a drink at any bar in the country yesterday were roaring drunk on champagne today and had hosts of warm personal friends in a town where they had forgotten how to bow or shake hands from long-continued want of practice. Johnny Morgan, a common loafer, had gone to sleep in the gutter and waked up worth a hundred thousand dollars, in consequence of the decision in the "Lady Franklin and Rough and Ready" lawsuit. And so—day in and day out the talk pelted our ears and the excitement waxed hotter and hotter around us.

I would have been more or less than human if I had not gone mad like the rest. Cart-loads of solid silver bricks, as large as pigs of lead, were arriving from the mills every day, and such sights as that gave substance to the wild talk about me. I succumbed and grew as frenzied as the craziest.

Every few days news would come of the discovery of a brand new mining region; immediately the papers would teem with accounts of its richness, and away the surplus population would scamper to take possession. By the time I was fairly inoculated with the disease, "Esmeralda" had just had a run and "Humboldt" was beginning to shriek for attention. "Humboldt! Humboldt!" was the new cry, and straightway Humboldt, the newest of the new, the richest of the rich, the most marvelous of the marvelous discoveries in silver-land, was occupying two columns of the public prints to "Esmeralda's" one. I was just on the point of starting to Esmeralda, but turned with the tide and got ready for Humboldt. That the reader may see what moved me, and what would as surely have moved him had he been there, I insert here one of the newspaper letters of the day. It and several other letters from the same calm hand were the main means of converting me. I shall not garble the extract, but put it in just as it appeared in the *Daily Territorial Enterprise*.

But what about our mines? I shall be candid with you. I shall express an honest opinion, based upon a thorough examination. Humboldt County is the richest mineral region upon God's footstool. Each mountain range is gorged with the precious ores. Humboldt is the true Golconda.

The other day an assay of mere *croppings* yielded exceeding *four thousand dollars to the ton*. A week or two ago an assay of just such surface developments made returns of *seven thousand* dollars to the ton. Our mountains are full of rambling prospectors. Each day and almost every hour reveals new and more startling evidences of the profuse and intensified wealth of our favored county. The metal is not silver alone. There are distinct ledges of auriferous ore. A late discovery plainly evinces cinnabar. The coarser metals are in gross abundance. Lately evidences of bituminous coal have been detected. My theory has ever been that coal is a ligneous formation. I told Col. Whitman, in times past, that the neighborhood of Dayton (Nevada) betrayed no present or previous manifestations of a ligneous foundation, and that hence I had no confidence in his lauded coal-mines. I repeated the same doctrine to the exultant coal-discoverers of Humboldt. I talked with my friend Captain Burch on the subject. My pyrhanism vanished upon his statement that in the very region referred to he had seen petrified trees of the length of two hundred feet. Then is the fact established that huge forests once cast their grim shadows over this remote section. I am firm in the coal faith. Have no fears of the mineral resources of Humboldt County. They are immense—incalculable.

Let me state one or two things which will help the reader to better comprehend certain items in the above. At this time, our near neighbor, Gold Hill, was the most successful silver-mining locality in Nevada. It was from there that more than half the daily shipments of silver bricks came. "Very rich" (and scarce) Gold Hill ore yielded from $100 to $400 to the ton; but the usual yield was only $20 to $40 per ton—that is to say, each hundred pounds of ore yielded from one dollar to two dollars. But the reader will perceive by the above extract, that in Humboldt from one-fourth to nearly half the mass was silver! That is to say, every one hundred pounds of the ore had from *two hundred* dollars up to about *three hundred and fifty* in it. Some days later this same correspondent wrote:

I have spoken of the vast and almost fabulous wealth of this region— it is incredible. The intestines of our mountains are gorged with pre-

cious ore to plethora. I have said that nature has so shaped our mountains as to furnish most excellent facilities for the working of our
mines. I have also told you that the country about here is pregnant
with the finest mill sites in the world. But what is the mining history
of Humboldt? The Sheba mine is in the hands of energetic San Francisco capitalists. It would seem that the ore is combined with metals
that render it difficult of reduction with our imperfect mountain
machinery. The proprietors have combined the capital and labor hint-
ed at in my exordium. They are toiling and probing. Their tunnel has
reached the length of one hundred feet. From primal assays alone,
coupled with the development of the mine and public confidence in
the continuance of effort, the stock had reared itself to eight hundred
dollars market value. I do not know that one ton of the ore has been
converted into current metal. I do know that there are many lodes in
this section that surpass the Sheba in primal assay value. Listen a
moment to the calculations of the Sheba operators. They purpose transporting the ore concentrated to Europe. The conveyance from Star City
(its locality) to Virginia City will cost seventy dollars per ton; from Virginia to San Francisco, forty dollars per ton; from thence to Liverpool,
its destination, ten dollars per ton. Their idea is that its conglomerate
metals will reimburse them their cost of original extraction, the price of
transportation, and the expense of reduction, and that then a ton of the
raw ore will net them twelve hundred dollars. The estimate may be
extravagant. Cut it in twain, and the product is enormous, far transcending any previous developments of our racy territory.

A very common calculation is that many of our mines will yield
five hundred dollars to the ton. Such fecundity throws the Gould &
Curry, the Ophir and the Mexican, of your neighborhood, in the dark-
est shadow. I have given you the estimate of the value of a single
developed mine. Its richness is indexed by its market valuation. The
people of Humboldt County are *feet* crazy. As I write, our towns are
near deserted. They look as languid as a consumptive girl. What has
become of our sinewy and athletic fellow-citizens? They are coursing
through ravines and over mountain-tops. Their tracks are visible in
every direction. Occasionally a horseman will dash among us. His
steed betrays hard usage. He alights before his adobe dwelling, hastily exchanges courtesies with his townsmen, hurries to an assay office
and from thence to the District Recorder's. In the morning, having
renewed his provisional supplies, he is off again on his wild and
unbeaten route. Why, the fellow numbers already his feet by the thousands. He is the horse-leech. He has the craving stomach of the shark
or anaconda. He would conquer metallic worlds.

This was enough. The instant we had finished reading the above article, four of us decided to go to Humboldt. We commenced getting ready at once. And we also commenced upbraiding ourselves for not deciding sooner—for we were in terror lest all the rich mines would be found and secured before we got there, and we might have to put up with ledges that would not yield more than two or three hundred dollars a ton, maybe. An hour before, I would have felt opulent if I had owned ten feet in a Gold Hill mine whose ore produced twenty-five dollars to the ton; now I was already annoyed at the prospect of having to put up with mines the poorest of which would be a marvel in Gold Hill.

Hurry, was the word! We wasted no time. Our party consisted of four persons—a blacksmith sixty years of age, two young lawyers, and myself. We bought a wagon and two miserable old horses. We put eighteen hundred pounds of provisions and mining-tools in the wagon and drove out of Carson on a chilly December afternoon. . . .

We were fifteen days making the trip—two hundred miles; thirteen, rather, for we lay by a couple of days, in one place, to let the horses rest. . . .

It was a hard, wearing, toilsome journey, but it had its bright side; for after each day was done and our wolfish hunger appeased with a hot supper of fried bacon, bread, molasses, and black coffee, the pipe-smoking, song-singing, and yarn-spinning around the evening campfire in the still solitudes of the desert was a happy, carefree sort of recreation that seemed the very summit and culmination of earthly luxury. It is a kind of life that has a potent charm for all men, whether city or country bred. We are descended from desert-lounging Arabs, and countless ages of growth toward perfect civilization have failed to root out of us the nomadic instinct. We all confess to a gratified thrill at the thought of "camping out."

Once we made twenty-five miles in a day, and once we made forty miles (through the Great American Desert), and ten miles beyond—fifty in all—in twenty-three hours, without halting to eat, drink, or rest. To stretch out and go to sleep, even on stony and frozen ground, after pushing a wagon and two horses fifty miles, is a delight so supreme that for the moment it almost seems cheap at the price. We camped two days in the neighborhood of the " Sink of the Humboldt." We tried to use the strong alkaline water of the Sink, but it would not answer. It was like drinking lye, and not weak lye, either. It left a taste in the mouth, bitter and every way execrable, and a burning in the stomach that was very uncomfortable. We put molasses in it, but that helped it very little; we added a pickle, yet the alkali was the prominent taste, and so it was unfit for drinking. The coffee we made of this water was the meanest compound man has yet invented. It was really viler to the taste than the unameliorated water itself. Mr. Ballou, being the architect and builder of the beverage, felt constrained to indorse and uphold it, and so drank half a cup, by little sips, making shift to praise it faintly the while, but faintly threw out the remainder, and said frankly it was "too technical for *him*."

But presently we found a spring of fresh water, convenient, and then, with nothing to mar our enjoyment, and no stragglers to interrupt it, we entered into our rest.

After leaving the Sink, we traveled along the Humboldt River a little way. People accustomed to the monster mile-wide Mississippi, grow accustomed to associating the term "river" with a high degree of watery grandeur. Consequently, such people feel rather disappointed when they stand on the shores of the Humboldt or the Carson and find that a "river" in Nevada is a sickly rivulet which is just the counterpart of the Erie canal in all respects save that the canal is twice as long and four times as deep. One of the pleasantest and most invigorating exercises one can contrive is to run and jump across the Humboldt River till he is overheated, and then drink it dry.

On the fifteenth day we completed our march of two hundred miles and entered Unionville, Humboldt County, in the midst of a driving snow- storm. Unionville consisted of eleven cabins and a liberty pole. Six of the cabins were strung along one side of a deep cañon, and the other five faced them. The rest of the landscape was made up of bleak mountain walls that rose so high into the sky from both sides of the cañon that the village was left, as it were, far down in the bottom of a crevice. It was always daylight on the mountain-tops a long time before the darkness lifted and revealed Unionville.

We built a small, rude cabin in the side of the crevice and roofed it with canvas, leaving a corner open to serve as a chimney, through which the cattle used to tumble occasionally, at night, and mash our furniture and interrupt our sleep. It was very cold weather and fuel was scarce. Indians brought brush and bushes several miles on their backs; and when we could catch a laden Indian it was well—and when we could not (which was the rule, not the exception), we shivered and bore it.

I confess, without shame, that I expected to find masses of silver lying all about the ground. I expected to see it glittering in the sun on the mountain summits. I said nothing about this, for some instinct told me that I might possibly have an exaggerated idea about it, and so if I betrayed my thought I might bring derision upon myself. Yet I was as perfectly satisfied in my own mind as I could be of anything, that I was going to gather up, in a day or two, or at furthest a week or two, silver enough to make me satisfactorily wealthy—and so my fancy was already busy with plans for spending this money. The first opportunity that offered, I sauntered carelessly away from the cabin, keeping an eye on the other boys, and stopping and contemplating the sky when they seemed to be observing me; but as soon as the coast was manifestly clear, I fled away as guiltily as a thief might have done and never halted till I was far beyond sight and call. Then I began my search with a feverish excitement that was brimful of expectation— almost of certainty. I crawled about the ground, seizing and examining bits of stone, blowing the dust from them or rubbing them on my clothes, and then peering at them with anxious hope. Presently I found a bright fragment and my heart bounded! I hid behind a boulder and polished it and scrutinized it with a nervous eagerness and a delight that was more pronounced than absolute certainty itself could have afforded. The more I examined the fragment the more I was convinced that I had found the door to fortune. I marked the spot and carried away my specimen. Up and down the rugged mountainside I searched, with always increasing interest and always augmenting gratitude that I had come to Humboldt and come in time. Of all the experiences of my life, this secret search among the hidden treasures of silver-land was the nearest to unmarred ecstasy. It was a delirious revel. By and by, in the bed of a shallow rivulet, I found a deposit of shining yellow scales, and my breath almost forsook me! A gold-mine, and in my simplicity I had been content with vulgar silver! I was so excited that I half believed my overwrought imagination was deceiving me. Then a fear came upon me that people might be observing me and would guess my secret. Moved by this thought, I made a circuit of the place, and ascended a knoll to reconnoiter. Solitude. No creature was near. Then I returned to my mine, fortifying myself against possible disappointment, but my fears were groundless—the shining scales were still there. I set about scooping them out, and for an hour I toiled down the windings of the stream and robbed its bed. But at last the descending sun warned me to give up the quest, and I turned homeward laden with wealth. As I walked along I could not help smiling at the thought of my being so excited over my fragment of silver when a nobler metal was almost under my nose. In this little time the former had so fallen in my estimation that once or twice I was on the point of throwing it away.

The boys were as hungry as usual, but I could eat nothing. Neither could I talk. I was full of dreams and far away. Their conversation interrupted the flow of my fancy somewhat, and annoyed me a little, too. I despised the sordid and commonplace things they talked about. But as they proceeded, it began to amuse me. It grew to be rare fun to hear them planning their poor little economies and sighing over possible privations and distresses when a gold-mine, all our own, lay within sight of the cabin, and I could point it out at any moment. Smothered hilarity began to oppress me, presently. It was hard to resist the impulse to burst out with exultation and reveal everything; but I did resist. I said within myself that I would filter the great news through my lips calmly and be serene as a summer morning while I watched its effect in their faces. I said:

"Where have you all been?"

"Prospecting."

"What did you find?"

"Nothing."

"Nothing? What do you think of the country?"

"Can't tell, yet," said Mr. Ballou, who was an old gold-miner, and had likewise had considerable experience among the silver-mines.

"Well, haven't you formed any sort of opinion?"

"Yes, a sort of a one. It's fair enough here, maybe, but overrated. Seven-thousand-dollar ledges are scarce, though. That Sheba may be rich enough, but we don't own it; and, besides, the rock is so full of base metals that all the science in the world can't work it. We'll not starve, here, but we'll not get rich, I'm afraid."

"So you think the prospect is pretty poor?"

"No name for it!"

"Well, we'd better go back, hadn't we?"

"Oh, not yet—of course not. We'll try it a riffle, first."

"Suppose, now—this is merely a supposition, you know—suppose you could find a ledge that would yield, say, a hundred and fifty dollars a ton—would that satisfy you?"

"Try us once!" from the whole party.

"Or suppose—merely a supposition, of course—suppose you were to find a ledge that would yield two thousand dollars a ton—would *that* satisfy you?"

"Here—what do you mean? What are you coming at? Is there some mystery behind all this?"

"Never mind. I am not saying anything. You know perfectly well there are no rich mines here—of course you do. Because you have been around and examined for yourselves. Anybody would know that, that had been around. But just for the sake of argument, suppose—in a kind of general way—suppose some person were to tell you that two-thousand-dollar ledges were simply contemptible—contemptible, understand—and that right yonder in sight of this very cabin there were piles of pure gold and pure silver—oceans of it—enough to make you all rich in twenty-four hours! Come!"

"I should say he was as crazy as a loon!" said old Ballou, but wild with excitement, nevertheless.

"Gentlemen," said I, "I don't say anything—*I* haven't been around, you know, and of course don't know anything—but all I ask of you is to cast your eye on *that*, for instance, and tell me what you think of it!" and I tossed my treasure before them.

There was an eager scrabble for it, and a closing of heads together over it under the candlelight. Then old Ballou said:

"Think of it? I think it is nothing but a lot of granite rubbish and nasty glittering mica that isn't worth ten cents an acre!"

So vanished my dream. So melted my wealth away. So toppled my airy castle to the earth and left me stricken and forlorn.

Moralizing, I observed, then, that "all that glitters is not gold."

Mr. Ballou said I could go further than that, and lay it up among my treasures of knowledge, that *nothing* that glitters is gold. So I learned then, once for all, that gold in its native state is but dull, unornamental stuff, and that only low-born metals excite the admiration of the ignorant with an ostentatious glitter. However, like the rest of the world, I still go on underrating men of gold and glorifying men of mica. Commonplace human nature cannot rise above that. . . .

from *Desert Challenge*
An Interpretation of Nevada (1942)

Richard G. Lillard

Writing in 1942, the environmental historian Richard G. Lillard concluded that "Nevada is the 'Old West' streamlined," as he connected the state's unique culture to the mining frontiers that dominated the first 75 years of the state's history: "Nevadans have held to the philosophy of the American frontier: a belief in individualism, an optimistic attitude, and a faith in men's future together, whatever their divergent pasts." According to Lillard, the unique spirit of the state's residents lay firmly rooted in the boomtowns that were built, operated, and often abandoned by the footloose miners who came from across the United States in search of gold and silver ore, and who moved from one mining camp to another in response to news of a new discovery. After spending months traveling across the state, Lillard concluded that Nevadans exuded a common spirit readily traceable to the days when mining dominated the state's economy and politics. Nevadans "have the idea that a man can make his own terms with destiny. . . . They consider their government best when it governs least. They say, 'Live your life, but don't try to live mine.'"

In the following excerpts from his classic Desert Challenge; An Interpretation of Nevada, *Lillard describes the culture of the mining camps, which were established by fortune hunters eager to exploit the gold and silver deposits that lay beneath the surface of the vast expanses of desert terrain. This fluid society of immigrants came from many backgrounds but quickly melded around the arduous and often frustrating life in which luck as well as skill counted for something.*

"Behind all the surface turbulence of mining camps," he writes, "sober citizens were setting up a stable society," creating governments, organizing political campaigns, building schools and churches, and founding theaters, debating clubs and libraries to counterbalance the effects of the many saloons and brothels that also served the needs of a largely male, transient population.

Lillard's engaging narrative ends with Nevada standing on the precipice of a major transformation. He could not have anticipated the sudden development of enormous hotel-casinos in Las Vegas and Reno, but he clearly understood that Nevada was home to a society open to change and innovation: "Only a few blocks apart, sometimes across the street from each other, are village homes, modern public schools, sophisticated hotels, efficient chain stores, churches, gambling clubs, grassy parks, noisy bars, and courthouses that use assembly-line methods to assemble and disassemble marriages. Filling these buildings and the streets that join them are Americans who represent all the strata and cross-strata of the nation's life." Nevada, he concluded, was unique, distinguishable from all of its neighboring western states. World War II would produce an economic renaissance in the state, stimulating a much larger in-migration of fortune seekers who would create a New Nevada, one founded upon the same spirit of aggressive individualism and stark capitalism that he described during the heyday of the mining boomtowns.

Often enough, after an excitement had produced a stampede and a mushroom town, men found that there was no excuse for a town. There were a mayor and a fire department, a politician aspiring to the United States Senate, a gun-sporting badman and a fire-eating editor, but the all-essential ore failed to extend downward or sideways. It declined in richness until it was low-grade that would not pay for its own mining and milling. Or it pinched out before it got any distance at all. What a competent geologist could have predicted in a brief, sane exploration of the area had been discovered only after several hundred or thousand people had gone through the process of setting up a community. Worse, sometimes the mines were all right, but "richer" mines were heard of somewhere else near.

Whichever way, the camp died without getting within gunshot of permanency. The citizenry moved to prosperous camps or joined the rush to the new strike. Everyone left, taking the portable possessions he had brought not so long before. The editor took his Washington hand press, the merchant his canvas walls and iron cashbox, the constable his notched gun, the miner his pick and shovel and dynamite caps. The huts of mud and sagebrush remained behind, as did the stone houses and the skeletons of frame buildings, but many one-room frame shanties were put on runners and dragged away to the new camp. The camp of Gold Creek, in the Owyhee region near Idaho, was established on the mere rumor of gold. A town was set up and immediately abandoned. One fire plug still remains. In some camps there were elaborate mills to leave behind—built before the limited ore supply was known—and roasting furnaces with tall chimneys of solid masonry, put up at great expense to extract precious metals that were never found. Generally not enough remained in a few years for the camp to be called a ghost town. It was merely a former site, a dimly remembered name—Yandleville, Yankee Blade, Pizarro, Geneva, Coral City.

If a strike made good, however, the camp took on the appearance of a real town. Excess population drifted away. The wild manners of the days of roughing it toned down. Law, comforts, conveniences were fully established. Tents became houses; booths, stores. Real-estate values leveled off and general property taxes became possible. Mining stocks were less a matter of wild speculation, more a matter of sober investment. Families arrived and good schools went up, staffed by well-paid teachers. Several newspapers competed for subscribers and influence over state politics. Churches were built, with special features in redwood. Marble shafts and family plots with ornamental iron fences appeared in the graveyards; the epitaphs named men, wives, and children. Sure of their town's future, citizens put up sandstone courthouses strong enough to last a century. Stage and freight lines settled down to regular schedules. . . .

Climax in Virginia City

Of all the mining towns that have been sensations in the West, the most famous is Virginia City. Its mines were the richest yet discovered in the United States, and a whole set of circumstances gave it a crucial importance no other mining camp has ever had. Successive ore finds and delirious stock gambling kept it at a higher pitch for a longer time than any other Western camp. It made precedents galore. Good fortune gave it a half dozen unusual journalists who won it regional fame at the start and later began a tradition of literary glorification of the town on a national scale. The history of Virginia City is to a very considerable degree the history of Nevada. It is part of the economic and political history of the United States. It is both a representative and a unique part of the history of the frontier.

The depth of the veins gave Virginia City a permanence that the California placer camps and most Nevada hard-rock camps never knew. By 1864, five years after the original rush, a complete city pattern of life had been established. Streets were straight and business was centered on C Street. Land had been subdivided into lots, with preferred frontages of forty to fifty feet selling for $10,000 to $20,000. Above C Street were residences of merchants and mining officials. Below were a Chinese section and the rickety huts of Washoes and Piutes, who throve peacefully on the wastes of town. Near by was a section of whitewashed cabins, gaudily furnished, with inmates sitting in uncurtained windows. Throughout the town, in hotels, rooming house, and shacks, the mineworkers lived. Livery stables were common. Saloons were everywhere. There were established schools, churches, and courts. The mine shafts were just downhill from town, but tunnels ran in all directions beneath the streets. According to the Bureau of the Census, the number of permanent residents in 1860 was only 2,500; 7,000 in 1870; and at the peak, in 1880, about 11,000. Estimates of reliable visitors during the booms between census years give a top total of 25,000 persons in town. . . .

Dan De Quille, and hundreds of his fellow citizens, obscure or prominent, lived through extraordinarily unstable years. For two decades there were excitements that came and went, wrecking some individuals but never dismaying the general public. The rush of 1859, encouraged by the original Ophir and Gold Hill ore bodies, flattened out during the next year. New discoveries came along, and in 1863 the second boom arrived. Many mines flourished. Freaks of fortune were both exciting and commonplace. A miner named Plato paid an Irish prostitute with the title to ten feet near the Bowers claim. Miners uncovered rich ore, the ten feet rose to $150,000 or $200,000 in value, and Plato had to marry the woman to get back the fortune. Once six tons from the Belcher mine yielded $770 per ton. Mine officials in Virginia City received the highest salaries in the United States. Superintendent Palmer of the Gould & Curry got $40,000 a year. Virginia City was rich and great, and the population reached 15,000. But the ore bodies terminated at five hundred feet, the boom deflated later in the year, and continued flabby for two years, ending in an acute panic in late 1865, when the population was down to 4,000. Early in 1866 new ore bodies revived the town and gave a year of prosperity. In 1870 this third boom subsided. No new ore was being found below a thousand feet. Pumping was stopped in most mines. Perhaps the Comstock was through.

Then toward the end of the year an unprecedented bonanza came to light 1,100 feet down in the Crown Point Mine in Gold Hill. Once again the Comstock became enormously busy. . . .

Closed mines reopened and new operations commenced. The fourth boom reached its height in 1872 and began to quiet down. Low-grade ore turned up in the Consolidated Virginia at the 1,200-foot level. And then, early in 1873, came the biggest cache of all, the Big Bonanza, which by 1880 produced $135,000,000 in gold and silver and paid $78,000,000 in dividends. Stock of the "Con Virginia" went up as did the values for all Virginia City mines. But at last the Comstock reached its superclimax. By January 7, 1875, according to Grant Smith, the market value of all Comstock mines reached about $300,000,000, an absurd value. On January 8 a panic set in that ruined thousands of people. The Crown Point ceased to pay dividends, the rich Belcher stopped in 1876, and thereafter only the Con Virginia and the California, which also tapped the Big Bonanza, paid dividends; and they stopped in 1880. In 1881 the market value of all the mines on the lode was only $7,000,000. Great hopes were in the past. Ghosthood loomed in the future.

During the gilded twenty years prospectors and stock-holders and merchants often made large amounts and lived well, and the daily laborers had a standard of living possibly unparalleled in its day. For two decades the strong Miners' Union kept the wage at $4. It forced the Nevada legislature to pass America's first eight-hour law for mine work. Workers as well as capitalists could afford the luxuries of life. The stores sold quantities of raw oysters on ice from San Francisco, fresh beef, California fruits, wines and liquors, fresh milk, potatoes, and green vegetables. Boarding tables set bounteous repasts. Drinking was universal and respectable. The saloonkeeper was an important member of society, powerful, often for the good, in politics. The world's finest liquors were served in all the mixtures and concoctions for which Americans are noted, and behind handsome mahogany bars were glasses and bottles of all shapes and sizes. Sawdust Corner, the Roadside Club, Hennessey & Breen, the Crystal Bar—and richly appointed gambling-rooms such as Gentry and Crittenden's lured miners from lonely cabins and rooming houses. They played faro, monte, vingt-et-un, rouge et noir, and roulette. . . .

For by the middle sixties laissez-faire competition had snarled Comstock business. More than a hundred stamp and amalgamation mills had been built on insufficient capital. The cream of the lode crop-pings had been skimmed. Property rights were tangled in litigation.

Little local banks were loaning more money, at three to five per cent a month, than they could collect. Speculators still dealt in "feet," linear measurements along ledges. Miners were going unpaid. The important banking house of Stateler and Arrington failed when some ore bodies petered out and market values fell from $6,000 to $700 per foot. It owed $40,000 to W. C. Ralston's Bank of California. At this time William Sharon, small, quiet dandyish, and calculating, appeared in Virginia City, established a branch of Ralston's bank. He subtly replaced Bill Stewart as boss of the Comstock and began calmly to acquire a mining monopoly for the bank. The capitalism of the expert businessman had reached the Washoe frontier and taken the place of the democracy of the inspired leader. Sharon established regular paydays for miners and a standard interest rate of two per cent per month. He introduced speculation in shares. He made loans to mines, encouraged additional borrowing, foreclosed, and got mines cheaply. He organized a monopoly milling company for the syndicate's mines, fought the building of Sutro's tunnel because he would have to pay it royalties for ore carried out through it, and in 1869 brought a railroad up a tortuous grade from Carson City, thus ending a picturesque business of wagoning and stagecoaching. Mining became a comparatively sober business, although the Sharon ring had opponents and big operators competed for huge spoils. In 1871 John P. Jones and Alvinza Hayward took advantage of a fall in stocks to buy under the Bank of California faction and get control of important mines, notably the Crown Point. About the same time John W. Mackay and James G. Fair, ex-superintendents and genuine mining experts, and James Flood and William O'Brien, saloon-keepers, began buying into mines and purchasing the hardly developed strip, between formerly rich mines, that held the dazzling ore casket, the Big Bonanza.

Here, on a desolate and barren range of mountains, by the mid-seventies, had grown up a city in which extraordinary things happened. Underground were the most extensive tunnelings yet made in America, and in them a quarter of the city's population was always at work. The streets of the town were the roof of a subterranean building that grew downward and was seventeen levels down by 1877, or the equivalent of about two Empire State Buildings. There was said to be as much lumber underground in Virginia City as there was in the whole city of Chicago. The size of the machinery and the ore dumps showed what great things were done. On top were the buildings that symbolized the wealth and energy of the place. Piper's Opera House cost $50,000. The Storey County Courthouse, sturdy to this day, was a $117,000 building on ground that cost $30,000. The Catholic Church,

St. Mary's in the Mountains, with its rose window, its redwood columns and arches, its Italian marble and Spanish bells, was commodious and beautiful. The International Hotel, six stories high, contained 160 large, high-ceilinged rooms, and the first elevator west of Chicago. Its elegant appointments symbolized the metropolitan pattern of life in the camp. In it was the bed occupied—on separate occasions—by General Grant, Dom Pedro of Brazil, Adelina Patti, and President Rutherford B. Hayes. In this hotel, according to the story, the Bonanza Kings entertained the Duke of Sutherland with five hundred bottles of champagne.

Social distinctions became more pronounced than in other camps. The elaborate Victorian homes of mineowners, superintendents, brokers, and merchants were furnished with the best that money could buy in an age of ornate interior decoration. Ladies and gentlemen dressed exceedingly well. Prince Albert coats, stovepipe hats, and Paris gowns were as abundant, proportionately, as in San Francisco and New York. Private card and dinner parties were gay and stylish. Millmen's wives and daughters exhibited diamonds and laces to their rivals as did social leaders in Eastern cities. Common were the phrases "high-toned," "genteel," and "the haut ton." Elegant ladies in silks and corals liked Virginia City for its cloudless skies, that were a contrast after their visits to "the bay," and for the bustle and activity of the town, which electrified and invigorated them. While the lords of creation gave their lives to money-making, their wives read novels, played Boston-made pianos, sang at the Choral Society on Thursday nights, went on picnic excursions where they ate chicken and ices and drank champagne, and peddled gossip. Occasional grand balls sponsored by fraternal organizations, and governor's levees and balls in Carson, had all the elegance and display and courtliness of a reception at Mrs. Vanderbilt's. There were the Ivy Social Club, the Washoe Club for the leaders of the Comstock, and the exclusive Entre Nous Club, noted for its waltzes, quadrilles, and mazurkas.

The generous production of the mines enabled Nevada to play its significant role of building San Francisco, helping to win the Civil War, giving America its first mineral kings, and upsetting the silver standard in the Western world. In the struggle to obtain the bullion, the mines and mills of the Comstock added to the technological knowledge of the time. There were tough problems to solve. There were no big trees on the Virginia Range to timber the mine workings. There was no pure water in or under the town. What water was there was unhealthfully if not poisonously filled with chemicals. Tunnels caved in. Clay earth swelled and snapped off uprights or sank and compressed twelve-inch yellow-pine planks into three-inch slabs as hard and dark as teakwood. Whitish sulphate masses—epsomite and pickeringite—grew like cauliflower heads and shredded, displaced, and broke the lagging, the side boards in the drifts and tunnels. Hidden lakes poured into the shafts, and Cornish pumps had to labor to lift out the water. Fires burst out and trapped clambering men in smoke and crashing timbers. The Crown Point-Yellow Jacket fire in 1869 was the most terrible metal-mine disaster in America up to the time. Between thirty-five and forty-nine miners were burned, smothered, and crushed to death. Dynamite caps blew too soon or too late. Workers and animals fell into shafts and winzes. Cables parted and tumbled miners down shafts in cages. Most continually perplexing was the ventilation problem caused by steaming mineralized waters from hot springs at the bottoms of the deep mines. Hot water was struck at about 1,200 feet. The farther down the hotter, generally one degree for every twenty-eight feet. At 2,100 feet the temperature miners worked in was about 120 degrees. Below 3,000 feet it was 138 degrees. Miners worked in seven-minute shifts, dousing themselves with ice water and sucking the ice liberally provided, while sweat ran down and filled their loose shoes.

"By the contest waged in this district," wrote a federal expert, "against the forces of nature, contributions of the first importance to mining science have been furnished; the foremost practical miners of America have been trained." Among the inventions developed or experimented with were compressed-air drills in tunneling, electric signals, giant powder cartridges, pressure ventilation, steam hoists, safety elevator cages, and the largest and most efficient water pumps known at that time; the Deidesheimer square-set system of timbering, honeycomb-wise, tunnels in loose ore, which took millions of board feet of timber into the mines and made them "the tomb of the Sierra forests" east and west of Tahoe; the V-shaped flume, for floating logs fifteen miles from the Sierras to Washoe Valley; processes of ore crushing and reducing that far surpassed those used for centuries in Mexico and Peru, including variations of the trip-hammer quartz mill. A great feat in its day, completed in 1873, was the piping of water 38,000 feet from Lake Marlette in the Tahoe Alps, down through Washoe Valley, and up around Mount Davidson to Virginia City, which is about 1,500 feet above the valley. Adolph Sutro ran his celebrated tunnel from the Carson River to the 1,640-foot level of the Virginia City mines. The railroad from Carson City was an engineering triumph. It rose nearly 1,600 feet in thirteen and a half miles of track so curving that its aggregate curves would make seventeen full coils. Across Crown Point Ravine in

Gold Hill was a sensational trestle 390 feet long, 90 feet high, containing about 20,000 tons of steel, bolts, pins, and cables. This fifty-two mile narrow-gauge railroad from Reno, owned by William Sharon and Darius Ogden Mills, was for a time the most prosperous railroad in the United States. Forty or fifty trains a day carried loads at monopoly rates. . . .

The style is irrelevant to the purpose of the buildings, their site, their destiny as monuments to the "Old West," but it does have all the fascinating ugliness of the General Grant period, which architects now label "The Reign of Terror." The climate has been at work to counteract its effrontery. Fronts are weather-beaten, and paint has faded or peeled off. Porches and balusters sag. Shingles are loose and ruffled. But the board walks remain fairly busy thoroughfares. The thresholds of granite or cast-iron plate await the further use of millions of feet. Hinged iron shutters bearing aged green paint give their medieval protection to windows. The wooden porches with their balustrades keep off the bright Nevada sunlight, and the rise of the street south over the horizon toward the Gold Hill divide suggests what once was there, a metropolis continuing on out of sight. The Presbyterian Church, built in 1867, is still in service. The obsolete, baroque public school bulks on South C. Isolated and paintless is the firehouse of Company No. 2. In the middle of town the Enterprise Building remains. The Tahoe House serves meals. Numerous dark, cramped shops offer goods. Decorating their windows are potted geraniums and succulents and sunflowers. A half dozen bars, including the Wonderlode and the Old 62, sell liquor superior to the lightning-rod rotgut of 1860 and inferior to the imported delicacies of 1875. The Masonic Hall on North C is intact, although propped up on the north side, where a neighboring structure has vanished. The one really jarring note is struck by a self-conscious novelty and "antique" shop, advertising itself as "The Museum of Memories" and an occupant of the building once the Bloody Bucket Saloon. Here the spirit of the Comstock has sunk to the level of cheap commercialism and still cheaper souvenirs.

Up the mountain on B Street are the Miners' Union Hall, a flagpole atop its gable, the county courthouse, and the Knights of Pythias Temple, with a cast-iron railing framing the top of the disintegrating porch. The skeleton of Piper's Opera House stands like a great barn, its shingles a loose thatch. When no longer a Mecca for the talent of the American theater, it became a silent-movie theater and a floor for high-school basketball games. Now it is a monument of scrap lumber waiting for fate to set it on fire. Its floor is warped like an accordion bellows. The stage slants dangerously. The galleries are propped up. The ceiling and roof are slatted. Positive weather and negative repairs have made them a mere latticework to strain snow and rain before they drip on the floor and swell it into further contortions.

Below C are the Episcopal Church, weathered brown and nailed shut, and, the width of a street away, St. Mary's in the Mountains, built in 1868, burned in the great fire of 1875, and rebuilt in 1876 with a water pipe installed in the cross on the steeple. The railway station is boarded up. No more receptions for Ulysses Grant, Rutherford Hayes, and Herbert Hoover! Dirt filters into the unused roadbed and covers the rails.

Scattered about the town are many pleasant homes set off by picket fences and shaded in summer by locusts, Lombardy poplars, and cottonwoods. In the gardens are apple and pear trees, sunflowers, golden glows, and bachelor's-buttons. Hop vines clamber along the fences and over the verandas. The WPA has built several public buildings and new high-gear roads to replace the steep Gold Canyon road up from Carson City and the dangerous Geiger Grade up from Reno. . . .

Present-day inhabitants of Virginia City, seasoned mining men among them, retain a faith in the lode. There are huge fortunes yet undiscovered, they feel, especially in the unexplored lower levels. The creed of the sixties is still alive: Once a silver mine, always a silver mine. There is always more to be found. "There's many a good mine in the sneer zone of an old ore." . . .

Virginia City made Nevada famous yesterday. Transitory residents came, obtained their fortunes, and crossed on, eastward or westward. The city is the state's most important name, its greatest antiquity. Nowadays Reno and Las Vegas are the cities in the publicity, as again transients come, to stay awhile, before journeying on into the horizons. They are notorious today, but one can doubt that they influence history as Virginia City did or that eighty years from now they will be the thriving tradition that it is after eight decades. The story of Virginia City, queen city of the Comstock, is a chapter in the history of the American Dream. . . .

from *The Conquest of the Arid West*
(1900)

William E. Smythe

By 1880, the great bonanza on the Comstock had been reduced to a steady but unspectacular mining operation. The state's population leveled off—it stood at 62,266 in the census of 1880—and then declined swiftly. By the mid-1890s, near-desperate state leaders were forced to search for other economic opportunities. The lack of water loomed as a formidable obstacle to economic development, but optimistic Nevadans embraced bold new plans to use the Carson and Truckee rivers to make "Nevada bloom." Visions of a ranching and agricultural bonanza inspired hope, but any meaningful irrigation project was far beyond the means of state government. In 1889, the State Board of Reclamation and Internal Improvements implored the federal government to fund a major irrigation project. Could the U.S. government, it plaintively asked, "refuse to render assistance or will it allow one of its sovereign states to languish?" Congressman Francis G. Newlands, the driving force behind the promotion of water projects, was rewarded in 1902 when Congress passed the Reclamation Act that authorized construction of the Truckee-Carson Project, which led to the irrigation of thousands of acres of land in Churchill County. In advancing his solution to Nevada's economic future, Newlands and his supporters drew heavily upon the writings of journalist William E. Smythe, whose book, The Conquest of the Arid West, *was published in 1900. While these programs were lauded as distinctly "progressive" at the time, most environmentalists have come to view them as destructive because they fundamentally altered the ecology of water systems, while historians have suggested that they sought to place a nineteenth-century small farm settlement pattern upon the land rather than anticipate the economic realities of the twentieth century.*

The Better Half of the United States

The ninety-seventh meridian divides the United States almost exactly into halves. East of that line dwell seventy-five million people. Here are overgrown cities and overcrowded industries. Here is surplus capital, as idle and burdensome as the surplus population. West of that line dwell five or six millions—less than the population of Pennsylvania, and scarcely more than that of Greater New York. And yet the vast territory to the West—so little known, so lightly esteemed, so sparsely peopled—is distinctly the better half of the United States.

The West and East are different sections, not merely in name and geographical location, but in physical endowments and fundamental elements of economic life. Nature wrote upon them, in her own indelible characters, the story of their wide contrasts and the prophecy of their varying civilizations. To the one were given the advantages of earlier development, but for the other were reserved the opportunities of a riper time. It was the destiny of the one to blossom and fruit in an epoch distinguished for the accumulation of wealth, with its vast possibilities of evil and of good. It was the destiny of the other to lie fallow until humanity should feel a nobler impulse; then to nurse, in the shadow of its everlasting mountains and the warmth of its unfailing sunshine, new dreams of liberty and equality for men.

That this is not the popular conception of the mission of the Far West may be frankly acknowledged. The region is little known to the great middle-classes in American life. It has been demonstrated by actual statistics that only three per cent of our people travel more than fifty miles from their homes in the course of a year. Those who make extended pleasure tours gravitate not unnaturally to Europe, drawn by the fascination of quaint foreign scenes and the fame of historic places. But the comparatively few whose business or fancy has taken them across the continent fail, as a rule, to grasp the true significance of the wide empire which stretches from the middle of the great plains to the shores of the Western sea.

It is a common human instinct to regard unfamiliar conditions with distrust. The first settlers in Iowa engaged in desperate rivalry for possession of the wooded lands, thinking that no soil was fit for agricultural purposes unless it furnished the pioneer an opportunity to cut down trees and pull up stumps. "Land that won't grow trees won't grow anything," was the maxim of the knowing ones. Their fathers had cleared the forests on the slopes of the Alleghenies to make way for the plough and the field, and the new generation could not conceive that land which bore rich crops of wild grasses and lay plastic and level for the husbandman to begin his labors, could have any value. A great deal of hard work was wasted before it was discovered that nature had provided new and superior conditions in the land beyond the Mississippi.

So it generally happens that the casual Western traveler, looking at the country from car-windows in the intervals between his daily paper, brings back more contempt than admiration for the economic possibilities of the country. One must live in the Far West to begin to comprehend it. Not only so, but he must come with eager eyes from an older civilization, and he must study the beginnings of industrial and social institutions throughout the region as a whole, to have any adequate appreciation of the real potentialities of that half of the United States which has been reserved for the theatre of twentieth-century developments. To all other observers the new West is a sealed book.

The West is divided from the East by a boundary-line which is not imaginary. It is a plain mark on the face of the earth, and no man made it. It is the place where the region of assured rainfall ends and the arid region begins. . . .

The superiority of the western half-continent over its eastern counterpart may not be expressed in a word. It is, rather, a matter for patient unfolding through a study of natural conditions over wide areas, and a scrutiny of the human institutions which are the inevitable product of this environment. Aridity, in the elementary sense, is purely an affair of climate. That it is also the germ of new industrial and social systems, with far-reaching possibilities in the fields of ethics and politics, will be demonstrated further on in these pages. But the first item of importance in the assets of the new West is climate. . . .

The Rising State of Nevada

Nevada, after a period of stagnation and decline, is moving along the upward path with steady strides and stands well to the front among States which are conspicuously prosperous.

No mining camps are attracting wider attention than Tonopah, Goldfield, and Bullfrog. No new agricultural district is more prominently in the eye of the home seeker than Carson Valley, watered by the first government canal to reach completion. No railroad developments now in progress promise more revolutionary results in opening rich, but hitherto idle, natural resources to human conquest, than the "Clark Road," which traverses the neglected empire of southern Nevada, the Western Pacific, which is to cross the State from east to west, and the lines which have been extended into the new and flourishing mining camps near the southwestern border. And few indeed are the towns which show a stronger pulse-beat than Reno, the commercial capital of the State.

No division of the Union has been so persistently and grossly misunderstood as the big sage-brush commonwealth which lies between Utah and California—two States of unusual human interest. The popular impression of Nevada has been largely created by those whose opinion of its scenery and resources is based on their experience of a railroad flight across its wide expanse. They glance impatiently out of the car window, inhale some alkali dust, and then denounce the region as "only fit to hold the earth together." If they happen to be literary artists, they vent their disgust in some such striking phrases as these, employed by a popular writer in a recent novel:

> "For beauty and promise, Nevada is a name among names. Nevada! Pronounce the word aloud. Does it not evoke mountains and clear air, heights of untrodden snow and valleys aromatic with the pine and musical with falling waters? Nevada! But the name is all. Abomination of desolation presides over nine-tenths of the place. The sun beats down on a roof of zinc, fierce and dull. Not a drop of water to a mile of sand. The mean ash-dump landscape stretches on from nowhere to nowhere, a spot of mange. No portion of the earth is more lacquered with paltry, unimportant ugliness."

What a difference in human souls! The man who sees a "spot of mange" in God's handiwork only reflects the spot of mange within himself, and shows how his own intelligence is "lacquered with paltry, unimportant ugliness." John C. Van Dyke looks upon the same scenes and then writes, in that classic, "The Desert:"

> "Not in vain these wastes of sand. And this time not because they develop character in desert life, but simply because they are beautiful in themselves and good to look upon whether they be life or death. In sublimity—the superlative degree of beauty—what land can equal the desert with its wide plains, its grim mountains, and its expanding canopy of sky! You shall never see elsewhere as here the dome, the pinnacle, the minaret fretted with golden fire at sunrise and sunset; you shall never see elsewhere as here the sunset valleys swimming in a pink and lilac haze, the great mesas and plateaus fading into blue distance, the gorges and canyons banked full of purple shadow. Never again shall you see such light and air and color; never such opaline mirage, such rosy dawn, such fiery twilight. . . . Look out from the mountain's edge once more. A dusk is gathering on the

desert's face, and over the eastern horizon the purple shadow of the world is reaching up to the sky. The light is fading out. Plain and mesa are blurring into unknown distances, and mountain-ranges are looming dimly into unknown heights. Warm drifts of lilac-blue are drawn like mists across the valleys; the yellow sands have shifted into a pallid gray. The glory of the wilderness has gone down with the sun. Mystery—that haunting sense of the unknown—is all that remains."

The difference between these two authors is only a difference in development. The one beholds a sealed book; the other understands. Nevada is typical of the whole desert region between the Rockies and the Western Ocean. To those who cannot comprehend its strange ensemble it is undeniably ugly, but to those who can comprehend, it is a land stamped with a beauty full of endless surprises. These latter are not necessarily cultured Van Dykes. They may be men who have never studied art or even read a book. Many a Piute Indian has looked upon the deserts and mountains of Nevada with a comprehension utterly denied to the novelist who beholds nothing in the scene except a "mean ash-dump landscape."

Even the fleeting railroad tourist might correct his superficial impression of Nevada's worthlessness by getting out of the car occasionally. Let him step off for a few moments to enjoy the cool fragrance of the little oasis at Humboldt, to walk within the shade of its trees and hear the music of its waters. The little patch of green which a hillside spring has spoken into being is a sample of what millions of desert acres will become. Farther on, the west-bound traveler catches a twilight glimpse of the thriving farms of Lovelock or the green Truckee meadows. But the larger examples of irrigation lie off the beaten path. Such an instance is the Carson Valley, hidden between the sheltering shoulders of the Sierras. To appreciate the possibilities of the region, the critic should visit that valley in the perfect Nevada springtime and look upon its farms, its homes, and its villages. There he would behold a memorable picture of thrift, of beauty, and of peace, from the white blossoms in the dooryards to the white summits of the mountains, and there he might read the true prophecy of Nevada's future.

Nevada farmers are very prosperous on the average, taking one year with another, and probably much more so than the farmers in more pretentious localities. For the most part, they were poor when they came and have grown steadily better off. The climate is perfectly adapted to the production of all the cereals and hardy fruits. The wheat is perfect, with a full, rich kernel and a clean, golden straw, free from smut and rust. It has taken prizes at all the great expositions. With a variety of soil, on the different slopes of hillside, plain, and valley, there are conditions to meet almost every requirement in an agricultural way within the limitations of climate. It seems absurd to explain that Nevada does not produce oranges, yet the question is sometimes asked by those who only know that Nevada is the next-door neighbor of California. Speaking broadly, Nevada is an elevated plateau in the Great Basin enclosed by the Wasatch Range on the east and the Sierra on the west, having an average altitude of about four thousand feet. Its climate is that of the north temperate zone. The winter is cold, the summer hot, the springtime marked by showers and high wind, the autumn long and golden. As in other parts of the arid region, the dry air moderates cold and heat, giving man and vegetation the benefits arising from the vigorous qualities of these extremes without the unpleasant effects which are felt in humid districts.

The national irrigation projects in Nevada are described in a later chapter, but it is important to note here the influence which this development must inevitably exert upon the whole social, political, and commercial life of the State. There will be a steady influx of population for many years to come. Farms will be smaller and more intensively cultivated. There will be a corresponding expansion in all lines of business. Social life in the country will lose its frontier characteristics, and political power will gravitate largely into the hands of the hosts of newcomers, drawn from many different parts of the United States. Owing their opportunities to the first great national experiment in the public ownership of utilities essential to industrial development, it would be strange indeed if this new population—the dominant element of the future—does not favor very advanced ideas in politics. . . .

Standing on the height above the roaring Truckee at Reno, in the midst of fragrant alfalfa fields and well fruited orchards, but little imagination is required to behold the Nevada of the future which is now rapidly rising on the Nevada of the past. A big, splendid, American State, blest with the climate in which English-speaking man has won nearly all his triumphs, except that its skies are cleared by aridity and its sunshine brightened by altitude, a land full of prosperous little farms, tilled by their owners, mountains pouring out their annual tribute of gold and silver, towns large enough to offer the refinements of modern life yet small enough to escape the awful contrasts between superfluous wealth and hopeless poverty, and a people so economically freed and politically untrammeled that they may make their institutions what they will,—this is the Nevada of the future. . . .

Truckee-Carson Project, Nevada

What is known as "the Truckee-Carson project" will ultimately irrigate 375,000 acres at a cost of about $9,000,000. Nine years will be required to bring it to completion. The portion of the works put into operation on June 17th, 1905, will distribute water to about 50,000 acres and represents a cost of about $1,750,000.

The main canal now in operation diverts the water from the channel of the Truckee at a point twenty-four miles east of Reno and conveys it through the divide to the Carson River, a distance of thirty-one miles. This canal has a capacity for the first six miles of its course of 1400 cubic feet per second, or 70,000 miner's inches under a four-inch pressure, and, for the remainder of its course, of 1200 cubic feet per second. There are three tunnels, all lined with concrete, as are two miles of the canal outside of the tunnels. The main canal discharges its water into a natural reservoir on the Carson and flows thence four and one-half miles to the diversion dam at the head of the distributing system, where it is led out upon the land in two wide-reaching canals, one on each side of the river. The canal on the north side has a capacity of 450 cubic feet per second. With their main branches, these waterways will ultimately have a total length of over 90 miles, while the laterals and drain-ditches to be constructed in Carson Sink Valley alone will aggregate fully 1200 miles.

The dam in the Carson at the head of the distributing system is something to bring a smile of satisfaction to the faces of those who have known the crude brush dams of the pioneers and the endless difficulties which arose from them. This government dam is a solid concrete structure, built for a thousand years. It furnishes an absolute guaranty of a permanent water supply to the settlers. This, indeed, is the character of all the work the Government has done.

The land to be irrigated is located in a number of valleys along the Truckee and Carson Rivers, extending on each side from the Central Pacific Railroad, the greatest distance from the road being twenty-five miles. The soil is adapted to alfalfa and other forage crops, potatoes, onions, beets, and other vegetables, apples, pears, berries, and similar hardy fruit.

Nearly all the land now irrigated was public property until recently filed upon, after the works were undertaken. Some of it is still open, but this condition will not continue long. No price is charged for the land, except filing fees, which are nominal. But the settler must repay the cost of irrigation in ten annual installments, without interest. This amounts to $26 an acre, of which about $10 an acre has been incurred by the provision of drainage facilities, made imperatively necessary as a means of removing the heavy alkali deposits. The settler is fortunate to be able to make his home where conditions have been scientifically ascertained in advance and where the best engineering skill, together with abundant capital, have been available to make the most thorough preparation for his success. . . .

from "Jeffries vs. Johnson"
(1910)

Arthur Ruhl

The first sports "star" in American history was arguably the charismatic prizefighter John L. Sullivan. In 1891, his career nearing an end, Sullivan issued a famous challenge to "all comers" in hopes of landing a large final payday. His challenge, however, was explicit: "In this challenge I include all fighters—first come, first served, who are white. I will not fight a negro. I never have and never shall." Sullivan considered himself the "Champion of White America." Thus it was only fitting that when the first heavyweight championship bout featuring an African-American pugilist was held in the United States, Sullivan was in the audience. Because prizefighting remained illegal in most states, Reno was one of few locations where this much-proclaimed "Fight of the Century" could be held. Warmly welcomed by state and city leaders, promoter Tex Rickard constructed a 20,000-seat pavilion near the railroad tracks on the east edge of Reno, and on fight day it was filled to capacity. In 1908, Texas native Jack Johnson had easily won the championship from Tommy Burns in a one-sided mismatch in Sydney, Australia. Race-conscious Americans were appalled that an African American had captured the symbolically important title, and a frantic search for a "Great White Hope" who could wrest the crown from Johnson was launched. That quest ultimately settled upon retired former champion Jim Jeffries, then living on a farm in northern California. The massive pre-fight media coverage emphasized racial angles, with many "experts" employing crude stereotypes to predict a Jeffries victory. However, Johnson was a superb boxer, much younger than the ex-champ and in better physical condition. For fourteen rounds he pummeled his prey and Jeffries did not come out for the fifteenth round. As journalist Arthur Ruhl reported, Johnson's major foe that day was not Jeffries, but rather the hostile racial environment in which he found himself. Fearing retribution, between rounds Johnson instructed one of his assistants to book train tickets for that evening. When reports of the fight reached several southern towns, white thugs attacked blacks to vent their frustrations. In Reno things remained calm as the distraught Jeffries fans consoled themselves in the taverns that dotted the downtown district of the small, frontier western town that, for a day at least, was the focus of the nation's attention.

RENO, NEVADA, JULY 4, 1910. The battle about which whole wood-pulp libraries have been written during the past few months is over, and the great Jeffries myth has vanished into the bright Nevada sunshine. As Mr. Jeffries himself and innumerable experts have stated repeatedly that one-time champion was never fitter in his life, one novice hesitates to dim the luster of his rival's achievement by concluding that he didn't "come back." Nevertheless, the fact remains whether or not the result was the due to Mr. Johnson's admittably exquisite technique or to his possession of that divine fire of youth which once lost is never found again, that in the fifteenth round the "hope of the white race, "with his crouch and his glare and all his hairy brown bulk, hung over the ropes by his knees in a position quite primordial enough to satisfy even the red-blood novelists who have written so eloquently of late in the sporting pages of neolithic men and the jungle-born. And above him, with superb muscles of that terrifying left arm and shoulder taut and trembling to continue the battle if need be, stood the black man, Johnson—"Lil' Artha," with the queer, flat-footed shuffle that only masked the quickness of a cat, "Lil' Artha" of the bass-viol and the crap-shooting and the half-puzzled, pleading, rather wistful smile —the undoubted champion.

As a mere fight, this battle for the greatest purse that two boxers ever fought for was, I suppose a pretty sad affair; but as an event, a drama of temperaments, an example of the phenomena possible in this year of grace 1910, it was as strange and as wildly romantic as any one child could desire. . . .

Every night for a week before between 100,000 and 150,000 words— two popular novels—to be doubled many times before they reached the newspapers to which they were telegraphed—went out to the world from Reno.

In addition to the regular war correspondents, most of the prize-fighters temporarily disengaged from the practice of their profession were also writing daily critiques for the papers. Some, to be sure, merely contributed the color of their signatures and photographs while weary but more articulate reporters did the actual work; but there was at least one shining exception and the sight of Mr. Battling Nelson, with his cauliflower ears growing redder and redder as he struggled nightly in the intricacies of the literary art with the public stenographer in the crowded lobby of the Hotel Golden, was one of fight's most fascinating pictures.

And this had been going on more of less similarly not only for days but for months. Several newspapers had regular office headquarters, as at a political convention. One San Francisco paper had fourteen fabulously-paid special writers, including two red-blood novelists, one of whom was accompanied by a manager at least, if not by a trainer, and all trying to say each day the same thing in fourteen different ways. One of its rivals, not to be outdistanced, threw its papers off the train into an automobile on the west side of the Sierras and shot through the night over Nevada and to Reno two hours ahead of the train. These two newspaper automobiles raced over the same course, and after that another paper loaded its papers into an automobile as they fell from the presses in San Francisco at two o'clock in the morning, flew clear across California and over the mountains, and arrived in Reno the next afternoon considerably ahead of the train.

There were correspondents from London and Australia, and even M. Dupuy, of the Paris "Figaro," traveled across those American deserts, mysterious and immeasurable, "to observe M. Jeff and M. Jack Johnson make the box." One overland train, white with alkali dust, would pull in with Big Tim Sullivan of New York or Charlie Millet of Mullen Centre, Iowa, and his friend Bill. Another would come in from the West and out would step a little band of Australians, speaking a quaint, modified cockney of the colonies.

And fighters were so thick that as you pushed through the mob in front of the Golden, with the faro chips and roulette wheels clicking in Jim May's and the Fafner-like bellowing of the megaphone filling the street with betting odds, you always looked first at each man's left ear to see whether it was lopped over and grown together like an oyster or the ordinary non-fighting man.

No one who was not there can easily understand what a curiously enthralling drama a simple fight can be made into when thus isolated in a quiet little desert city and analyzed, colored, and vitalized by the nervous cumulative intelligence of two or three hundred keen and imaginative men with nothing else to do. All the raw material was there. They only needed to be made interesting.

On the one hand was this brown Colossus of a white man, not a fighter in the "scrappy" sense of the word, rather a sort of grizzly bear, bored by people and photographers and noise, and much preferring to bury himself in the mountains and fish. He didn't want to fight again. Public clamor made him.

And yet you had but to look at that vast hairy body, those legs like trees, the long projecting jaw, deep-set scowling eyes, and wide, thin, cruel mouth, to know that here was an animal who would stand up and give battle as long as it could see, whom cleverness could not ruffle, nor blows dismay.

A Caged Bear

There was nothing winsome about Jeffries. He was as surly and ugly as a caged bear. He would ride past you on a country road, returning alone from a fishing trip crouched in the rear seat of his automobile, swarthly, glowering, chewing gum, and never so much as notice your greeting by the flicker of an eyelid. After the machine had stopped at the gate of his training quarters and a crowd of harmlessly demented admirers had gathered about it, he would sometimes sit there without moving for five or ten minutes, still glowering straight ahead, chewing gum and seeing only, as it seemed, the vision of his black rival coming to meet him across the ring. There was something peculiarly sinister in this static ferocity, and he did not lessen the impression when he climbed down at last and walked slowly away, seeing no one, with his huge right arm partly contracted and slowly sawing the air as if aimed for a blow. . . .

"Lil' Artha" Johnson, the negro, was as different as could be. About twenty pounds lighter than Jeffries, with a rather lathy underbody and superb shoulders and arms, he was as smooth and sleek and supple as a seal just coming out of the water. Light-hearted, humorous, witty even as he showed—even during the thick of the battle—when any one ventured to engage him in repartee, he yet had the good sense or cleverness to keep the respectful ingratiating ways of the Southern darkey. He was quiet, well-mannered, generous in what he said of his opponent, and, indeed, not without an almost winsome charm.

In the ring he at once became fascinating. There was mystery in that slow, flat-footed shuffle, in the way his gloves, moving slowly about his opponent's biceps, turned like lightning either to block a lead or shoot in a blow. With seemingly indolent grace and his drowsy smile, he would stand up before George Cotton, his big black sparring partner, and catch and turn aside a rain of blows as easily as a big brother might play pease-porridge-hot with his little sister, Once during the fight, when Jeffries started a left swing for the wind that looked enough to fell an ox, the negro caught it in just the same way, and Jeffries's arm stopped as his biceps met the black man's right as neatly as if it were a ball settling into a catcher's glove.

The Impulse of Traditions

But what it was thought he didn't have—and this is what made the fight between the mature thinking white man and the light-hearted, seemingly careless, negro most interesting—was that dogged courage and intellectual initiative which is the white man's inheritance. For in any supreme effort there comes a moment when cleverness and technique count for nothing and the issue is decided by that something which goes down through panting lungs and beating heart and straining muscles and calls for the very core and soul of the man. And it is here, other things being equal, that a negro is always at a disadvantage. He has no traditions behind him. He stands alone. The white man has thirty centuries of traditions behind him—all the supreme efforts, the inventions and conquests, and whether he knows it or not, Bunker Hill and Thermopylae and Hastings and Agincourt.

You should have seen Mr. Mike Murphy throw back his head, close one eye tight shut, and with just a crack showing in the other like the eye of some curious withered, wise old bird, and with insight gained from training generations of runners and football men, go straight to the heart of things in his crackling, half-quizzical drawl. He didn't believe even when the talk was wildest, that Jeffries could come back. "No man ever did," he would say, "and no man ever will. There are three things you can't beat—nature, instinct and death."

Fighting with the Mind

He thought the negro ought to win. He had the strength and skill, yet he couldn't quite make himself sure of that seemingly vague good-humored will.

"*Mind!*" he said to me one day, squinting through the half-opened eye and tapping his temple with one finger, "it's all mind. If you go into a contest with your mind right, you've got the other man beaten already. And that negro," he waved his hands vaguely, "loose! No concentration. If he don't wake up, he might get knocked out in the first round. Look at Jeffries. He's going into a fight. Temperament, that's the whole thing. Give me eleven men and time enough and I'll put into their hearts the idea that they are going to win and you can't beat 'em. That's what training is. Roosevelt would make a good trainer."

"Ha!" he crackled, "that's the way we used to beat Harvard—we had 'em beaten when we came onto the field." He tapped his chest mysteriously. "Here."

Here was a man of the imagination and parts. In the contagious bite and snap of his words was the very mysticism and poetry of fighting. . . .

The betting was 10 to 6 or 7 on Jeffries and the talk about 1,000 to 1. You couldn't hurt him—Fitzsimmons had landed enough times to kill an ordinary man in the first few rounds, and Jeffries had only shaken his head like a bull and bored in. The negro might be a clever boxer, but he had never been up against a real fighter before. He had a yellow streak, there was nothing to it, and anyway, "let's hope he kills the coon."

A Scowling Brown Colossus

That was about the mental atmosphere as Lil' Artha, wrapped in a dressing-gown and smiling his half-puzzled, rather pleading smile, climbed into the ring. Old Billy Jordan, who has been announcing fights for fifty years or so, was just introducing the negro to the buzzing, hostile audience, when Jeffries, with a cloud of seconds and camp-followers behind him, climbed through the ropes.

I had a seat at the ringside, directly opposite him, and I can unhesitatingly state that I have never seen a human being more calculated to strike terror into an opponent's heart than this scowling brown Colossus as he came through the ropes, stamped like a bull pawing the ground before his charge, and chewing gum rapidly, glared at the black man across the ring.

If looks could have throttled, burned and torn to pieces, Mr. Jack Arthur Johnson would have disappeared that instant into a few specks of inanimate dust. The negro had his back turned at the moment, as he was being presented to the crowd on the opposite side. He did not turn round, and as he took his corner and his trainer and seconds, crowding in front of him, concealed the white man a sort of hoot, wolfish and rather terrible, went up from the crowed. "He darsen't look at him! O-o-o! Don't let him see him! Don't let him see him!" And when Jeffries pulled off his clothes with a vicious jerk, and standing erect and throwing out his chest, jabbed his great arms above his head once or twice, I don't suppose that one man in a hundred in that crowd would have given two cents for the negro's chances.

Nor did many suspect until Johnson's left shot across to the white man's right eye in the sixth round and closed it—so strong and convincing was the Jeffries tradition, the contagion of the atmosphere, and that crouching, scowling gladiator—that the negro's finish was anything but a matter of time.

They had all seen or heard of that short, rather slow, piston-rod-like punch which the white man knew how to send with a tremendous, if not spectacular, force into his opponent's side just under the lower right ribs. They saw him send it in, time and again apparently, and each time the crowd gave a sort of subdued, exultant grunt. When Johnson supposed he must be shamming, and when those uppercuts of his shot up like lightning, they thought it was merely pretty, but didn't hurt.

When that blow got across in the sixth round, however, the cynicism of the white man's glare suddenly went dead and changed. His right eye blackened and closed, and the blood began to run down from his right nostril. He was fighting after that not to finish his opponent, but to save himself, to stave off what he probably knew, if the crowd did not yet suspect, nothing but chance could save him from. Mr. Jim Corbett, who as Jeffries second and following the quaint sportsmanship of the ring, had gone across to the corner nearest the Negro between each of the earlier rounds to fix him with a sneering eye and wittily taunt and terrify him lost his bright vaudeville smile. Once, when he called out to Johnson during a round, the negro laughing across Jeffries shoulder, gave him as good as he sent. Once a man far up in the seats called down to Johnson, "Why don't you smile now?" and the negro, who seemed to know everything that was going on in and out of the ring without at any time paying close attention, deliberately turned his head and smiled. He looked fierce occasionally, but that was only when he feinted. When something real and dangerous was to be done, he was apparently dreaming placidly as the flowers of May.

A Mirage for the Multitude

The rest is an old story now—how the big man, bleeding, beaten, but glaring stubbornly out of his one good eye, bored steadily in as the bull charges the matador toward the end of his fight: how suddenly, the main drama about which had gathered such a curiously, modern and top-heavy mountain of accessories, rushed to its swift and unexpected conclusion. In the thirteenth round the crafty black turned loose for a moment, and it was all over then but the shouting.

In the fourteenth and fifteenth rounds, however, the old champion came crouching back, groggy but willing: in the fifteenth there was a quick clash, and all at once his tree-like legs caved-in, and the great hairy-brown hulk, which had never been knocked down before nor beaten, sank close to the ropes. The crowd didn't cheer. It rose and stood and stared as if the solid ground beneath it were turning to a mirage.

At the count of nine Jeffries got to his feet, only to be sent back again, this time between the ropes. His camp followers forgetting themselves in the desperation of the moment, pushed him to his feet, but it was only to stagger across the ring and go down again, and for the last time on the other side.

They lifted the fallen idol and slapped his big shoulders and led him away; men rushed down and hopped over the sputtering telegraph instruments to cut the ropes and floor canvas into souvenirs, and Mr. Jack Arthur Johnson, with only a slightly cut lip, rode back to camp in his automobile with a harder road ahead of him than any he ever yet has traveled—the gilded, beguiling pathway of him who is not climbing but has arrived.

The After-Effect

The white race, whose supremacy this contest was going to establish, must, naturally, have been as dead as the Aztecs or the Incas; but the representatives of it in Reno seemed to battle their way into the overflowing restaurants to-night with their usual interest to smoke their black cigars with their customary zest, and gaze out at the pink and lavender lights turning to purple and ashes the distant mountains with the usual air of equanimity. They reasoned, I believe, that there hadn't been any fight, that Jeffries was only a shell of a man, and it wasn't certain that they were convinced that he even had any arms.

That was all very well after the event and for those who forget how things stood and when the battle opened. But any one who happened to see from Johnson's corner, the face of Jim Jeffries as he climbed into the ring, and felt the focused mind and heard the taunts and jeers of the hostile crowd, knows that it took something more than boxing skill for that black man to go out and meet his fate; that he had concentration right enough if it didn't show on the outside, and stood on his own feet and thought for himself, and fought and vanquished a brave opponent cleanly and like a brave man.

"These United States—VIII"[1]

"Nevada: Beautiful Desert of Buried Hopes" (1922)

Anne Martin

Anne Martin was born in 1875 in the small mining town of Empire, located on the banks of the Carson River near the present-day town of Dayton. Her father relocated the family to the emerging railroad town of Reno in 1883 and operated a thriving mercantile store. She received the best of educations available, eventually taking a master's degree in European History at Stanford University before returning to Reno in 1897 to teach at the recently opened state university. Intensely inter-ested in political affairs, she gravitated to the major woman's issue of the day: securing the right to vote. After several years in England, where she participated in the feminist activities led by Emmeline Pankhurst, Martin returned to Reno in 1911 and became a leader of the Nevada Equal Franchise Movement. In 1914, the state's male vot-ers approved an amendment to the State Constitution granting women the right to vote. In 1918, Martin shocked traditionalists by launching an independent campaign for the United States Senate. Her progressive platform included support for organized labor, pro-tections for women workers, expansion of child welfare programs, and educational reform. She wanted to demonstrate that women could succeed in politics, but won only 25 percent of the vote when the anticipated "sex solidarity" behind her candidacy proved unfounded. She ran again in 1920 with the same result. Hurt, if not angered, by the sexist newspaper editorials and "news" stories that maligned her campaigns, Martin moved to Carmel on the California coast. From a self-imposed exile, in 1922 she joined a long list of distinguished writers who wrote extended essays in The Nation *examining life in each of the 48 states. Her bluntly critical appraisal of Nevada's political and economic situation completed her estrangement from her native state. Until far-reaching economic reform took place in "the weakling in the family of States," she predicted, Nevada would remain "inert and hopeless like an exhausted Titan in the sun—a beautiful desert of homeseekers' buried hopes." The response from leading Nevadans was predictably vitriolic, and Martin lived in Carmel until her death in 1951.*

Nevada to most Easterners suggests divorces, or gambling in mining shares of doubtful value on the New York or Philadelphia stock exchanges. Some, more informed, have heard of our "big bonanza" mines which produced nearly a billion dollars in silver after the Civil War, thus helping to restore national credit, and incidentally producing a crop of millionaires and adventurers, some of whom have won seats in the United States Senate. The "wild and woolly" character of the pioneer mining State fixed on her by Mark Twain in "Roughing It" still clings in the popular mind and is confirmed by most of the news that seeps through the press. Few outsiders have ever heard of her agriculture or any constructive activities, and no one with eyes can see her as anything but a vast, exploited, undeveloped State with a meager and boss-ridden population. Those who wish more information will find in reference books that Nevada began well. She was admitted into the Union in 1864 as the "battle-born State," to give President Lincoln additional support in the Senate, and with her vast domain and natural resources gave great promise. Almost as old as Kansas, Minnesota, and West Virginia, and older than Nebraska, Colorado, the Dakotas, Montana, and all other Far Western States except California and Oregon, "youth" cannot explain away her backwardness and vagaries, her bizarre history, her position as the ugly duckling, the disappointment, the neglected step-child, the weakling in the family of States, despite her charm and beauty and great natural advantages.

The casual railway traveler who has crossed Nevada remembers with wonder or weariness, according to temperament, her twelve hours of "desert" plain, her endless chain of sunny sage-brush valleys surrounded by opalescent mountains, all fertile land but valueless without water, and all without sign of water or habitation, excepting a few railroad tanks and straggling towns, or the drying bed of a river. Reformers know her as perhaps the most "wide-open" State of the West, where prize-fighting, gambling, and saloons have been encouraged greatly to flourish, and where the six-months' divorce still reigns, backed by legal and business interests of Reno. They remember her as the last Western State to adopt woman suffrage, and one of the last to accept State prohibition. She is the despair not only of reformers but of case-hardened lawyers, who must be agile indeed to keep pace with the rapid and contradictory changes in laws made every two years by servile legislatures, at the command of the selfish interests which elected them. To national political leaders she is known as a "doubtful" State, a "pocket-borough," which can be swung more easily than any other into the Republican or Democratic column, according to the amount of money used by either side. (She should therefore not be called "doubtful," but *sure*.) She is known as a State where politicians, irrespective of party, cynically combine every campaign to elect congressmen and legislatures pleasing to the "interests." These legislatures so chosen are largely migratory. Some members have been known to leave the State, pockets bulging, by the midnight train after adjournment. I recall the difficulty experienced by a former governor in securing a quorum for a special session, as many of our itinerant legislators were already far afield in other States, or in Mexico, Alaska, South America, and South Africa.

It must be admitted that there are other Western States which differ only in degree. But what makes Nevada an extreme example? Why has she a larger proportionate number of migratory laborers (as of legislators), of homeless men, than any of her neighbors? Why is she the most "male" State in the Union, with more than twice as many men as women, and the smallest proportionate number of women and children? Why has she the smallest and sparsest population of any State, and why has it decreased since 1910? Why has she a peripatetic male electorate nearly half of which has vanished by the next election, with new voters taking their places who will themselves soon vanish? Why is she perhaps the most backward State in precautions against the spread of venereal diseases, the most shameless in her flaunting of prostitution and red-light districts, surrounded by high board fences, to the children of the towns? With no large cities and a largely rural population, why has she a greater percentage in her jails and prison, her almshouses and insane asylum than certain of her neighbors? How can we account for these extreme peculiarities of her industrial, political, and social life?

The migratory character of mining and railway labor has some influence, but the fundamental cause of every one of these conditions undoubtedly lies in the monopoly by the live-stock industry of the water, the watered lands, and the public range lands of the State. At first blush this may sound like saying that sun-spots cause insanity, or that there is an epidemic of pellagra in the South, of small-pox in China, or of cholera in Russia because Wall Street governs us in Washington. But the relation of cause and effect in Nevada is clear. Some may insist that her backwardness is due to her exploitation from the very beginning by the railroads; others, that the mining interests have picked the vitals from her, have taken everything out and given nothing back: witness San Francisco's and even some of New York's finest structures built largely with bullion from her "ghost cities," the Postal Telegraph and Cable system which girdles the globe by means of the Mackay millions taken from the quickly gutted Comstock lode, the Guggenheim and other similar interests still picking the bones for all that is left! True; but mere exploitation by railroads and mine owners does not account for the condition in which we find her today. Other Western States with comparable natural resources have been similarly exploited, and are not a "notorious bad example" of political, economic, and social degeneration.

The livestock industry, established as a monopoly in Nevada under very extraordinary conditions, is responsible. It has prevented the development of small farms, of family life, of a stable agricultural population, and has produced instead an excessive proportion of migratory laborers and of homeless men, larger than any State in the Union. The 1910 census figures give 220 men to every 100 women. The number of married women in the State is about one-third the number of men. The number of children from six to fourteen years is less than two-fifths of the usual average in other States. Utah, for example, with natural resources not much larger than Nevada, has more than eight times as many school children. (The 1920 census figures so far received show an improvement in these proportions more apparent than real, due chiefly to the reduction of the homeless male population since 1910 by the migration of thousands from dying mining camps.) It appears that practically one-half of the men of Nevada, or nearly 20,000 out of our total population of nearly 80,000, are living under bad social conditions outside the home environment, as cowboys, sheepherders, hay-hands, miners, and railwaymen, sleeping in company bunk-houses or on the range, and dependent for their few pleasures and social contacts on the frontier towns the traveler sees from the train window. These afford a movie, perhaps, certainly a gambling house with bootleg whiskey, and a "restricted district" behind a stockade, in which the woman are "medically inspected" (for a price) while the men are not.

A characteristic Nevada sight, and to those who know its signifi-cance one of the most pathetic, is the large groups of roughly dressed men aimlessly wandering about the streets or standing on the street corners of Reno, Lovelock, Winnemucca, Battle Mountain, Elko, Wells, Ely, Tonopah, Goldfield, and other towns, every day in the year. They are in from the ranches and mines for a holiday with hard-earned money, and the only place they have to spend it is in the numerous men's lodging houses, gambling dens, or brothels. In our suffrage cam-paign in 1914 and in later campaigns we found it always possible to gather these men into a quick, responsive, and generous street audi-ence. But a large proportion of them are wanderers, and are, of course, prevented from voting by the election laws. Of those who can vote many have most naturally no sense of civic responsibility and are eas-ily corrupted by the political machine. If instead of the land and water monopoly by the live-stock interests for the almost exclusive produc-tion of hay, cattle, and sheep, this same land with water, now manned chiefly by "ranch-hands" and in the hay-making season by a large influx of migratory hay-hands, were subdivided into small farms for diversified and intensive agriculture, Nevada would soon have many new homes with women and children in them, she would soon have a large and growing farm population, larger towns and community cen-ters, and greater social stability, instead of languishing on as an exhausted weakling in the sisterhood of States. But the strangle-hold of the livestock interests continues as the cause of the mortal illness from which she is suffering, and to grasp the case we must consider some physical features.

Nevada's area is 110,000 square miles, more than twice as large as New York or Pennsylvania. Her population is 77,000, or about one per-son to every one and one-half square miles. Her *land* area is more than 70,000,000 acres, of which nearly 90 per cent is still owned by the National Government. The remainder is chiefly land granted by the Government to the railroad, with the exception of a little more than 3 per cent, or about 2,300,000 acres, which are reported in privately owned farms in 1920. Of this amount nearly 600,000 acres, or less than 1 per cent of the total land area, are under irrigation. The water for this purpose is supplied chiefly by Nevada's four rivers, the Truckee, Carson, and Walker, which rise in the Sierra Nevada Mountains, and the Humboldt, which rises in the northeast. The snow-fall in the mountain ranges which traverse the State north and south produces in addition a few small springs and streams. These water part of the valley lands. It has been estimated that the State has enough water, if carefully conserved and used, to irrigate 2,000,000 acres, or about 3 per cent of her area. But owing to the great cost of constructing the necessary dams and reservoirs for the storage of flood waters, and the dams and ditches for its distribution, and because of waste of water by many users, the irrigated area is not increasing. According to the 1920 census it has decreased. The vital fact is that about 97 per cent of the State's enormous area has no agricultural value except as grazing land for cattle and sheep (unless water can be developed from new sources such as artesian wells), and that the National Government owns nearly all of the grazing land. Uncle Sam owns it, but a few live-stock companies monopolize its use for their herds. This is made possible by the fact that the law under which government grants of school lands to Nevada were administered enabled certain stockmen to select practically all the land with water, so as to control all water available for irrigation and drinking purposes for livestock. Unlike other States, the Nevada law controlling the sale of the millions of acres granted by the Government enabled a stockman to pick out only the forty-acre tracts with water on them. He could buy 640 acres directly, and get as much more as he wanted by using the names of relatives and employees—"dummies." The price of the land was $1.25 an acre, but only 25 cents had to be paid down, with long time for the balance. So a man with $5,000 could buy 25,000 acres, carefully selected in forty-acre tracts along the banks of rivers and streams, and through this water monopoly he could secure the exclusive control of a million acres of public range land as free pasture for his herds. In other states the government land grants consisted of numbered sections according to United States surveys, and buyers could not pick out exclusively the areas with water. (The bill granting 7,000,000 acres of government land to Nevada, which passed the United States Senate in 1916 through the efforts of Senator Pittman, was drawn on similarly vicious lines. It would have increased the hold of the land and water monopolies and large-scale live-stock producers on the people.)

Thus was fixed the strangle-hold of the live-stock interests on Nevada. A few families and corporations control nearly all her many million acres of range land (97 per cent of the State's area) through their control of the water, and own most of the watered land. Trespassers are kept off by the laws of nature, as they cannot use the pasture unless they have drinking water, or if necessary, by the "law of the range," as shown by many past conflicts of stockmen with their small competitors. With rare exceptions like the Newlands irrigation project at Fallon, Truckee Meadows, and a few other valleys early settled in small and fertile farms by the pioneers, this monopoly has made Nevada practically one large and desolate live-stock ranch. But deliberately or unconsciously its population of homeless workers has taken its revenge, as told by Nevada's overflowing jails and prison, her almshouses and insane asylum, by her lack of political, economic, and social stability, by the most backward position of all the States. No society can allow its natural resources to be monopolized and neglect its workers without paying a heavy price. As Professor Romanzo Adams points out,[2] in no other State is there such concentration of land ownership in a few families, or are there so few farmers. In no other State is the average size of farms, and the average number of cattle or sheep on each farm, so large. And in no other State are there so many migratory farm workers in proportion to the number of farms. "Nevada has from two to six times as large a percentage in prison, jails, almshouses, and hospital for the insane as certain neighboring States where farms and farm homes are numerous and migratory workers few."[3] Paupers, insane, and prisoners are largely recruited from the migratory workers. But the sorry population of her institutions does not tell the full story of damage done. Thousands more must have been maimed in body and soul, and roam free to spread the social canker, while the State continues to decrease in population and to deteriorate in nearly all that increases human welfare.

What is the remedy? Will the live-stock interests subdivide their holdings? Will pigs fly? The stockman's motto is "What I have I hold," down to the last drop of water. I have seen large quantities of it overflowing the ditches and running to waste on the fields and roads of company ranches, producing a rich crop of willows and tules after irrigating the wild hay lands. Across the road were scattered "dugouts" and cabins of settlers who under great difficulties had cleared a few acres of sage-brush land. They were struggling to "prove up" and sustain life for their families and themselves on a "dry" farm, as their entire water supply was from a well. Staring at us through the sage-brush or clinging to their mother's skirts were two or three eerie little children, timid as jack-rabbits, growing up without school or toys, in ignorance even of children's games. Sooner or later these settlers are starved out, as Nevada is literally the "driest" State in the Union (as regards rainfall), and dry-farming is hopeless. These failures please the large owners; they do not want homesteaders "fussing about," fencing the land on their own government range, and breaking the continuity of their holdings. I know intrepid settlers who have hoarded trickles from mountain streams and seepage that would otherwise be wasted, and used it to water crops on their homesteads, into which they had put years of work and all their meager capital. But they were enjoined at the behest of the neighboring live-stock company from using the hoarded water, on the ground of "prior rights." I have seen them denied its use and lose everything in court. Only their cabin home and the parched land with its withered crops were left them. The manager of this company replied to my protest: "This is *our* country, and we don't want any damned squatters and water stealers around interfering with our water and range and settling it up. We'd *run* them out if we couldn't get rid of them any other way!" However, it is generally not necessary "to run them out," as under our big-business system of government, national and State, the natural resource monopolists, the banks, and the courts are of course in cahoots, and the verdict is to the strong.

We have in Nevada some laws that automatically keep water away from the land and the settler. On one of my campaigns I met a sturdy young fellow climbing out of a tungsten mine in the Humboldt Mountains, who told me with pride of his wife's work as school-teacher to help him in his struggle for a farm and home for their children. "This is no sort of life for a man to lead," he admitted, wiping the yellow dust from his face, and gazing off at the desert. "I've got to live on top of this mountain in a company bunk-house (and pay $40 a month extra for board) instead of having a home. We can't have it until I get water on my land. The water's there in the Humboldt River, but I can't get it." He had filed on 320 acres under the Desert Land Act, "proved up on it" by making the necessary improvements and payments, cleared the land of sage-brush, dug ditches, secured a water right to certain river waters from the State engineer, and put in a crop of wheat which sprouted well but died, because he was not allowed to run water to his ditches. Instead of the profit of $2,000 he was counting on to pay his debts and build a house, he lost several hundred dollars and all his work, and was now struggling as a miner for a fresh start. He took from his pocket a letter from the agent of a land and live-stock company owning adjoining land. It curtly refused his request for a ditch right of way over its land to his. Another company had filed a protest in the State engineer's office against granting his water right because the company "believed" a dam built at the point of diversion of his ditch from the river would back up the water and flood its land, and because his ditches would have to cross numerous company ditches and thereby prevent it "from enjoying the free use of its vested water and ditch rights." Only by winning lawsuits against neighboring land owners—and both cards and courts were stacked against him—could he fill his ditches. "And with water running to waste in the Humboldt Sink," he said bitterly. "We fellows haven't a man's chance, and all we want is a fair show to live by our own work." He held out his large, muscular, calloused hands. "And with the Government wasting billions on airplanes and shipyards and railroads and foreign loans! We're doing some thinking for ourselves!" The tungsten mine has since shut down and he has joined the army of homeless men looking for work, while one of the neighboring land companies has filed on his water right, on the ground that he never put it to beneficial use by raising crops.

I have seen families stoically enduring life in little hot cabins in the heart of a burning desert. A well, a few scraggly chickens, a cow perhaps, and a sparse and parched field of rye or wheat were their only visible means of subsistence. The father of one of these families confessed almost apologetically: "I ain't one of these dry farmers, ma'am. I've got some good wells located and could grow fine crops if I could only get a few hundred dollars for a pump." Throughout the State I found it: on the one hand, men and women who had shown energy and hardihood and a pioneer spirit in their struggle against nature for a meager existence, asking only for water; on the other hand the Government, national and State, indifferent to the crying need for farms, homes, and jobs, doing nothing. The settlers struggle on until they lose everything, the land remains barren and unproductive for lack of a "few hundred dollars for a pump," while underground rivers flow beneath the floor of Nevada's driest looking valleys, and undeveloped artesian water abounds. (Senator Pittman's underground waters bill, recently enacted, reserving the right to any citizen or "association of citizens" to drill for water for two years on land areas of 2,560 acres, thus securing a patent on 640 acres if water is developed, does not help the settler; as a director in one of these water-drilling corporations recently told me: "Only big companies can afford to drill and get land and water on these terms." Several companies have already done so, thus increasing the monopoly in the hands of a few.)

I have seen rivers flooding their banks on their way through barren valleys which in the language of congressmen would "blossom as the rose" with the storage and distribution of this water. The Humboldt River spreads out into a lake at one point, owing to a bad channel, and loses 300,000 acre feet in a few miles, due to evaporation and absorption. This is enough to irrigate 200,000 acres through the season, and provide homes for 2,000 families. Fertile sage-brush lands, but water-less, spread on both sides of the river for miles to the foot of distant mountains, waiting for the homemakers.

Utah has shown our bosses both in Washington and Nevada how to manage large land and water holdings for the public good. It was the policy of the Mormon church to divide good land into small farms. And Utah, with nearly equal agricultural resources, has a much larger population and greater economic and social stability than her neighbor. The Mormon church carried out this policy in Nevada, when a large cattle range of several thousand acres in the eastern part of the State accidentally came into its possession. It planned at once to divide it into a large number of small farms. The Mormon bishop there tells me the church was warned that the colonists would starve, as "the ranch was only fit for cattle." But the colonists came, and the land today supports two villages of more than one hundred families, which are producing diversified crops under sound social conditions, instead of wild hay for cattle at great social cost to a lot of homeless men and to the State.

What is the solution for Nevada's problem? Undoubtedly the Government should end its long neglect of its vast public domain and administer these lands as it recently began the administration of its forest reserves, but in the interest of the small settler. The Government should extend its irrigation projects, providing credits and other necessary aid to settlers during the first difficult years, and, even more important, in cooperation with the State, should buy from the large stockmen tracts of land which control water for live stock. It should manage land, water, and public range with the definite purpose of increasing the number of small farms, of small stockmen, and range users. As Professor Adams suggests, it should also reduce the number of animals pastured on the public range by large owners, which would of course reduce their yearly production and profit and thus lessen the value of their watered lands. Thus the natural operation of economic laws would lead to the subdivision of their holdings. But this will never be done until the people make their bosses see that government, national and State, if it is to endure, must develop natural resources for the good of all, instead of gutting them for the enrichment of a few, to the ultimate injury of all. Until it is done, Nevada's stable population cannot increase; despite the efforts of boosters' clubs and chambers of commerce. She will continue to lie, inert and helpless, like an exhausted Titan in the sun—a beautiful desert of homeseekers' buried hopes.

from *Mining Illusions:*
The Case of Rawhide, Nevada
(2004)

Peter Goin and C. Elizabeth Raymond

Nevada's second major mining boom began in 1900 with discovery of large silver and gold deposits in south-central Nevada. The rush to Tonopah and Goldfield followed the same pattern that had occurred forty years earlier on the Comstock. These mining booms created outlandish expectations and speculations, and without adequate state and federal laws and regulations they produced many examples of fraud in the sale of mining stock. Confidence men found gold-crazed men easy pickings. One of the notorious instances of abuse resulted from the work of George Graham Rice, who arrived in Goldfield in 1904 and promptly created a stock promotion and trust company in which he and his partner, "Shanghai" Larry Sullivan, sold worthless stock hyped by inspired promotional schemes. When the company failed in 1906, he and Sullivan fled to Reno to escape angry investors. From that safe distance, Rice launched another scheme, promoting a new company that he claimed controlled vast gold reserves near the new town of Rawhide. In 1908, a national mining journal exposed Rice and his company for the fraud that it was, and a fire—not an unusual event in mining towns where rickety wooden structures were hastily constructed—wiped out much of the town. Two University of Nevada, Reno scholars have examined the speculative shenanigans that occurred in Rawhide as many an unwary investor was separated from his money.

Mining Illusions

The Case of Rawhide, Nevada

At Rawhide, Nevada, as in Bingham Canyon, a mine has transformed a landscape almost beyond recognition and displaced a town in the process, but there the similarities end. In contrast to Bingham Canyon, where mining has been steady and profitable, Rawhide is an extreme example of mining's capriciousness. Famed as a mining town for a few years in the early twentieth century, when it was touted by newspapers as "The Youngest and Richest Gold Camp on Earth," Rawhide never managed to live up to its reputation until the 1990s. The active mine depicted in this chapter, by contrast, is just over a decade old, and mining ceased in 2003. Reclamation work is scheduled through 2005.[1]

Rather that Bingham's semipermanence, Rawhide exemplifies the relentless boom-and-bust cycle that has stigmatized the mining economy. It is a prime example of mining speculation and promotion, a place that was the self-conscious creation of resident press agents seeking to sell stock rather than the creation of "mining men." Analysis of both historical and contemporary images of Rawhide reveals an interesting case of the mining landscape being used as a self-reflexive promotional device.

The modern Denton-Rawhide Mine in Rawhide is a typical open-pit operation where few of the original contours remain. This gold and silver mine is owned by Kennecott Corporation and two partners. In a story that has become familiar in recent years throughout the western United States, low-grade ore, with gold values averaging only .04 ounces per ton, has become profitable to mine by means of a new cyanide-based, heap-leaching technology. The technique is particularly widespread in Nevada, which has extensive deposits amenable to this form of treatment. As a result, Nevada is the state with the largest percentage of personal income and employment derived from the mining industry.[2]

In heap-leach mining, low-grade ore is removed systematically from a huge open pit. After blasting to loosen it, the rock is crushed, treated, and then piled on a leach pad. There a drip irrigation system distributes a cyanide solution over the heap to extract the precious metals, which are then precipitated out of the solution and processed in an electric induction furnace. A system of liners and drains captures the cyanide solution for reuse and keeps it from contact with the local watershed. The Kennecott Rawhide Mining Company, which operates the Denton-Rawhide Mine, anticipated moving and processing eighty to one hundred million tons of ore and waste rock at this site.[3]

The ratio of waste to ore is tremendous and the physical transformation of the landscape absolute. Disorientation is almost inevitable.
The town and its original canyons have disappeared as entire hillsides
are fed into the crushers. As part of the mine's reclamation plan, new
artificial hillsides are being created nearby from waste rock. Yet
straightforward dislocation is not the only consequence. The town of
Rawhide had atrophied long before the arrival of the current mine
operation and seems to have assumed more importance in retrospect
than it ever held in actual fact. Richard Francaviglia has observed this
phenomenon: "If every culture needs ruins to emphasize its past
accomplishments and its relationship to nature, then our once-
prosperous mining towns are among the most powerful of our cultural symbols."[4] Rawhide, Nevada, a boom town that didn't experience a
genuine boom until eighty years after its founding, and long after its
physical disappearance, is surely among the more curious of such cultural symbols.

Due to spotty and refractory deposits, mining in early Rawhide never
produced much gold. Instead the town was largely the product of
ambitious promoters. Men seeking to encourage investment in
Rawhide capitalized on early discoveries of rich gold ore to position
their camp as the next Tonopah or Goldfield, more distinguished and
genuinely wealthy Nevada towns that had boomed nearby in 1901 and
1904 respectively. As a London geologist tartly summarized the matter
in 1909, when the district was already in decline, "In the wild excitement of its younger days Rawhide won fleeting and intermittent fame
that rose alternatively from gold production and ink consumption."[5]
　　Rawhide, in short, was famous for being famous, depicted almost
from the moment of its establishment as a stereotype, the quintessen-
tial western mining boom camp. In contrast to the process described
by Duane Smith, however, in which glamorous images of the mining
industry were created by outside observers, Rawhide's myth was cynically produced by men and women intimately involved in the industry and the place. It was not a creation exclusively by or for touring
outsiders.[6]
　　In an extraordinarily short life cycle—from its birth in late 1907,
through a heady period of crowding so great that people could barely
move in its streets, to its virtual demise only three years later following
a serious fire and then a flood—Rawhide achieved neither great nor
permanent production from its ground. Yet the tantalizing lure of
wealth, sustained by perplexing deposits of jewelry-grade ore scat-

tered amid generally unpromising rock, enticed skilled promoters such as George Graham Rice. Rice was imprisoned for a fraudulent Nevada stock selling scheme in 1910, and he recounted his escapades from prison in a book entitled *My Adventures With Your Money*. In concert with several partners, his efforts made the town into an overnight sensation, a locus for consumption and desire vastly disproportionate to the actual yield of the mines.[7]

Rawhide was, in fact, a mining boom town in which relatively little mining occurred, but it was impossible to know that from any published accounts. Rice championed his Rawhide properties by means of what he called "press agenting," arranging to place in newspapers stories that prominently featured the camp and its potential richness. In one widely circulated tale, for example, it was reported that a chunk of ore loosened by a random dynamite blast in Rawhide broke a window in a nearby bank and was worth enough that the banker accepted it in payment for the broken glass. Rice, the probable source of this and other such stories, reported himself "pleased in contemplating the fact that very little false coloring, if any was resorted to."[8]

Instead he used occasions like the visit of popular British novelist Elinor Glyn, then infamous for her risqué book, *Three Weeks*, which had been banned in Boston. Glyn was invited to visit Rawhide by Tex Rickard, a well-known saloon and gambling house operator who later went on to manage the original Madison Square Garden in New York City. Rickard had earlier operated in Goldfield, where he promoted the famous 1906 Gans-Nelson championship prize fight and built the Northern Saloon. When the 1907 panic struck the latter town and news arrived of a new gold strike at Rawhide, Rickard departed in search of new opportunities. As a contemporary reported it:

> When Rickard heard that gold had been discovered at a place called Rawhide, he along with his partner Nat Goodwin decided to dramatically publicize and promote the strike in order to create the kind of boom psychology that had so recently boosted places like Goldfield and Tonopah. In this way he hoped to draw in new hordes of fortune hunters and thereby bring profits to his various ventures. . . . Which is to say that he understood more clearly than anyone else that on the mining frontier there was at least as much money in alcohol and cards as in gold. Stock companies were, as usual, created in large numbers by exciting and inflated stories which were given out to newspapers all over the country about the enormous riches presumed to lie beneath the desert around Rawhide.[9]

Nat C. Goodwin was the third member of Rawhide's publicity triumvirate. A popular comic actor from New York City who had also invested in Goldfield, he headed a brokerage house—Nat C. Goodwin & Co.—that boosted mines owned or controlled by Rice.

Glyn was already touring the U.S. and was visiting in Goldfield, accompanied by Raymond T. Baker and Utah mining magnate Sam Newhouse, one of the developers of the mine at Bingham Canyon. Seeking to capitalize on her notoriety, Rickard, Goodwin, and Rice invited her to experience the new camp in addition to the more established, four-year-old metropolis to the south. She arrived on May 27, 1908, to witness a staged high-stakes poker game that ended in an apparent double murder and an elaborate ceremony in which she was appointed a deputy sheriff and presented with a pistol. According to one skeptical resident, the publicity machine was operating at its best: "No one recorded whether Miss Glyn's tongue was in her cheek, or a twinkle in her eye, as she thanked them for an unforgettable experience. But the bash has gone down in history as the ultimate in histrionics."[10]

Glyn's adventures in Rawhide (which was disguised as the town of Moonbeams) were duly reported in her subsequent book, *Elizabeth Visits America*, published in 1909. There she makes clear that her tongue was, indeed, planted firmly in her cheek, as she recalls how the Nevada men told her "delightful things of shootings and blood-curdling adventures, and all with a delicious twinkle in the eye as much as to say, 'we are keeping up the character of the place to please you.'" Nevertheless, her highly romantic novel climaxes with the excitement of a robbery and deadly shootout in Moonbeams/Rawhide. And because Glyn was a celebrity, her travels were also widely reported in the press. As Rice blithely declared, accusations of fakery made no difference: "Every knock's a boost. Just the fact that we could get anyone as prominent as Elinor Glyn to visit us will impress people with Rawhide's growing importance."[11]

As predicted, Rawhide gained national prominence in the aftermath of Glyn's visit. Throughout 1908 it attracted what Rice described as "an ever shifting kaleidoscopic maelstrom of humanity," made up of "fashionably tailored Easterners, digging-booted prospectors, grimy miners, hustling brokers, promoters, mine operators, mercantile men, with here and there a scattering of 'tin horns.'"[12] All of them contributed to the town's aura of feverish excitement and self-proclaimed importance, as well as its escalating need for commercial services such as saloons, hotels, and banks.

But Glyn wasn't the only source of publicity for the young camp. Rawhide in 1908 was the subject of popular music. ("In Rawhide

Where Young and Old Are Finding Gold" by Glenn W. Ashley and Fred E. Jones), of promotional poetry ("Rawhide" by William Tompkins, the Rawhide Booster), and, most notably, of Riley Grannan's Funeral Oration, delivered by one-time Methodist preacher W. H. Knickerbocker. Grannan was a noteworthy gambler whose exploits "furnished sensational headlines for newspapers for many years," due to the remarkable size of his wagers. When he died in Rawhide in April, 1908, of pneumonia, the event was of national interest to the sporting set. His funeral, reportedly bankrolled by Tex Rickard, was held in the back room of a saloon. The eulogy was reprinted in numerous pamphlet and text versions, reportedly based on the shorthand notes of a California reporter who conveniently happened to be present (although a contemporary observer says that no one took any notes at the time, and that Knickerbocker spoke extemporaneously).[13]

In any event, the resulting paean to the efforts of a less-than-perfect man, who did the best that he could, proved to be far more enduring than the town itself. Grannan's eulogy was reprinted as recently as the 1970s and exists in numerous versions in archival collections. The net effect of these various publicity efforts was to keep Rawhide's name constantly before the public and to lure both the attention and the money of eastern capitalists. Not coincidentally, Rice and Goodwin were poised to sell stock to anyone who might desire to participate personally in the excitement of Rawhide.

Visual images were also an important, though sometimes neglected, part of that promotional effort. Views of Nevada's newest mining district, which Rice and Rickard hoped would be a successor to Goldfield, were circulated in numerous mining publications but also in general periodicals. A special photographic booklet by Ned Johnson, *Souvenir Views of Rawhide Nevada* was published in Los Angeles in 1908, at the height of the promotional frenzy. Another collection, *Rawhide Nevada, Where the Gold Glitters*, was published by the same photographer around the same time. The photographs of the mining landscape contained in these volumes depicted Rawhide as the prosperous mining community it aspired to be rather than the evanescent boom town it was in fact.[14]

In a series of carefully selected views, Rawhide was revealed to the viewer as it progressed with lightning speed from camp to fully developed town. Rawhide's status as a "real town" was perpetually at issue, and newspaper articles frequently recited the number of businesses, frame houses, and leases in operation, in order to distinguish the settlement from a mere camp that might flourish temporarily but would then wither and die. The foreword to *Souvenir Views*, for example, assured the reader that "the publishers . . . have no other object in view than to show the public at large, the marvelous growth of the camp from the time of its inception to the present day." One of the most thorough journalistic accounts of the town placed considerable emphasis on its acquisition of "the forms and institutions of settled life," including public utilities such as a water company, an electric light franchise, and a railroad (the latter planned but never built). All of these were considered to be symbols of a permanent town, a place that warranted further attention, even financial investment. In the words of the Rawhide City Directory for 1908-1909, "The influx into Rawhide goes on record as a worldbeater in the history of mining camps."[15]

The difficulties of visualization were manifold. Even the most prosperous mines were difficult to glorify visually, as few viewers could be expected to understand the complicated interplay of headframes and hoists, development work and active mining for shipment. In Rawhide, as in most Nevada desert mines until recently, familiar elements of the technological sublime were missing. Absent an impressive mill, the mechanical works of individual mines actually seemed rather puny. Even the most impressive technical accomplishments at Rawhide scarcely registered in the immense surrounding landscape. Frail and apparently temporary, they failed to evoke the sense of mastery over nature that was the essence of the celebratory sublime.[16]

This representational dilemma in mining photography gave rise to a new repertoire of visual symbols to convey the meaning of Rawhide's mining landscape. A few examples suggest the nature of that vocabulary. The St. Ives Lease reveals few signs of mining beginning to emerge on the landscape. Instead it prominently features the principals in the company, clustered to admire what is presumably an extremely rich sample of ore from their ground. Their rapt attention makes what is otherwise nondescript rock into an object of apparent significance. Similar ore had actually created several millionaires in Goldfield a few years earlier, but Rawhide's deposits were notoriously shallow and unreliable. As one mining observer cynically commented: "It is not uncommon to see very rich hornings on any and all of the principal leases. When one knows the streaks and seams, the richest kind of rock is readily found for the visitor. Many a visitor leaves the camp with the most glowing yarns of the horning that have been made for him."[17]

The ploy was remarkably successful. Although a few critics remonstrated that they were never allowed to sample systematically at Rawhide, but shown only the jewelry-rock—the richest streaks that occurred without apparent pattern throughout the area—many were willing to believe that Rawhide was a new Goldfield in the making. Rawhide's population actually peaked at approximately four thousand people in 1908, but published reports claimed that as many as ten thousand had arrived in the town. As a local newspaper editor put it: "Rawhide is in the air. . . . Rawhide is bewildering. It is day all day in the daytime and there is no night in Rawhide. The streets in the chill of the dawn are as thronged as they are at midday. Everybody is in a hurry and everybody has a mysterious secret to whisper to everybody else. . . . Pockets are laden with specimens and location notices. Brains are full of air castles. No one is poor in Rawhide even if he hasn't a cent in his jeans."[18]

The photographs gave visual form to the spirit of excitement, dwelling on the huge teams and wagons devoted to hauling sacks of ore from Rawhide. Such canvas bags of ore were a kind of visual mining shorthand, signifying to the observer that the companies had located rock sufficiently precious to justify the labor and the considerable cost of transporting it out of the camp by wagon for processing and refining elsewhere. Only ore of substantial value would justify such expense. In written accounts of the mining districts, reporters were careful to specify the number of ore bags amassed on each lease they visited.

More careful observers questioned the prevailing pieties. One anonymous commentator in the industry journal, the *Mining and Scientific Press*, commented shrewdly: "I saw some twenty or thirty sacks of ore on the hill, but no claims are made that any has ever been shipped. . . . On one lease some twenty sacks are piled, and at two other places from five to ten sacks. These have been on the ground for several months. One lessee claimed $12,000 per ton for his six sacks—but no care was taken to prevent theft! This is a sample of the 'dope' that is handed out."[19] In fact it was true that, as soon became apparent, the bulk of Rawhide's ore was not of shipping quality. Even the construction of three small mills by 1909 didn't bring wealth. But the visual images promised prosperity in the form of those laboriously filled ore sacks.

More successful in representing mining success at Rawhide was the photograph of the Grutt Hill-Truitt Mining Company. Grutt Hill featured the first major producing mine of the district, and this prospect was intentionally juxtaposed against the urban growth that it had presumably spawned. Views such as this one magnified the importance of the small hillside shacks of the St. Ives Lease, instructing the observer about the crucial link between the mines above and the substantial residential and commercial development evident in the canyon below. In topographical views such as this one, Rawhide mining companies took on aspects of a commercial, if not a technological sublime.

Even at the height of the rush, in 1908, the most generous estimates of actual mining employment in Rawhide fluctuated between 250 and 500 men. Many observed that the masses of humanity attracted to Rawhide were hangers-on, not miners, "idle men" who filled the dozen gambling saloons to overflowing. Although Rawhide at the time boasted two exuberant newspapers, ten brokerage houses, two banks, five restaurants, and fourteen saloons—and competitors at Goldfield proclaimed it a "New World Wonder"—in the end it proved a mere flash in the pan. In the words of one of its residents: "in general the promoters were selling stock and not mining."[20]

Compressing the normal life span of mining town from years into months, Rawhide busted almost as quickly as it boomed. The townsite was laid out in September, 1907, and population peaked in March, 1908. In September, 1908, a disastrous fire nearly destroyed the entire camp, burning most of the business section. Stories quickly circulated of the miners who, lacking a resource of water to extinguish the fire, had attempted to save the timbering in one mine by pouring beer on the flames. Although many owners rebuilt, the economic depression and collapse of both banks dampened enthusiasm for potential riches in Rawhide. Some of the speculators and gamblers drifted away to more prosperous surroundings. In August of 1909 a cloudburst flooded the narrow canyon housing the town, sweeping buildings, tents, and equipment away in its path. From this disaster Rawhide never recovered. The steady population of five hundred dwindled to about fifty, and although some mining continued, the few remaining buildings gradually subsided into a state of decay or were moved away to be used elsewhere.[21]

For roughly seventy years, until the 1980s, Rawhide was quiescent. The last permanent resident moved away in 1966, and Reno newspaper headlines mourned the town's demise in 1950: "Rawhide Now Is Deserted and Barren."[22] Photographers lingered lovingly on the few physical remains of the boom period, which were themselves more speculative than solid. The aging equipment and stark headframes became prime visual examples of what Richard Francaviglia has labeled "technostalgia," a romanticization of the remains of the industrial past.[23]

Yet in the long period of "genteel decline," the romance of Rawhide's reputation as "the last mad camp of that mad decade" lived on. In a 1941 obituary for the town, occasioned by the announcement that its post office would be closed, the *Reno Evening Gazette* forthrightly admitted that Rawhide "was, in a truer sense, more of a promotion camp, founded on speculation and hope, than it was a bonanza."[24] That it failed as a mining proposition, however, did not affect its mythical status.

What the paper glorified in retrospect was the same thing that the town's backers promoted in its early prime—its potential, the promise of wealth that it represented to the many who flocked there, and to the many others who sent money to be invested. In the words of the *Gazette*: "These camps never die because there will always be prospectors who envision a discovery that will restore them to their former status. Sometimes these dreams are realized. Even Rawhide may rise again to some measure of the heights it reached for a few brief months in 1908."[25]

Prescient in ways that could scarcely have been imagined in 1941, the Reno paper was referring to nearby deposits of tungsten, which was a strategic wartime metal at the time. In fact it was precious metals, gold and silver, that finally brought Rawhide the mineral wealth that so many had confidently predicted in the first decade of the twentieth century. In the process, however, the earlier mining landscape that had been painstakingly created and exuberantly promoted as an icon of prosperity was completely obliterated. Indeed, the landscape that had once been Rawhide was so drastically altered during the 1990s that mine managers were uncertain about the identity of photographs only six years old.

Perhaps mindful of the ironies inherent in celebrating a heritage it prepared to obliterate, Kennecott invited several descendants of early Rawhide claimants to attend the dedication for the Denton-Rawhide Mine in October, 1990. One of them was Eugene Grutt, whose father named Rawhide's Grutt Hill and continued to operate there into the 1930s. According to the press reports of the event, Grutt pronounced himself satisfied that Rawhide would now experience, "for the first time, a sense of mining stability." A colleague, eighty-year-old Horace E. Dunning, declared that while Rawhide had " 'always been there,'. . . it is only with the recent mine development that he felt its mining future has been 'made.' " During the 1990s Rawhide at last became what its founders had always planned for it to be, a fabulously lucrative mining district. At that same moment, it began to vanish altogether from the face of the earth.[26]

The new mining technology of heap leaching involves the physical destruction of entire mountains, which are pulverized, stripped of their minute ore content, and redeposited in new configurations. The new landscape of Rawhide genuinely incarnates the technological sublime that its predecessors never manifested, but it simultaneously erases human scale altogether.

Indeed, the boom town that has now come to life after so many years of anticipation is no longer a town at all. In a final act of reconstituting identity, Rawhide's sole remaining building, a stone jail, was refurbished by Kennecott and removed to the county seat of Hawthorne, some forty miles distant. There it sits in splendid isolation, in the corner of a parking lot, one last example of Rawhide reinventing itself for public consumption. A commemorative marker proclaims the place, against all odds, "one of the most authentic western mining towns in the state of Nevada."

By now the "authentic" Rawhide is no longer the physical setting in which profitable mining currently occurs, but the spectacular image that was self-consciously created to represent that place. As the archaeologists who assessed the district for the Bureau of Land Management remarked in 1993, Rawhide "was one of the highly publicized places that helped to form the present widespread notion of what a mining town in the 'old west' was like."[27] The fact that such a past never really existed—that it was a fiction of skillful promoters and that Rawhide never achieved the permanence or the prosperity it so desperately sought—is ultimately irrelevant. The landscape that once constituted Rawhide has been obliterated by the modern Denton-Rawhide Mine, but its multiple and incongruous cultural vestiges persist.

from *Twentieth Century Marvel*
(1988)

Joseph E. Stevens

Construction of Boulder Dam during the Great Depression of the 1930s inspired the American people. Journalists compared the project to the Pyramids or the Great Wall of China, although many a skeptic predicted that even the best of America's engineers could not block the fierce flow of the Colorado River where it ripped through the narrow rock-lined cliffs of Black Canyon twenty-two miles east of Las Vegas. Government engineers in the Bureau of Reclamation had dreamed for years of harnessing the incredible power of the river to generate hydroelectric power and divert water for urban development. On June 25, 1929, President Herbert Hoover signed the Boulder Canyon Project Act with an authorization for expenditures of $164 million. Upon completion he proudly announced that Boulder Dam would be the world's largest dam, a majestic symbol of man's engineering and technological prowess, tangible evidence of American "progress." Thousands of unemployed men and their families descended upon Black Canyon in hopes of finding work. By 1933, the project had become the largest employer in the state with approximately 5,500 men laboring under difficult and dangerous conditions. The once tranquil canyon became a frenetic scene as jackhammers banged away at the steep cliffs, air compressors and heavy equipment roared, train engines chugged and whistled, and booming echoes of exploding dynamite filled the air. Many workers collapsed as summer temperatures *reached 120 degrees. By the time the project was completed, 96 workers had died, some falling hundreds of feet to spectacular deaths. On September 30, 1935, President Franklin Roosevelt officially dedicated Boulder Dam, proclaiming it to be "a twentieth-century marvel." It reached a height of 727 feet, stretched 1,244 feet across the riverbed, and held back the surging river at its 660-foot-wide base. In 1947, Congress voted to change the name of Boulder Dam to honor the man whose leadership as a Cabinet member during the presidency of Calvin Coolidge had helped make it a reality, Herbert Hoover. Historian Joseph E. Stevens examines the lasting impact of the dam upon the American Southwest.*

Early on the morning of September 30, 1935, the normally sleepy downtown blocks of Boulder City were abuzz with activity. Women in their Sunday-best dresses, men in pressed trousers and white shirts, well-scrubbed boys and combed-and-curled girls moved along the sidewalks, pausing under the arched porticos to greet friends or to stare at the passing throng. The traffic on Nevada Highway, running through the business district, was nearly bumper to bumper, and more cars kept coming, funneling through the gate at the edge of the project reservation, creeping through town, then heading over the crest of the valley and down toward the dam. Anywhere there was a bit of empty shoulder along the road linking Boulder City and Black Canyon, automobiles were pulled over to the side. People sat or stood close by, fanning themselves, fiddling with Brownie cameras, chatting, waiting patiently. At the observation niches overlooking the dam, the tightly packed spectators pressed against the restraining masonry walls, and near the Nevada abutment, surrounding a bunting-draped platform, the biggest crowd of all, numbering in the thousands, milled about. Before the day was over, twelve thousand people would line the cliffs, cover the abutment area, and spill onto the dam's crest.[1]

The event was the dedication of Hoover Dam, the official culmination of four and a half years of prodigious labor. Like the opening of the Brooklyn Bridge a half-century earlier, completion of the dam was cause for public celebration and self-congratulation, not only in the Southwest but throughout the United States. Just as the span of granite and steel thrown across New York's East River had been heralded as a nineteenth century "wonder of science," an "astounding exhibition of the power of man to change nature," so had the vaulting arch of concrete, stark and gleaming in its desert gorge, been seized upon as a symbol of twentieth-century America's ability to shape a new and better world with technology. The "Great Pyramid of the American desert, the Ninth Symphony of our day," one writer called it. "A visual symphony written in steel and concrete—the terms of our mathematical and machine-age culture—it is inexpressibly beautiful of line, magnificently original, strong, simple, and as majestic as the greatest works of art of all time and all people, and eloquently expressive of our own as anything ever achieved."[2]

For a nation deeply wounded by the Great Depression, the symbolism was doubly important, linking as it did the traditional American free-enterprise values of private initiative, ingenuity, and risk taking with the more recent New Deal policy of government planning, funding, and supervision of public-works projects.

Hoover Dam was a triumph of individuals: of visionaries like Arthur Powell Davis, Herbert Hoover, and Phil Swing, who helped create the legislative blueprint for developing the Colorado River; of entrepreneurs like Warren Bechtel, Harry Morrison, and Henry Kaiser, whose financial acumen, organizational talent, and gambler's luck forged the managerial team needed to run the job; of engineers like Walker Young and Frank Crowe, whose resourcefulness and leadership overcame all obstacles and transformed paper plans into action; and of workers—miners, muckers, high scalers, and all the others—whose sweat and blood literally made a dream reality. But Hoover Dam was also a collective national triumph, a stunning example of what private industry, government, and labor, and working together, could accomplish for the betterment of all.

If after five years of the Depression, with all its hardships and rending uncertainties, there was doubt about the country's capacity to recover and build for the future, the dam offered powerful reassurance, tangible affirmation that the American dream of limitless possibility still lived. Twelve thousand people had come in person, and millions more would tune in on a nationwide radio hookup, to celebrate that dream and participate in a rite of national self-renewal.

At 9:30 A.M., at the Union Pacific Station in Las Vegas, the doors of a private railroad car opened and the president of the United States was helped to the platform and then into an open touring automobile. Accompanied by his wife, his personal aide, several Secret Service men, and Construction Engineer Walker Young, he rode down Fremont Street, through the outskirts of the city, and southeast into the desert, heading towards the rugged escarpment of the River Mountains. One thousand six hundred and fifty three days earlier, a tall, stoop-shouldered engineer had made this same journey, but under vastly different circumstances. On that spring morning in 1931 the lawn of Union Pacific Park had been populated by ragged scarecrows, not the well-dressed citizens to whom the president smiled and waved. Fremont Street had been dusty, run down, and dreary, a pale shadow of the bustling thoroughfare along which the presidential limousine glided. The edge of town had been marked by tents and shacks, not neat new construction, and the smooth ribbon of pavement angling up the desert slope had been a rutted and treacherous desert track. Beyond Railroad Pass, where the desolate Eldorado Valley had stretched empty to the horizon, Boulder City sat on its irrigated green island, and at the foot of Hemenway Wash, where the Colorado had plowed its muddy course, a glittering sheet of water covered the sand flats. In the four and a half years since Frank Crowe first made his way along this route, the geography, both physical and human, had been changed almost beyond recognition.

Shortly after 10:30 the motorcade arrived at the dam, and while the thousands of onlookers applauded and snapped pictures, the president's car slowly crossed the crest into Arizona and then came back to the speaker's platform on the Nevada side. Already the dais was crowded with an impressive array of officials: Harry Hopkins and Interior Secretary Ickes from the presidential entourage; Elwood Mead, Raymond Walter, and Jack Savage of the Bureau of Reclamation; Senators Key Pittman and Pat McCarren, Representative James Scrugham, and Governor Richard Kirman representing Nevada; the governors of California, Arizona, Utah, Wyoming, and Mexico representing five other Colorado Basin states; Harry Morrison, Steve and Kenneth Bechtel, Felix Kahn, Charlie Shea, and Frank Crowe of Six Companies; and in the back, Ragnald Fyhen and James Farndale of the Boulder City and Las Vegas central labor councils.

"Gee, this is magnificent," the president exclaimed with a broad smile as he was seated, and then Harold Ickes stepped forward to deliver the first address.[3]

"Pridefully, man acclaims his conquest of nature," began the pudgy, bespectacled secretary, but his words, amplified by the microphone, were garbled and then drowned out by thunderous echoes off the canyon walls. The horns of the public-address system were turned off and the secretary continued, although many in the audience now had a hard time understanding what he was saying. The subject of his speech was conservation and the importance of developing the nation's natural resources for public rather than individual benefit. "Here behind this massive dam is slowly accumulating a rich deposit of wealth greater than all the mines of the West have ever produced," he said, "wealth to be drawn upon for all time to come for the renewed life and continued benefit of generations of Americans."

Having spoken eloquently of the dam's purpose and of the role it would play in nation's future, Ickes turned to politics and his personal obsession with the structure's name. He repeated *Boulder Dam* again and again—five times in a half-minute passage—and finally concluded his address with a thinly veiled dig at Herbert Hoover: "This great engineering achievement should not carry the name of any living man but, on the contrary, should be baptized with a designation as bold and characteristic and imagination stirring as the dam itself."[4]

Key Pittman followed Ickes, and then, finally, it was the president's turn to speak. Franklin Delano Roosevelt, his dark double-breasted suit buttoned in spite of the ninety-degree heat, put down the pages of his speech, gripped the edge of the podium, and looked out at the upturned faces of the crowd. "This morning I came, I saw, and I was conquered as everyone will be who sees for the first time this great feat of mankind," he ad-libbed, and his listeners smiled at the sound of the patrician eastern accent familiar from so many radio broadcasts. More amusement was provided by Secretary Ickes, who dropped a handful of coins on the floor of the platform and then blushed beet red while the press section snickered at his discomfiture.[5] But the president did not seem to notice the disruption behind him. He was gazing across the lip of the dam at the cerulean waters of the new lake miraculously growing in the midst of a wilderness of sand and rock. Then his eyes dropped to the text in front of him, and his powerful voice rolled out over the crowed: "Ten years ago the place where we are gathered was an unpeopled, forbidding desert. In the bottom of a gloomy canyon, whose precipitous walls rose to a height of more than 1,000 feet, flowed a turbulent, dangerous river. The mountains on either side were difficult of access, with neither road nor rail, and their rocks were protected by neither trees nor grass from the blazing heat of the sun. The site of Boulder City was a cactus-covered waste. The transformation wrought here is a twentieth-century marvel."

The crowd stirred and applauded politely, but for those who had been in Black Canyon from the start, the president's introductory remarks had special meaning. Looking at the spreading lake, they could easily visualize the Colorado as it had been when they first glimpsed it: a dirty red-brown ribbon snaking along between the cliffs. The blink of an eye removed all the roads and footpaths, the cables and transmission lines that crisscrossed the canyon, and once again the walls were the soaring, unbroken barriers of 1931, awaiting the bite of steel and the shock of dynamite. Somewhere beyond the looming bluff of Cape Horn, under a fast-deepening blanket of water, lay the remains of Ragtown and the River Camp, cleansed out of existence, but not out of memory.

"All these dimensions are superlative," the president continued, referring to the size of the dam and to the vast quantities of water and electric power it would harness. "When we behold them it is fitting that we pay tribute to the genius of their designers. We recognize also the energy, resourcefulness, and zeal of the builders. . . . But especially we express our gratitude to the thousands of workers who gave brain and brawn to work of construction."

Almost directly across from the rostrum, three-quarters of the way up the Arizona wall, was the spot where Jack Russell had slipped from his scaler's chair and tumbled to his death. To the left of that point, somewhere in the middle of the dam, was the place where W. A. Jameson had been buried under a hundred tons of concrete. Deep in the breast of the Nevada cliff, six hundred feet under the president's shoes, was the tunnel section where Carl Bennett had been killed by a premature explosion and Bert Lynch had been crushed by a rockslide. It was hard for the workers at the ceremony to look at any part of the dam site and not recall moments of fear, horror, sadness, and anger. But it was also hard for them to look about and not feel a surging pride of accomplishment, a dawning realization that the long days of discomfort, drudgery, and danger had been great days, that their labor at Hoover Dam was an experience that would loom ever larger with the passing of time until it became an integral part of the their identity, one of the touchstones of their lives. Most had come here thinking only of making a living; now, for the first time, they began to sense that they had made history, too.

The president's voice rose as he began his peroration. "This is an engineering victory of the first order—another great achievement of American resourcefulness, skill, and determination." He drew a breath and looked squarely into the faces of his audience as if trying to establish eye contact with each individual. The pitch of his voice fell again, and his words were measured and sincere. "That is why I have the right once more to congratulate you who have created Boulder Dam and on behalf of the nation to say to you, 'Well done.'"[6]

* * *

"There's something peculiarly satisfying about building a great dam," Frank Crowe said in 1943. "You know what you build will stand for centuries."[7]

Hoover Dam has stood now for more than half a century, while all around it cities and states—in fact, an entire region—have been transformed by the revolution it sparked. Water and power, dispensed at the push of a button, have turned the "profitless locality" of the arid Southwest into America's new technological and agricultural promised land, ushering in an era of material wealth and physical comfort that was undreamed of, even by the visionaries who conceived the development of the Colorado River.

This transformation did not occur overnight, nor was it all directly linked to Hoover Dam, but just as the buried steel and concrete footings of a skyscraper hold up the glass aeries a thousand feet above, so did the concrete wedge in Black Canyon undergird the elaborate network of reservoirs and aqueducts, substations and transmission lines, that nourished the Southwest's oasis civilization into being.

The flood protection provided by Hoover made possible the construction of Parker Dam and the creation of Lake Havasu, the reservoir from which the cities of Southern California and Arizona draw their share of the Colorado's flow. The Colorado River Aqueduct, an incredible system of tunnels, canals, siphons, and pumping plants stretching across 240 miles of mountains and deserts to the Pacific coast, was built by the Los Angeles Metropolitan Water District with Hoover Dam power and began delivering water to Los Angeles and surrounding communities in the spring of 1941.

Work on the third phase of the Boulder Canyon Project—the All-American Canal and Imperial Dam—began in 1933. An immense 650-ton dragline chewed its way through the sandy waste of the Walking Hills eighty miles into the heart of Imperial Valley while at the same time Imperial Dam, a low concrete barrier that raised the river level twenty-three feet, and a series of desilting basins were built eighteen miles north of Yuma. On October 13, 1940, water coursed down the bed of the new canal and the long-standing dream of Imperial Valley farmers—an assured irrigation supply beyond the reach of Mexican officialdom—was finally realized.

Power generation, the Boulder Canyon Project's third major function began at Hoover Dam when the first of four generating units installed in the Nevada wing of the powerhouse in 1936–37 was turned on. All of the Nevada units, plus one Arizona unit, were operating by 1937, producing electricity for Los Angeles, Glendale, Burbank, and Pasadena, California as well as for Boulder City and Las Vegas. Two more generators went on line in 1938, powering the Metropolitan Water District's Colorado River Aqueduct project, and another pair was installed in the Arizona wing in 1939 to supply energy for the Southern California Edison Company. With nine turbines cranking out over more than seven hundred thousand kilowatts by the end of 1939, the powerhouse in Black Canyon was the world's largest hydroelectric facility.[8]

Hoover Dam's immediate impact was substantial: water and power for the Los Angeles metropolitan area, water and flood protection for the fertile agricultural lands of Southern California and Arizona. But even more important was its long-term impact on the way westerners thought about their region and its future.

Since its settlement in the nineteenth century the West had been an economic colony of the East, exporting minerals, timber, petroleum, and other raw materials to eastern factories and importing finished manufactured goods. Lack of electric power and reliable supplies of water stunted industrial development, discouraged immigration, and kept the region commercially and politically weak.[9] In this atmosphere of dependency and stagnation, Hoover Dam came as a revelation; in one stroke it freed Southern California from its economic fetters and made possible virtually unlimited growth. In Northern California, in Oregon and Washington, in Idaho and Montana, in Colorado and western Nebraska, farmers, businessmen, and politicians studied this example of large-scale reclamation, saw the economic potential it had unlocked, and began clamoring for similar projects of their own.

No less inspired by Hoover Dam were President Roosevelt and Interior Secretary Ickes, who saw it as a compelling demonstration of the social and economic benefits they believed would flow from centralized resource planning, public-power development, and federally funded public-works projects. The political popularity of the Hoover Dam undertaking was not lost on them, either. They embraced multipurpose water projects as the central element of their economic and natural-resources policy for the West: Grand Coulee, Bonneville, Shasta, Hungry Horse, Fort Peck, Granby, and scores of smaller New Deal dams, canals, tunnels, and power plants, stretching from the hundredth meridian to the Pacific shore and from Canada to Mexico, were all children of Hoover Dam.[10]

Less than a decade after the last bucket of concrete was poured in Black Canyon, an extensive water and power network was in place in the West, ready to support rapid expansion of agricultural production and operation of new factories. All that was needed was a catalyst to ignite an explosion of industrial growth, and the Japanese attack on Pearl Harbor provided it. Overnight America was at war in the Pacific and in desperate need of guns, ships, and airplanes that eastern and midwestern plants, already committed to supplying the European theater, could not produce in sufficient quantities. With its new power grid the West was prepared to mobilize, and in a remarkably short time shipyards, aircraft plants, and other war industries were up and running, churning out the flood of weapons that would ultimately crush the Japanese.

Hoover Dam played a vital role in this speedy defense buildup. The electricity it generated flowed to Los Angeles, where it powered steel and aluminum mills and the Douglas, Lockheed, and North American aircraft plants, which built approximately sixty-two thousand fighters, bombers, and cargo planes—a fifth of the nation's entire aircraft production—between 1941 and 1945.[11] When the war was over, Hoover Dam power and water continued to sustain the aerospace industry and to attract new plants, fostering a robust cycle of growth in Los Angeles and surrounding communities that in the span of two decades turned Southern California into one of the nation's leading centers of population and commerce.

The postwar economic explosion in the Los Angeles metropolitan area was not surprising, given its climate and coastal location; the same could not be said for the boom that took place in southern Nevada. When the Boulder Canyon Project's benefits were apportioned, few anticipated that the Silver State would become a major market for Hoover Dam water and electricity. Reno, the only urban center of any size in Nevada in the late 1920s, was too far to the north, and the south was deemed too barren and hot to attract industry or significant numbers of settlers. Las Vegas, it was thought, would enjoy a modest spurt of growth while construction went on in Black Canyon, then slip back into its former desert somnolence.

The authors of this scenario could not foresee the effects of three important developments, however: the legalization of gambling in Nevada in 1931, the beginning of the New Deal in 1933, and the emergence of Hoover Dam as a tourist attraction in 1934 and 1935. In 1931, as the project began, dozens of casinos and clubs opened to cater to dam workers, and the profitability of gaming was demonstrated dramatically. Starting in 1933, the city received the much-needed facelift, courtesy of the New Deal, as government-paid work crews paved city streets, laid sewer lines, landscaped parks, and constructed new public buildings. Then came the wave of tourists—an astonishing three-quarters of a million visitors in 1934–35 to see the dam and visit Las Vegas—and the revelation that Six Companies workers were not the only ones who liked to gamble.[12]

A steady flow of tourists continued to come to southern Nevada even after work in Black Canyon was finished, and in 1941 Las Vegas confounded the forecasters who had said it would never house heavy industry when it attracted Basic Magnesium Industries with the promise of abundant water and power from Hoover Dam. Where the Squatters' community of Midway had stood on Boulder Highway, a sprawling light-metals complex was built and a new town called Henderson sprang up. Shortly after Basic Magnesium located in southern Nevada, the U.S. Army Air Force established a large training school and gunnery range in the area, pumping even more defense dollars into the Las Vegas economy.[13]

After the war, power from the Black Canyon kept the gaming industry expanding by running the air conditioners and neon displays of resorts that sprouted up and down the Las Vegas Strip and by supporting the population surge in Southern California, the area from which Las Vegas casinos drew many of their customers. Water was added to the growth formula in 1971 when the first stage of a project to pump a portion of Lake Mead over the River Mountains and into the Las Vegas Valley was constructed. The second stage was built in 1982, completing a system that can deliver 299,000 acre-feet a year, freeing southern Nevada from its dependence on diminishing supplies of groundwater.[14] Today, seemingly against all odds, the dusty desert village of five thousand souls that Frank Crowe saw in 1931 has become one of the great gambling and entertainment meccas of the world, a thriving city with a metropolitan population exceeding half a million.

* * *

The dam itself has changed very little since the day in 1936 when Frank Crowe presented it to the government. The concrete in its body is still slowly curing, growing stronger with each passing year. Faint brown, beige, and white water stains streak the once-unblemished downstream face, but the effect is not unpleasing, adding a measure of warmth and contrast to the otherwise stark and austere facade.

Alterations have been made in the powerhouse: four generators were installed during World War II, three more in 1952, and one in 1961, completing the power plant and bringing the dam's nameplate generating capacity to 1,344,800 kilowatts. In the early 1980s a program to uprate the plant was begun; as part of this program, the original cast-steel turbine runners were replaced with more efficient, lower-maintenance stainless steel runners, and new, thinner insulation was installed in the generators, increasing their capacity to more than 2 million kilowatts.[15]

Diversion-tunnel repairs and modifications were made necessary by the most dramatic event in the dam's working life: the flood of 1983. It began in late spring when snowstorms in the Rocky Mountains were followed by a heat wave and heavy rains. Runoff between April and July was 210 percent of normal, and the Colorado River reservoirs filled rapidly. On June 6, 1983, Lake Powell behind Glen Canyon Dam was full, and emergency water releases began through its spillways. By late June ninety thousand cubic feet of water per second was rushing through the Grand Canyon toward Lake Mead, and it was apparent that Hoover Dam's flood-control capacity would be put to a severe test.

Late in the evening of July 2, the dam's giant steel gates were lifted and a foaming wave crashed into the spillway channels and was sucked into the diversion tunnels. A cloud of mist rose into the hot desert night, and after a hiatus of fifty-two years, the wild freight-train roar of the Colorado River was heard again in Black Canyon.

The flood crested on July 24 when more than fifty thousand cubic feet of water per second was discharged through the diversion tunnels; the spill was continued until September 6, when the drum gates were closed. Millions of dollars' worth of damage occurred in the river corridor downstream from Hoover Dam, but the destruction was only a fraction of what it would have been if Lake Mead had not cut the peak from the flood.[16]

At Glen Canyon Dam, built in the late 1950s, the emergency discharges virtually destroyed the diversion tunnels' linings. Cavitation—the forceful collapse of partial vacuums in fast-moving water—chewed through the concrete as if it were cardboard and gouged large holes in the tunnel floors. Inspection of the Hoover Dam diversion tunnels revealed a much different outcome: the water, racing along at speeds up to 120 miles per hour had caused slight pitting and abrading, but the concrete linings were still intact—a tribute to the design and construction expertise of the men who had built them fifty years earlier. In spite of the minor nature of the tunnel damage, the Bureau of Reclamation decided in 1985 to patch the concrete and install air slots to prevent cavitation during spillway discharges.[17]

The flood of 1983 demonstrated the fundamental soundness of Hoover Dam's design and the high quality of its construction. Frank Crowe and his work crews not only built fast, they built well; with proper maintenance the dam's life should be indefinite.

* * *

Although it is no longer the tallest dam in the world (Nourek Dam in the Soviet Union is 314 feet higher), Hoover Dam is still the most famous. The number of sightseers touring the dam and power plant has risen steadily since World War II, with yearly visitor totals now approaching three-quarters of a million. On busy summer days, as many as three thousand people come to see the huge structure, walk across its crest, and ride elevators down into its body to see the tunnels and generators.

The experience, especially the first glimpse of the dam from one of the hairpin turns in the road zigzagging down through the red and black cliffs, seldom fails to elicit a visceral response. The sight is unearthly, particularly at night, when recessed lamps illuminate the expanse of concrete and the tailrace below in a blaze of dazzling golden light. Confronting this spectacle in the midst of emptiness and desolation first provokes fear, then wonderment, and finally a sense of awe and pride in man's skill in bending the forces of nature to his purpose. In the shadow of Hoover Dam one feels that the future is limitless, that no obstacle is insurmountable, that we have in our grasp the power to achieve anything if we can but summon the will.

Some try to suppress this feeling, thinking that it is naïve to be enthralled by an engineering marvel, dangerous to be seduced by twentieth-century technology, which cynics say is untrustworthy, exploitative, and destructive of the environment and the human spirit. But in the clear desert light of Black Canyon, guilt about the deeds of the past and doubt about the promise of the future shrivel. The romance of the engineer still lives in the graceful lines and brute strength of Hoover Dam. The courage of the construction worker is written in concrete and steel across the face of the towering cliffs, and a generation's belief in the destiny of the next is proclaimed by the deep-throated hum of the generators. Let poet May Sarton describe it:

> But here among the hills bare and red,
> A violent precipice, a dizzy white curve falls,
> Hundreds of feet through rock to the deep canyon-bed;
> A beauty sheer and clean and without error
> It stands with the created sapphire lake behind it,
> It stands, a work of man as noble as the hills,
> And it is faith as well as water it spills.
>
> Not built on terror like the empty pyramid,
> Not built to conquer but to illuminate a world:
> It is the human answer to a human need,
> Power in absolute control, freed as a gift,
> A pure creative act, God when the world was born!
> It proves that we have built for life and built for love
> And when we all are dead, this dam will stand and give.[18]

from *Reno's Big Gamble*
Image and Reputation in the Biggest Little City
(2008)

Alicia Barber

Walter Van Tilburg Clark grew up in Reno during the 1920s when his father served as president of the University of Nevada. His autobiographical novel, A City of Trembling Leaves, *was published in 1945 and became a national bestseller. Clark had attracted national literary attention five years earlier with publication of* The Ox-Bow Incident *that became a classic Western novel and the basis for a popular motion picture. In* Trembling Leaves *Clark attempted to recapture the Reno he had known as a youth—a pleasant town where its residents lived in modest but comfortable homes, sent their children to good schools and attended friendly churches on Sundays. His description of his hometown provided a sharp contrast to the "other Reno" that took shape while Clark was a teenager. In this other Reno, city leaders openly embraced a libertarian lifestyle designed to attract tourists to the community. By the 1920s, at any given time, the city hosted several hundred persons who were part of the "divorce colony," mostly affluent women who spent six months in town to establish residency to obtain a "quickie divorce." These individuals became an essential part of the local economy. Many of the women found outlet from boredom by patronizing nightclubs and dude ranches that catered to their interests. In Reno, Prohibition was widely disparaged, and bootleggers operated openly and without fear of arrest. A large brothel, The Stockade, did a thriving business and was one of several such businesses that operated on the edge of downtown. In 1931, Reno's political and economic establishment spearheaded passage of legislation that created wide-open casino gambling in Nevada. Reno's open embrace of divorce, liquor, prostitution, and gambling set it apart from all other communities in the United States, and attracted heavy journalistic attention. The driving force for mak-*

ing Reno "The Biggest Little City in the World" was George Wing-
field, a multi-millionaire with multiple business interests across the
state. Wingfield owned and operated twelve banks in Nevada, and
effectively controlled both political parties, whose state offices were
conveniently located in his downtown Reno bank. One of his many
associates was Reno mayor E. E. Roberts, a divorce lawyer whose
many colorful statements embracing a "live and let live" lifestyle
made him a subject of national ridicule by moral reformers, but
enabled him to win three consecutive elections. In the following selec-
tion, historian Alicia Barber explores the creation of the Reno that
Walter Van Tilburg Clark lamented.

Tensions came to a head in the mayoral election of 1923, a turning point
that single-handedly may have determined the course of Reno's future
growth and development and established the lasting nature of its
national reputation. The incumbent, Harry E. Stewart, had been mayor
of Reno since 1919. Stewart shared the Progressive impulses of Francis
Newlands, who died in 1917, and devoted much energy to civic
improvement initiatives like street paving and the construction of
schools and parks. His major effort was backing the "Redlight Abate-
ment Movement" to permanently abolish Reno's "restricted," "regu-
lated," or red-light district.[59] Reintroduced after a brief ban during
World War I, prostitution was becoming an increased concern to some
residents. Demand remained high due to the continuing numbers of
potential customers who kept passing through, men involved in the
railroad, mining, livestock, or other trades. After the war, prostitution
was scattered throughout the east side of downtown, in hotels and
clubs on East First and Second Streets, and in Chinatown's remaining
wooden shacks. In 1922, the League of Women Voters and various
reform-minded civic groups campaigned against prostitution, and
Mayor Stewart finally declared the red-light district closed through an
executive order that was backed by the city council in January 1923.[60]

   To Stewart, Reno's fame had done nothing to improve life in the little town. Reflecting on the priorities that had driven him during his
previous term as mayor—moral uplift and beautification—Stewart
told his constituents, "I knew that a City Attractive was bound to grow
far faster and longer than a City Notorious." His agenda brimmed with
civic improvement measures including street paving, the establishment of city parks, and banning vice from the downtown area. He was
also very aware of what outsiders were saying about Reno. Referring
to a recent article in *Collier's* that had lauded his ban of the red-light
district, Stewart was emphatic that it not be reinstated.[61]

In his reelection campaign of 1923, Stewart made his philosophy clear, asserting his belief "that it is the desire of the majority of the people that Reno continue to progress in civic betterments, both physical and moral."[62] He faced competition from two parties: Frank J. Byington, who had served as Reno's mayor from 1914–1919, and Edwin E. Roberts, a colorful divorce lawyer who had served as the Republican U.S. congressman from Nevada from 1911 to 1919. With his experience in the position, Byington was a serious contender, but Roberts was not considered a factor in the election by most. Two days before the election, the *Nevada State Journal* dismissively editorialized, "Roberts as a candidate was invented to take enough votes from Byington to elect Stewart."[63]

The election prompted the largest voter turnout in Reno history, and to the surprise of many, ended with Roberts "smothering his opponents in an avalanche of votes," three times more than either competitor. After his victory, Roberts told an audience in an impromptu speech at a Kiwanis Club luncheon, "We must . . . pull together and do something to make Reno a bigger city, a more hospitable city, and a place where people will long to come and hate to leave." Like many others, he favored growth and finding new ways to put Reno "on the map"; unlike many, Stewart in particular, he opposed legislating reform. That August, speaking to the Sparks Lions Club, he clarified his position on the subject, telling his audience, "A minority of paid reformers in the United States are trying to legislate morals into the people. I am not in favor of such an attempt. You can't make a man good by law. . . . If you will use your influence for common sense and bring up your children with common sense training there will be less disrespect for law and less fool laws passed."[64] For his part, Roberts continued to practice divorce law from his office in city hall, the walls of which were decorated with "pack upon pack of playing-cards," as *Pictorial Review's* Genevieve Parkhurst noted. The national press delighted in the western demeanor and pithy comments of such a colorful and outspoken character, but the reform community was not amused.[65]

In supporting Roberts, the voters of Reno had moved decisively away from Senator Francis Newlands' Progressive philosophies to the more profit-driven vision shared by George Wingfield, Roberts, and others. Reno was already notorious for bucking convention, and it was about to go much further. After Roberts won the 1923 mayoral election, the new city council passed Bill No. 893, an amendment to the new antiprostitution law, permitting brothels to operate "at a distance of 250 feet or more distant from any public street or alley in the City of Reno, now being actually used as a public thoroughfare." With this new requirement, brothel operators were required to relocate, but could remain in business. As a result, most brothels moved further east from downtown, but not very far.[66]

In fact, a few new houses of prostitution were built, with names like the Green Lantern and the Cottage, but the best known and longest running in Reno history was the "Crib," built off Second Street in 1923. The principal operators of the Riverside Securities Company, which constructed it, were "Jimmy the Cinch" McKay and "Curly Bill" Graham, owners of the Willows. Nicknamed the "Stockade" for the tall wooden fence at its entrance, the compound featured two rows of "cribs," twenty-five on each side, with a dance hall, the Pastime Club, at the end. Up to three shifts of women per day rented the cribs, registered with the police, and were tested regularly for venereal disease. Mayor Roberts voiced his approval of the arrangement, claiming that it kept prostitutes off the streets.[67]

Roberts was reelected in 1927, in a campaign openly backed by George Wingfield, and embarked upon a term in which some of the most decisive and far-reaching decisions about Reno were made. In a divorce guidebook published in Reno after Roberts's initial victory, James H. Bolin praised the mayor as a kind of "Moses" who had made Reno "the widest open town in the United States" by encouraging licensed poker games, public dance halls, book-making and even "an occasional Chinese lottery."[68] His impatience with national Prohibition echoed that of many of Nevada's leaders, a rebellious perspective that made national headlines. In 1926, a *New York Times* special correspondent reported that "Of the States west of the Rocky Mountains, Nevada alone has the hardihood to take a positive stand on prohibition. She is 'agin' it without equivocation or compromise, and is not only willing but eager that the world shall know it." Reflecting latent national support for repeal, he continued, "At a time when pretty much everybody else is singing low on prohibition, Nevada's attitude brings a certain sense of moral refreshment." A few months later, the same reporter described Roberts himself as "a rip-roaring wet" with the "character of a 'helluva feller'" who, as Reno's mayor, had "advocated and sustained the wide-open principle, illustrating in his own character and practice a fairly complete exemplification of his publicly declared views."[69]

In addition to his liberal views on these other social issues, mayor Roberts, along with George Wingfield, was among a group of politicians who conspired to have the required residency period for divorce shortened from six months to three, legislation that passed in March of

1927. A few years later, Roberts told a reporter from *Pictorial Review* how it was done. The original bill introduced to legislators was purportedly intended only to amend the standing divorce law by adding "insanity" to the accepted grounds for divorce. However, an amendment to the law required that the law first be repealed and then resubmitted with the new language. After receiving a copy of the bill, which mentioned the six-month residency requirement twice, Roberts and a group of lawyers replaced each "six" with a "three" and then took their version to George Wingfield, who arranged to have it taken to the floor by a collaborating legislator. The amendment passed just before dawn, surprising sleepy legislators once they were informed of precisely what they had signed. "I had no compunctions about it," Roberts asserted, after the fact.[70]

Those who did have compunctions were seemingly in the minority. The day after the bill passed, H. R. Cooke, the president of the State Bar Association, criticized both the method and the result. He said, "I regard the enactment of this three months bill as nothing more nor less than a cold-blooded bid for the dollars of the divorcées of other states," a motivation that many others were perfectly willing to admit. The president of the Washoe County Bar Association approved of the move, reasoning, "It seems to me that if people are to be divorced there is no moral question in whether the divorce be granted in Reno or Paris." He continued, "Economically I believe it is to the advantage of Reno to have the residential period for divorce three month. I am not touchy over the adverse criticism of Reno which arises from some sources. In my travels I have found more favorable comment than unfavorable." A political cartoon appearing in New York's *Herald Tribune* the following month translated public opinion of Nevada into a single image. In it, a miner figure labeled "Reno" emerged from a hole in the ground, lifting up a large prospecting pan dripping with gold coins; next to him, a sign read "New Divorce Law, Quicker and Easier" while a "Legislative Badger" exclaimed, "I found it for him!" From one jackpot to another, Nevada's motives seemed clear.[71]

The legislative change made the front page of the *New York Times*, as more people than ever before started traveling to Reno for the new ninety-day divorce. Five days later the *Times* reported a "divorce suit every hour," or forty-eight suits filed in the past forty-eight hours, remarking that "Even when Reno, under the advantages of the six months' residence law, was famous as a divorce centre, the filing of separation suits never reached such numbers as now." Indeed, the number of divorces granted in Nevada courts nearly doubled that year, from 1,021 in 1926 to 1,953 in 1927 and 2,595 in 1928. They included high-profile socialites like heir and writer Cornelius Vanderbilt, Jr., who headed to Reno just four months after the new legislation passed to pursue a heavily publicized divorce.[72]

The association of Reno with celebrities like Vanderbilt, as well as intrigue with the legislative shenanigans of such a brazen state, kept Reno in the public eye. Gustavus Swift Paine, a professor of English at the University of Nevada who wrote for the *North American Review* in 1930, argued that celebrity patronage had granted Reno enough social cachet that its residents need not be ashamed of its reputation. Comparing 1930s Reno to the heady days of the Comstock Lode, when Nevada contributed to the fortunes of the Comstock silver barons, he wrote,

> Now Nevada has been of vital service to such other splendid names as Vanderbilt, Morgan, Gould, Rhinelander, DuPont, and Whitney. Three of the foremost American writers of the present time have been divorced in Reno—Sherwood Anderson, Sinclair Lewis, and Eugene O'Neill. Names that are household words, such as Church (soda, not seats), Colgate (soap), Durant (automobiles), Hoover (vacuum cleaners), Pratt (Standard Oil), Fargo (express), and Clark (both thread and copper) have all appeared in the Reno news within the last few months.[73]

In a new consumer age, it seemed, what better way to assert the stature of a town than through association with consumer royalty? In a strange twist on Thorstein Veblen's theory of "conspicuous consumption," the manufacturers of consumer goods were functioning here both as "conspicuous consumers" who purchased for themselves what Reno had to offer, as well as commodities invoked to market the product that was Reno.[74]

Businessman George Wingfield was prepared to benefit personally from the new legislation and specifically from the new consumers it would attract. After a disastrous fire burned down the Riverside Hotel in March 1922, owner Harry Gosse was unable to secure the funds to rebuild. In 1924, Wingfield bought the property and soon began to construct a new and improved Riverside Hotel on the same site, designed specifically with the divorce trade in mind. The new six-story red brick structure opened in May 1927, just two months after the new legislation passed, with sixty luxurious hotel rooms and forty corner suites suitable for extended stays, each with a combination living room/bedroom, dining room, and kitchen complete with tile-lined refrigerators and electric ranges. The lobby floor was made of Tennessee marble, and the lounge floor and all other woodwork of mahogany. In constructing the massive building, Wingfield obviously shared the opinion held by the *New York Times* that "Reno expects to come back under the new law and attract the divorce seekers of America."[75]

Wingfield's plan worked like a charm; travel writer Mary Day Winn reported in 1931 that the Riverside was "patronized almost one hundred per cent by divorce-seekers." Official city-sponsored publications did not mention divorce in relation to the Riverside, although they praised the hotel for its elegance and style. Residents were said to understand the unspoken references, however. Henry Pringle wrote that "The Riverside Hotel in Reno, Nevada, is invariably described as 'smart' or 'swanky' or 'ultra-fashionable' in the local newspapers; which means that the elite of the divorce trade register there."[76]...

With the completion of the Victory and Lincoln Highways, many locals saw the potential for even more tourist dollars. City officials predicted that "with the completion of improved transcontinental highways and the improvement of highways tributary to the main arteries in Nevada in 1926, there will pass across this state a flow of tourist travel from the East alone, that will be unprecedented in the history of modern methods of transportation."[78] To celebrate the momentous occasion, Reno hosted a Transcontinental Highways Exposition in June 1927 on the grounds of Idlewild Park, a 49-acre expanse on the south bank of the Truckee River, just west of downtown. For purposes of publicity and celebration, city officials constructed a metal arch that spanned Virginia Street near Commercial Row and brandished the word "RENO" with electrified torches above and lines below announcing the dates of the Exposition. The arch remained in place after the event ended and gained new wording in 1929, when hundreds of light bulbs set aglow the phrase that had now become the city's permanent slogan: "The Biggest Little City in the World."

With the coming of the Highways Exposition, increasing numbers of motor tourists, and the rise of auto camps in and around Reno, the Chamber of Commerce embarked on a new kind of outdoor-oriented civic promotion, specifically emphasizing the area's recreational opportunities and directing people to "Invite your Friends to spend their Vacation in Nevada's Wonderland." That wonderland had expanded from the shores of Lake Tahoe, the focal point of nineteenth-century recreationists, to sites closer to home. In the city's directories, the Chamber of Commerce wrote, "Nevada, vast state of mystery and dormant natural wealth, is rich in a history to be revealed to the hordes of visitors from every clime who will respond to the attractions of our Wonderland." An advertisement appearing in subsequent directories labeled Reno "The recreational Center of America" and depicted a man in golf clothes, a woman in riding jodhpurs, and a ranger standing beside a sleek convertible. Men and women alike, it seemed, could find a plethora of outdoor activities to fit their interests in and around Reno.[79]

Promotion of these attractions targeted mainstream tourists as well as members of the divorce colony eager for a change of scenery. The requirement that they remain within the state for the duration of their residency period increased the appeal of nearby attractions accessible by automobile. George Bond's divorce guidebook encouraged motor trips to Pyramid Lake and area hot springs. A brochure called "Ramblings through the Pines and Sage," published by the Nevada State Automobile Association in 1928 outlined a series of one-day motor tours out of Reno. Directed to "Mr. and Mrs. Average Visitor," it included detailed motor trips around the town itself; heading west to Lake Tahoe; "Following the Trail of Romance" to the Comstock; sampling four of the area's hot springs; exploring the so-called "Canyon-Land" area irrigated by the Newlands project; and even a northward visit to the "Vacation Land" of Lassen Volcanic National Park and northern California. For those unwilling or unable to drive themselves, arrangements could be made through the local branch of Pickwick Stages, a national company advertising itself as "the world's greatest stage line."[80] . . .

But the claim that the town valued income over all was never far from the thoughts of its chroniclers. A 1930 article in *American Magazine* stated that "The town has been made beautiful, largely as a bait for divorce seekers. They spend three to four million dollars a year in Reno." The author blamed Reno, at least in part, for the country's rising divorce rate, "because Reno has done its best to make divorce-getting as easy, as cheap, and as agreeable as possible." Of Reno's residents, she said "The people are delightful. But—they have given up a good deal in exchange for the divorce revenue which makes possible their boast of being 'The Biggest Little City in the World.' They think they have made a good bargain. But I wonder."[82] Others would wonder, too, as the state legislature took a number of rather shocking steps that oriented Reno's landscape even more toward the transient, tourist population.

Numerous strategies to channel more money into the state were proposed after the stock market crash of October 1929, although Nevada did not suffer major financial repercussions right away.

Nationally, the onset of the Depression brought a decrease in both weddings and divorces, as both cost money. In 1930, of forty states measured, thirty-three recorded fewer marriages than the previous year, and thirty recorded fewer divorces. Nevada was one of the few exceptions, reporting slight increases in both.[83] However, it was not long before the uncertainties of the incipient Depression, a major statewide drought in 1930–1931, and the imminent collapse of the city's banking institutions, including those of the formerly untouchable George Wingfield, all combined to increase anxiety about the state's future. Nevada's political leaders recognized the need for additional measures to ensure the state's financial health and to maintain Reno's hold on the lucrative divorce industry. . . .

The proposed legalization of gambling met with strong disapproval from a handful of citizens, including a philosophy professor from the University of Nevada, R. C. Thompson, one of those who had taken up the reform mantle of president Joseph Stubbs after his sudden death, reportedly of heart failure, in 1914. As Thompson declared, "Gambling, as a business, has no standing-ground whatsoever. It represents a parasitic business which preys upon the welfare of society."[85] However, most residents seemed accepting of the full legalization of a practice they well knew to have been continuing for years in various forms, some legally sanctioned, some not.

The announcement in March 1931 that Nevada governor Fred Balzar had signed legislation that not only reduced the state's residency period to six weeks but also fully legalized gambling prompted a national uproar. Although other states permitted some casino gaming, Nevada was the only one to legalize "full-scale, public casino gambling," and no other state would match the forty-two-day divorce. As the largest city in Nevada, Reno would be the primary beneficiary of both new pieces of legislation.[86]

As the national response suggested, the two bills were in many ways intertwined. Up to that point, divorce had been the bigger business by far, and many observers saw the legalization of gambling as the means by which Reno hoped to save it. As the *San Antonio Light* wrote, "Nevadans are old hands at gambling and when their big divorce trade stake was threatened, they did not hesitate to throw enough chips into the pot to scare the other fellows out." With these new laws, they wrote, Nevada would "probably keep the bulk of the very profitable Eastern divorce business."[87] As Carol W. Cross, a Central Press correspondent, reported, "Divorce is recognized as a social necessity in Reno, but it also is recognized as a profitable business and for that reason Nevada's key city welcomes the unhappily wed with 'open arms.'" She continued, "'Come here,' Reno seems to say, 'Come here for your divorce, but don't forget to spend your money.'"[88] The American public had been familiar with Reno's "quickie" divorces for decades now, and with the increasing acceptability of divorce, even the passage of such a short residency period provoked more satire than outrage.

The new divorce law would not grant any six-week divorces until the first week of May, but the gambling law became effective immediately. Among the legal games now were roulette, keno, faro, monte, blackjack, twenty-one, craps, draw poker, and more. With reporters already on the scene, the *New York Times* announced, "In the flush of wide-open gambling the new forty-two-day divorce law virtually was forgotten." Many gambling clubs had already been in operation, openly or not, but immediately upon legalization, as the *Times* reported of one establishment, "The hum and hubbub of gambling, the click-clack of machines and the clatter of poker chips were partly drowned by the staccato noise of a compressed air drill operated by a construction crew engaged in cutting through massive walls to enlarge the gaming room."[89] Mayor Roberts triumphantly stated, "For eight years I've been trying to make Reno a place where everybody can do what they please, just so they don't interfere with other people's rights. Now we can do lawfully what Nevada has always done under cover."[90] It was this spirit, this brash confidence in the value of what Reno had to offer, that later inspired historian Daniel Boorstin to characterize the town as a community of "Go-Getters"—American entrepreneurs who "exploited the federal commodity" with a competitive spirit that characterized the age.[91]

Within days, twenty-one clubs applied for their gaming licenses, at a monthly cost of $25 per social game (such as bridge, whist, and poker), $50 per mercantile game (such as faro or craps), and $10 per slot macine.[92] Located on Commercial Row, the Owl Club had already offered poker games and now was licensed for casino games including roulette, craps, 21, and slot machines. The operations of the Bank Club now moved to the ground floor and it quickly expanded to become the largest and most profitable casino in the state. A new façade and marquis drew the attention of passersby, while inside, an expensive electric keno board featuring 1,000 light bulbs dominated a gaming floor offering roulette, craps, 21, faro, hazard, keno, stud poker, pan, and one slot machine.[93] Other clubs flinging their doors open to the public included the Rex Club, also owned by Graham and McKay; the Wine House, a former site of cockfighting battles among other activities; and the Waldorf Club, on North Virginia. The Rex Club, Bank Club, and several others fronted Douglas Alley, located between Commercial Row and Second Street, which became a center of gambling in Reno.

As was true for the divorce trade, national publicity for the new attractions arose without any local effort. With no competition anywhere in the country, the casinos did not need to advertise; the press accomplished that for them, and the novelty alone drew enormous crowds to Reno. On the first national holiday following legalization, Memorial Day weekend, a local reporter wrote, "The crowds were the largest Reno has seen since the recent gambling and six-weeks' divorce law secured widespread 'free' publicity." He estimated that 5,000 visitors had descended on Reno and observed, "thousands of holiday visitors swarmed the streets to see for themselves the things which they have been told about Nevada's gay metropolis." Hotel rooms were booked to overflowing, and buildings in local parks and local residences were temporarily turned into hotels for the weekend, reminiscent of the 1910 "Fight of the Century." Men and women alike tried their luck at the tables, and "a carnival spirit prevailed," noted one writer, with the crowds undeterred by a Salvation Army preacher who reportedly stood on a downtown corner warning casino patrons to seek salvation. Two downtown casinos were still in the process of enlarging their gaming floors, and new neon lights glowed on the city streets.[94] . . .

Every paper from California to New York, it seemed, had something to say about the new legalized gambling. Many, like Ohio's *Portsmouth Times*, clearly recognized the financial motive, which was generally disparaged: "Unable to pull itself out of the doldrums by enterprise, the state has resorted to a common device—cheapening itself for the sake of money to be gained. It is fortunate, indeed, that there is only a handful of native Nevada citizens to share in the shame the state should feel."[98] Even criticism, from predictable quarters, provided publicity. Not surprisingly, religious leaders nationwide criticized Reno for its immorality, but supporting the old adage that no publicity is bad publicity, *Outlook*'s Henry Pringle wrote that

> Reno is well satisfied. Publicity such as has not come to her in decades has resulted from the new liberalism. Every knock, every denunciation, makes her that much better known. A few more divorce suits will be filed. A score of tin-can tourists, making their way across the continent to golden California, will plan their journey to allow for several days of sin. The role of sinner among the cities of America should be profitable.[99]

The new "wide open" policy took some of the more conservative observers aback. One visitor that summer noted disapprovingly that "there is no attempt to cover up Reno's open vice"; in fact, it was quite the opposite, as "certain features of it are blazoned to all the passing world. Center street, for example, after dark is a shrieking jungle of neon tube signs—those blazing reds and blues and greens that are so much more strident than any other form of outdoor signs—and practically all are advertising gambling 'clubs.'" And upon entering, he reported, "the scene inside these clubs is anything but glamorous. It is, in truth, almost unrelievedly sordid..."[100]

Those who disapproved of prostitution, gambling, divorce, prize-fighting, and the like could now single out Reno as the repository of all that was immoral and reprehensible in society. The city therefore became an immediate target for other ministers and moralizers. The leaders of the International Christian Endeavor Society convention in San Francisco that summer called Reno "a blot on civilization" and "a distinct menace to the American home." One minister announced, "The State is a disgrace to the nation, both in its divorce and gambling phases," and another agreed, "Reno and what it is doing presents a distinct menace to the ideals and concepts for which this country has always stood." Reverend Clarence True Wilson, head of the Methodist Church's board of temperance, prohibition, and public morals, promptly charged Nevada with advertising the state as "a three-fold compound of Sodom, Gomorrah and Perdition," to which the *Kansas City Star* confirmed, "it fits."[104]

Mayor Roberts defended Reno from the Methodist leader's charges in a speech to the Reno Lion's Club on March 26. Claiming that Nevada's motives had been misunderstood, Roberts stated his firm belief that morals should be instilled through education, not prohibition. Quoted in pieces and out of context by the national press, his words would be used for decades to come as an endorsement of drunkenness, debauchery, and the pursuit of vice. In its original form, however, his proposed solution, radical as it sounded, combined a libertarian belief in loose governmental regulation with a call for individual responsibility. To bring an end to bootlegging, he stated, "I would have the city of Reno go to the expense of manufacturing 1,000 gallons of good corn whisky at $2.50 per gallon and would place a barrel on every street corner in the city of Reno with a dipper attached labeled: 'Good corn whisky. Help yourself, but don't carry any away. Drink all you want, but do so openly and above-board.'"[105]

The result, he stated, would be to "take the profit out of the stuff," thereby removing any incentive for criminal activity. But this was not all. "I believe in letting every man do just what he wants to do so long as he does not interfere with the rights of others," Roberts continued, referring to the legislation of gambling as "tearing off the mask of hypocrisy and doing in the open what we know is going on all over our nation today behind closed doors." Roberts repeated these points a few days later to a packed house in a speech for "men's night" at Reno's Methodist Church, where he professed his support for temperance but repeated his claim that Prohibition was unenforceable. The combination of such liberal views delivered in a house of worship earned the speech national headlines along the lines of "Reno Defender Goes It Alone" and "Wants Free Whisky."[106]

Up for reelection that spring, Roberts repeated his philosophy again in interviews with correspondents from across the country. To the *Kansas City Star*, he stated, "I would repeal all blue laws. I would make Reno the playground of the world. . . . I would have gambling legalized, as it is here, because close contact with gambling will show any man with a lick of sense that he can't win, and in that way open gambling will kill itself."[107] Putting the onus of responsibility for self-regulation on the individual gambler and drinker, Roberts presented a vision of Reno not as greedy or mercenary, but tolerant and above all, realistic. The majority of locals apparently liked what they heard, reelecting him as their mayor, a position he held until his death in December 1933.

Although in the minority, at least publicly, a handful of commentators acknowledged that Nevada, although worthy of rebuke, was only tapping into a common, all-too-human impulse manifested in various forms throughout American society. While acknowledging that gambling was clearly a "fruitless, time wasting and evil influence," the *Helena Independent* reflected, "gambling on the spin of an ivory ball on a roulette wheel is no worse than gambling on the trend of the stock market," no worse than "going to any one of ten thousand places in the United States and buying race-track tickets or participating in baseball pools." In fact, the editorial continued, "We all gamble in a way, in our business, in our lives, but most of us gamble on our ability."[108] We might criticize Reno, the writer seemed to suggest, but perhaps we might question our own hypocrisy before doing so. Nevada's leaders had taken a radical step, staking Reno's economic future on Americans' willingness to follow their own natural impulses. It remained to be seen whether, and how far, the general public would buy into those impulses and what the ensuing consequences for Reno's reputation might be.

from *"Yes I Can": The Story of Sammy Davis, Jr.*
(1965)

Sammy Davis, Jr.

and

from *Fighting Back: A Life in the Struggle for Civil Rights*
(1997)

James B. McMillan

Although Nevada entered the Union in 1864 to buttress the reelection of President Abraham Lincoln and his plans for Reconstruction, abolition and racial equality did not resonate among many of its white residents. While the number of African Americans then in Nevada was minuscule, the state legislature passed legislation requiring black, as well as Native American and Chinese children, to attend segregated schools. (Small numbers of minority students and financial constraints precluded the actual opening of such schools.) Previously, the territorial legislature had prohibited such individuals from testi-

fying in court and had made cohabitation and interracial marriage illegal. In a telling moment, the original Nevada Constitution had limited the right to vote to white males. For decades the number of blacks in the state remained no more than a few hundred. The racial composition of Nevada—Las Vegas in particular—changed markedly during the Second World War. By 1950, nearly 3,000 African Americans lived in Nevada, which led to imposition of restrictions upon the rental and sale of real estate. These residential segregation policies produced a small black ghetto in the Westside neighborhood of Las Vegas. Although African-American patrons were initially welcomed in the small clubs, by the late 1940s the growing number of tourists from southern states prompted the segregation of the city's hotel-casinos. This uninviting environment confronted such black entertainers as Sammy Davis, Jr., during the 1950s. They could perform before appreciative all-white audiences in the lavish showrooms and lounges, but not stay in the same hotels, eat in the restaurants, or place a bet in the casinos. It was during this time that the state's first black dentist arrived in Las Vegas to establish a practice. Born in Mississippi and educated in Detroit, James McMillan had received his dental education while serving in the U. S. Army during the war. He opened his dental office in Westside and soon had a thriving practice that included many white patients. He took a leadership role in the Las Vegas chapter of the National Association for the Advancement of Colored People. In March 1961, inspired by the developments of sit-in protests at segregated lunch counters that had spread across the South, McMillan and the NAACP decided to confront Las Vegas mayor Oran Gragson and key casino managers. Fears of an impending racial crisis spread as plans for a protest march were announced. At that juncture, however, casino managers announced that their properties were now open to people of all races. Under pressure from state and city political leaders, they had apparently calculated that it was in everyone's best interests to accept black customers.

from "Yes I Can"

by James B. McMillan

In Seattle, after our fourth show, the musicians would sit in with a college band run by a kid named Quincy Jones. I went along with them and we played, sang, and experimented with new things until dawn.

There was a note under my door when I got home one morning. "Wake me whenever you come in. Don't worry. Everything's fine. Will."

I heard the springs of his bed creak, then his slippers swooshing across the floor. He opened the door, rubbing his eyes, smiling. "Go get Big Sam."

I looked from one to the other. "Okay, now we have a pajama party. What's it all about?"

Will said, "We're booked as the opening act at El Rancho Vegas in Las Vegas, Nevada. For five hundred dollars a week." He smiled, pleased. "Mose Gastin, *now* let me hear you say we're going to be buried."

The trade papers were bursting with news about Las Vegas. It was starting to become a show town. El Rancho and the Last Frontier were the first luxury hotels and there was talk about new hotels being planned to go up near them.

My father was heating coffee on the hot plate. "The word is they're payin' acts twice as much as anywheres else. Free suites and food tabs." Will said, "They're out to make it the number one show town." I listened to them like I was watching a ping-pong game.

"... flyin' customers in ..." "... *Variety* says ..." "The whole business is watching what's happening in Vegas."

I walked over to Will. "Massey, I'm going to do those impressions."

He got out of bed and stared out the window. I knew by his long silence that he wasn't going to fight me. Finally, "Sammy, I don't think you can get away with it. Still, you're a third of the trio and you've seen a lot of show business so I won't stop you. I'm just going to hope you're right."

I looked around backstage while we waited to rehearse. The band was the biggest we'd ever worked with, the floor of the stage was springy and slick, the lighting was the most modern I'd ever seen. I was standing next to the stage manager. I asked, "Do I have it right about our rooms, that they're part of our deal here?"

The manager came over to us as we finished rehearsing. "Sorry. We can't let you have rooms here. House rules. You'll have to find a place in the—uh, on the other side of town."

I picked up our suitcases. "Let's go, Dad, Will."

The hotels we'd passed in the town itself looked awful compared to El Rancho but even they were out of bounds to us. The cab driver said, "There's a woman name of Cartwright over in Westside takes in you people."

It was Tobacco Road. A three- or four-year-old baby, naked, was standing in front of a shack made of wooden crates and cardboard that was unfit for human life. None of us spoke.

The driver sounded almost embarrassed. "Guess y'can't say a lot for housing out here. Been hardly any call for labor 'round these parts. Just a handful of porters and dishwashers they use over on the Strip. Not much cause for you people t'come to Vegas."

The cab stopped in front of one of the few decent houses. A woman was standing in the doorway. "Come right in, folks. You boys with one of the shows? Well, I got three nice rooms for you."

When she told us the price Will almost choked. "But that's probably twice what it would cost at El Rancho Vegas."

"Then why don't you go live at El Rancho Vegas?"

"Pay her the money, Massey. It's not important."

Will counted out the first week's rent. My father smiled sardonically at her. "Looks like if the ofays don't get us, then our own will."

"Business is business. I've got my own troubles."

My father followed me into my room. "Not half bad." I nodded and started unpacking. He sat down and I could feel him watching me. I threw a shirt into a drawer and slammed it closed. "All right, Dad, for God's sake what is it?"

"*That's* what it is. Exactly what you're doin', eatin' yourself up, grindin' your teeth. Y'can't let it get t'you, Poppa. I know how you feels. But the fact is, when it comes time to lay your head down at night what's the difference if it's here or in a room at El Rancho?"

"Dad, I don't give a damn about their lousy rooms, I really don't. Right now, the only thing in this world that I want is their stage!"

As I danced, I did Satchmo. I shuffled across the stage like Step'n Fetchit. Then I spun around and came back doing the Jimmy Cagney walk to the center of the stage and stood there, facing my father and Will, doing Cagney's legs-apart stance, the face, and then "All right . . . you dirty rats!" For a moment there was no sound from out front—then they roared.

In the wings Will smiled warmly. "I'm glad I was wrong, Sammy." My father laughed and hugged me. "Poppa, you was *great!*" He put me down. "Whattya say we get dressed after the next show and go look around the casino. I got fifty dollars tha's bustin' t'grow into a hundred."

We went out the stage door and around the building. The desert all around us was as dark as night can be but the casino was blazing with light. The door opened and as some people came out there was an outpour of sounds such as I'd never before heard: slot machines clanging, dealers droning, a woman shrieking with joy—and behind it all, a background of the liveliest, gayest music I'd ever heard. As I held the door open for my father, my head went in all directions to slot machines, dice tables, waiters rushing around with drinks, a man carrying a tray full of silver dollars.

I saw a hand on my father's shoulder. A deputy sheriff was holding him, shaking his head.

We rode to Mrs. Cartwright's in silence. They got out of the cab and I continued on downtown where there was a movie theater, where for a few hours I could lose myself in other people's lives.

A hand gripped my arm like a circle of steel, yanking me out of my seat, half-dragging me out to the lobby. "What're you, boy? A wise guy?" He was a sheriff, wearing a star badge and the big Western hat. His hand came up from nowhere and slapped across my face. He'd done it effortlessly but my jaw felt like it had been torn loose from my head. "Speak up when I talk to you!"

"What'd I do?"

"Don't bull me, boy. You know the law."

When I explained I'd just gotten to town and had never been there before, he pointed to a sign. "Coloreds sit in the last three rows. You're in Nevada now, not New York. Mind our rules and you'll be treated square. Go on back and enjoy the movie, boy."

I had no choice but to go in. A Mickey Rooney picture was on. After a while I glanced up to catch a song he was doing and I looked away, still steaming. Then I looked up again and I forgot the cop and the theater and the rules and I was dancing across the campus in a college musical. An hour later I was Danny Kaye git-gat-gattling my way through the army. Then the lights went on and I was sitting in the last row of an almost empty movie theater, and again I was a Negro in a Jim Crow town.

I went back to Mrs. Cartwright's and slammed her dirty, gouging door and swore to myself that someday it would be different. I tried reading but I couldn't keep my mind on the book. I felt closed in so I went out for a walk but the sight of all the poorness drove me back to my room. I stared out the window at the glow of the lights from the Strip in the distance until it faded into the morning sun.

I should have been tired the next night but as eight o'clock drew near I was vibrating with energy and I couldn't wait to get on the stage. I worked with the strength of ten men.

We did our shows and went out to get a cab to Mrs. Cartwright's. I looked away from the lights of the casino but I couldn't avoid hearing the sounds. Night after night I had to pass that door to get a cab. Once, between shows, I stood around the corner where nobody would see me, and waited for the door to open so I could catch the short bursts of gaiety that escaped as people went in and came out. I sat on the ground for an hour, listening and wondering what it must be like to be able to just walk in anywhere.

My father looked into my room, smiling. "Hey, Poppa, you wanta come out and wrap yourself around some of the best barbecue you'll ever taste? Then after lunch we could look in on the bar. It's a real nice place. They got a Keeno game goin' and we can double our money." He was selling me, as he had been every day for a week.

"Thanks, Dad. You go ahead."

"Hell, son, come on and get some laughs outa life."

"I'm happy, Dad."

"No you ain't."

"The hell I'm not."

"The hell you is. You sit here all day listening to them records when already you sound more like them people than they do. Then you're blowin' the horn. . . ."

"And I'm getting pretty good. Here, listen. . . ."

"I know." He tapped on the wall, causing a hollow knocking sound, and smiled. "This ain't exactly made outa three-foot-thick cement." He sat down on the bed. "Poppa, you do impressions, you dance, you play drums and trumpet, but you don't know doodly squat about livin'. You're not havin' your fun."

"I will, Dad. Bet your life on it. I will!"

He gave me a frustrated look. "Okay, son. I don't know how t'help you. So just tell me. . . ."

I watched him walking down the street toward the commercial section of Westside. There were a few decent places over there and under other conditions I could have enjoyed them, but the idea that I was being told, "That's your side of town, stay there," that those were the only places I was allowed in, made it impossible for me to go near them.

He looked back and saw me in the window and waved, offering me a chance to change my mind. I waved back and he turned and kept walking. I picked up the trumpet and started playing.

* * *

In Vegas, for twenty minutes, twice a night, our skin had no color. Then, the second we stepped off the stage, we were colored again.

I went on every night, turning myself inside out for the audience. They were paying more attention and giving us more respect than ever before, and after every performance I was so exhilarated by our acceptance onstage that I really expected one of the owners to come rushing back saying, "You were great. To hell with the rules. Come on in and have a drink with us." But it never happened. The other acts could move around the hotel, go out and gamble or sit in the lounge and have a drink, but we had to leave through the kitchen, with the garbage, like thieves in the night. I was dying to grab a look into the casino, just to see what it was like, but I was damned if I'd let anyone see me like a kid with his nose against the candy store window. I wanted to believe "If they don't want me then I don't want them either," but I couldn't help imagining what it must be like to be wanted, to be able to walk into any casino in town. I kept seeing the warmth in the faces of the people we'd played to that night. How could they like me onstage—and then this?

My father spent his time around the Westside bars and casino but I went to my room trying to ignore the taunting glow of light coming from the Strip, bigger and brighter than ever, until finally the irresistible blaze of it drew me to the window and I gazed across at it knowing it was only three in the morning, which is like noon in Las Vegas, feeling as wide awake as the rest of the town which was rocking with excitement. I pictured myself in the midst of it all, the music, the gaiety, the money piled high on tables, the women in beautiful dresses and diamonds, gambling away fortunes and laughing.

It took a physical effort to tear myself away from the window. I forced it all out of my mind and kept telling myself: Someday . . . , listening to records and reading until I was tired enough to fall asleep, always wondering when "someday" would be.

* * *

It was a gorgeous crisp November morning as I stepped off the train in Las Vegas. My father and Will were waiting for me on the platform. I searched their faces. "Well?"

My father made a circle with his thumb and forefinger. "The best."

"No problems?"

Will shook his head. "They're bending over backwards." I put my arms around both their shoulders and we walked through the station.

They stopped in front of a beautiful brand new Cadillac convertible. I looked at my father. "Damn! You musta hit a eight-horse parlay to get your hands on this baby!"

He tossed me the key. "Well, seein' as you like her, she's yours. Will and me bought it for you as a sorta advance birthday present." I took a slow walk around the car and stopped in front of the "S.D.Jr." they'd had painted on the door. "Well, climb in, Poppa, and let's see if she drives."

They slid in alongside me and I put the top down. "Might as well let 'em see who owns this boat." I put it in gear and we rolled away from the station. I ran my fingers over a plastic cone which jutted out from the center of the steering wheel, enclosing the Cadillac emblem. "I don't know how to thank you."

Will said, "Don't thank us, Sammy. Thank show business. That's where it all come from."

I couldn't get serious if my life depended on it. We stopped for a light and I pulled out the ash tray. "Hey, fellas, whatta we do when this gets filled up?"

My father came right in on cue. "We throws this car away and gets us a *new* one."

Will smiled. "You boys keep doing old jokes like that and we'll be back riding buses."

As we got onto The Strip, I slowed down. "We just drive straight up to the front entrance, right?"

My father laughed. "Like we own the place." He was as giddy as I had been a minute before. "We don't even have t'bother parking the car. They got a man standin' there just to do that and all you do is slip him a silver dollar and he tips his hat and says, 'Thank you, sir.'"

As we approached the hotel I saw the big sign out front, "THE WILL MASTIN TRIO featuring SAMMY DAVIS, JR." I turned into the driveway and pulled up in front of the entrance. A doorman hurried over and opened my door. "I'll take care of it for you, Mr. Davis." I gave him a five and he tipped his hat. "Thanks, Mr. Davis." A bellman came over. "Take your luggage, Mr. Davis?" I pointed to a cab just pulling up. "It's in that one, baby. My valet will give it to you."

The door closed and we were alone in a huge, beautiful suite. I collapsed onto the bed, kicking my legs in the air. "I don't *never* wanta leave this room! I'd sign a contract to stay here for the rest of my *natural!*" I got up and looked around. There was a large basket of flowers in the living room. The card read: "Welcome to the Old Frontier" and was signed by the manager.

My father was standing behind a bar in the corner of the room. "Glasses, ice, soda, cokes, scotch, bourbon . . . hell, they didn't slip up on nothin'."

"Well, I guess this is about as First Cabin as anyone can ever hope to go."

Charley Head, the man I'd hired in L.A., came in leading four bellmen carrying my luggage. I walked my father and Will to the door. "How about your rooms?"

"Almost the same layouts. Right down the hall."

I inspected the suite while Charlie started unpacking. "Pretty nice, huh, baby?"

He didn't look around. "I'll let you know when I see where they put me."

Oh God, I hadn't thought about that. "Well, look, you let me know, and if it's not okay you'll stay here with me." He just kept unpacking. I could imagine how he felt. "Let me help you, baby, and we'll get it done faster."

Morty was rehearsing the band. I sat in the back of the room listening, and checked John out on the lights.

When Morty gave the guys a break I called him aside. "Baby, I'll open with 'Birth of the Blues.'"

"You're joking! What'll you go off on?"

"We'll use 'Fascinating Rhythm.' Look, we throw away all the rules here. The plotting of a show for a Vegas audience is different than anywhere else. For openers, the hotels are all but giving away the best shows that money can buy, so the average cat who comes in to see us has been in town for a few days and he's already seen maybe six or eight of the biggest names in the business. This same guy may never see a live show from one end of the year to the next when he's home but after a few days here he's Charley-Make-Me-Laugh. Now, above and beyond that, plus the normal nightclub distractions, if I don't hook that guy right from the start and hang on to him I'm dead, because he'll be watching me but he'll start wondering if when he leaves maybe he should try ten the hard way. So, it's like when we make records: we do or die in the first eight bars." He whistled softly. "And on top of that, where in a normal club if I start off a little slow I can always stay on until eventually I get 'em and they leave saying, 'Hey, isn't it nice the way he does those long shows,' in Vegas the headliner has exactly fifty-two minutes, including bows. They're in the gambling business here and everything's timed down to the split second: there's no dancing after the shows and your check is collected before the show breaks. Those doors lead into the casino and they want the people to walk through them *on time*! There are just so many minutes in each day and the hotel anticipates a certain amount of gambling revenue for each one of them. I can't steal any of that time to make sure I come off smelling like a rose. They pay me to bring customers *to* the tables, not to keep them away. So, watch me extra carefully for the cues, baby, 'cause once I'm out there it's fight-for-your-life time."

* * *

As we stood in the wings listening to them shouting for more my father cocked his head and sighed, "I hope the word don't spread that we're bad for the heart." The three of us walked arm in arm back to the dressing rooms. "You gonna take a look around the casino, Poppa? Maybe take yourself a few bows?"

"I don't know, Dad. I'll see."

I put on a black mohair suit, a gray and black striped tie, my platinum watch, folded a handkerchief into my breast pocket and took a last look in the mirror. I took out the handkerchief and went downstairs.

I stood outside the casino, afraid. A security guard passed me. "Anything I can do for you, Sammy?" I shook my head. A few people coming out spotted me. "Great show, Sammy . . . Wonderful!"

I lit another cigarette. I took two drags, stamped it out, pushed the door open and walked in.

The deputy sheriff standing just inside said, "Hi 'ya, Sammy."

I smiled back and kept walking. I was right in the middle of all the sounds I'd heard before and they took form even wilder and more feverish than I'd imagined them. People were playing blackjack and roulette and shooting craps with a deadly serious hilarity, dropping coins into hundreds of one-armed bandits which lined every wall and the sound was like we were inside a huge, tin piggy bank and somebody was shaking all the money around.

There was an empty seat at one of the blackjack tables. The faces around the table seemed pleasant enough, but how would they react to me sitting down to gamble with them?

I broke a hundred dollar bill at the cashier's window. The seat was still open. I went over to one of the machines and dropped a silver dollar in the slot. If I win, I go to the table. I pulled the handle and watched the spinning figures slow to a halt . . . cherries . . . cherries . . . orange. There was a sharp click and silver dollars poured out.

The dealer was in the middle of a hand as I put my money on the table and pulled up the chair. Someone said something about me but I couldn't catch what it was. I kept my eyes on the green cloth. People were gathering around. I looked up. They were smiling.

I pushed a silver dollar forward and played my first hand. I won. I let the two dollars ride—and won again. I pulled back my winnings and kept playing for two dollars. A woman at the end of the table smiled. "I loved your show." The dealer glared at her. "Would you like another card?" She giggled nervously and looked back at her hand. I lit a cigarette and he slid an ash tray toward me. He jerked his head toward the nightclub. "I hope you're as lucky in here as you are in there." The man next to me said, "That's not luck. That's talent." A cocktail waitress came by. "Would you like a drink, Mr. Davis?" "I'd love a coke, thank you."

I began to feel some of my audience drifting away. I handed the dealer a hundred dollar bill. "I'll take some of those five-dollar chips, baby." Without counting them I pushed a stack of blue chips forward. Someone said, "Yeah. Go, Sammy. Break the bank." I won. I let it all ride. A woman yelled, "Arnold, come over here. Sammy Davis is playing. Hurry, Arnold." The dealer was all but handling me the chips in a shovel. He looked at the mountain of them spilling over the whole table in front of me. "You want twenty-five-dollar chips for these, Sammy?" "No thanks, baby. These are doing fine for me." The crowd was three deep around the table now. I pushed the whole pile forward. "Shoot the works."

"Oh my God, Arnold, will you look what he's doing?" "It's peanuts to him. Do you know what he makes a week?"

The dealer flipped the cards around the table as casually as if he were dealing to silver dollars. The crowd was silent. The ace of diamonds slid face up in front of me. I opened my down card. The jack of hearts. There was a roar behind me as if I'd just gone off on "Birth of the Blues." Arnold's wife was going out of her mind and people were pounding me on the back as the dealer stacked hundred-dollar-chips against my bet and then added half again, the bonus for blackjack.

I wasn't going to top that moment. I pulled the mass of chips toward me and dropped a handful of them into the dealer's shirt pocket. "Thanks, Sammy." A woman moaned. "You're not stopping, are you?" I smiled. "It's a definite quit while I'm ahead." As the crowd opened up for me I heard, "Hurry. Sit there, Arnold. It's a lucky seat."

I walked through the casino, both hands holding the bundle of chips against my chest . . . "Hey, Sammy, y'want some help gettin' rid of those?" . . . "How much you sock 'em for, kid?" . . . "The rich get richer, don't they?" . . . A deputy rushed ahead of me to help me with the door.

Outside, alone, I had to fight an urge to throw the chips in the air like confetti. It was such a joke. Such a big, fat joke.

On my way to breakfast, I passed a couple of the chorus kids sunbathing around the pool. I did bits with them for a few minutes, had some coffee, wandered over to the casino and sat at the bar drinking a coke and watching the action. A middle-aged guy with a swinging-looking blonde raised his glass and smiled. "You're the greatest, Sammy."

The bartender said to me, quietly, "Now there's a guy who lives. Hits town every Friday like clockwork. But with a different wife every week."

The manager sat down on the stool next to me. "Sammy, I hope you won't mind, but, I'd consider it a favor if you'd try not to spend too much time around the pool."

I looked him in the eye, waiting for "It's not that *we* mind but you know how people are . . ."

Our cab moved slowly through the downtown traffic, past the Golden Nugget, Horseshoe Club, Jackpot, and onto Highway 91. Dave was Charley Tourist, twisting around, looking out of all windows. "Hey, is this The Strip?"

"Yeah, baby. This is it."

"Wow, what a wild-looking town! What's it like in those places?" I didn't answer.

I stopped off at my father's room to say hello. "Any word from Mama and Peewee, Dad?"

"They called from a gas station less'n an hour ago. Oughta be here by six."

"Great. I'll arrange a table for the dinner show."

"Hey, Poppa, you sure maybe you're not pushin' the horse a little faster'n he can run? Colored people sittin' out front in Vegas?" He was shaking his head. "I just hope you ain't stickin' your neck out too far."

"I'm not sitcking my neck out. But I ain't pullin' it in like a goddamned turtle, either. My grandmother is gonna sit and watch me perform or there ain't *nobody* gonna sit and watch me perform." I picked up the phone and asked to be connected with the Venus room. "Hello, this is Sammy Davis, Jr. . . . fine thanks. I'd like a table for six for my family, at the ringside, for the dinner show tonight."

"Well? What'd they say, Poppa?"

"They said, 'Have a great opening, Mr. Davis.' "

"Hell, don't me *me* that poker face. I taught it to you."

"Dad, they couldn't have been nicer and they're holding a table at *center* ringside. I'll invite Dave to sit with them, that way they won't feel like they're alone in the world." I stood up. "Catch you later."

* * *

The living room was jammed and I went from group to group, saying hello, soaking up the flattery. I sat down next to Mama. "You have a good time tonight?"

"Just seeing what people think of you and how they're treating you is a good time for me, Sammy. I'd better be getting my sleep, though. And don't you stay up too late neither. You need your rest."

I walked her to the door. "Don't worry about me, Mama. I never felt better in my life."

There were still about a dozen people left. I sat down, Charley handed me a coke, and I lit a cigarette and relaxed into their conversation. Dave said, "Hey, whattya say we start at one end of the town and hit every place along the way?" His face, turned toward me, was still reflecting the excitement of the evening. "I hear there's a wild lounge act over at the Desert Inn. We could start there and then . . . "

"Baby, we're comfortable, it's late, we've got everything we want."

"It's only four o'clock. Come on, let's really celebrate."

"I don't know about those places, Dave." He looked at me, not understanding. "Baby, this is Vegas. It's one thing for me here where I'm working, but I'm not so sure about those other hotels. Now do you wanta see a lounge act, or a lynching?"

Somebody else said, "Are you doing modest bits or don't you *know* how big you are? They'll roll out a red carpet anywhere you go."

Dave said, "He's out of his mind and I'll prove it." He picked up the phone. "Maybe years ago it was one thing . . . hello, may I have the Desert Inn, please."

Conversation stopped. Dave lit a cigarette, crossed one leg over the other and blew smoke rings at the ceiling. "Connect me with the Lounge, please, darling . . . Hello, I'd like to reserve a table for about twenty minutes from now for Sammy Davis, Jr. and a party of . . ." The burst of red across his cheeks was as though he'd been slapped. He lowered the phone back on the hook. "Sam . . . I did it again. I'm sorry."

I shrugged. "Let's not make a ninety-minute spectacular out of it." I could feel everybody looking at me, embarrassed for me. There were murmers of "Well if that's how they are then who the hell needs 'em . . ." "They're a hundred years behind the times . . . " The party was lying on the floor dead.

I stood up. "Charley, get hot on the phone with room service and have them bring over twenty steak sandwiches, and tell them we'll need a case of their best champagne, quick-style. Morty, do me a favor. Swing by the casino and find Sunny and the kids. Tell 'em it's a party. Invite everybody you see that we dig." I turned on the hi-fi set, loud. Within ten minutes the crowd of kids pouring in was drowning it out, and the room came alive like somebody'd plugged us in.

Dave came over to where I was standing. "You okay?"

"Thanks, baby. I'm fine."

I had the feeling of having waited all my life to own a raincoat and when finally I got one it wasn't working, the water was coming through.

I had to get bigger, that's all. I just had to get bigger.

from "Fighting Back: A Life in the Struggle for Civil Rights"

by James B. McMillan

It was 1960. Oran Gragson, was mayor and I was president of the NAACP. We had the Voter's League. Throughout the country there were sit-ins, and in the South people were fighting to eliminate discrimination.[1] The national NAACP office sent out correspondence to the presidents of all the branches saying that each branch should do everything possible to eliminate all vestiges of discrimination in its region. As I read it I asked myself, "What can we do to *really* start a movement here to eliminate segregation?"

Dave Hoggard and I got together that night and talked about it. I said, "Dave, we're going to write a letter to the mayor, tell him we've received instructions from national headquarters to take action against segregation in this community. I'm going to give him thirty days to respond, thirty days to tell us what he can do to help eliminate discrimination in the city of Las Vegas." We wrote the letter and I sent it to the mayor's office. I didn't expect an immediate response, but I thought the tone of the letter might shake up white people, get them to think that we were stirred up and that we might actually do something this time. Three or four days later Alan Jarlson, a reporter for the *Sun* who worked city hall, was in the mayor's office. He saw the letter and called me and said he wanted to use it as the basis for a story, to get the news out. I said, "Well, good. Be my guest."

At that time most of the newspaper people and the television and radio people were tight with the establishment in this town. Nothing got out that would rock the boat. Hank Greenspun, the editor and publisher of the *Sun*, was the exception, and he was our early salvation. Greenspun loaded his "Where I Stand" columns with civil rights issues. In contrast the *Review-Journal*, which John Cahlan and his brother Al ran, never had anything good to say about the blacks or eliminating segregation; in fact some people believe that the *R-J* went so far as to deliberately cover news about blacks in a negative way. We were lucky that there were two papers. If it hadn't been for Hank Greenspun and his son we wouldn't have had a chance to get anything in front of the public. Greenspun ran Jarlson's story the next day, and all of Las Vegas knew that the NAACP was threatening a boycott if something wasn't done immediately to end discrimination.

There was a national radio program broadcast from the Fremont Hotel, and this guy took the newspaper story and put it out that night on the radio: "The NAACP threatens a boycott on the Las Vegas Strip in thirty days if there is no response to their request to negotiate a desegregation agreement." When that went out on radio throughout the United States, all hell broke loose. Radio and television stations and newspapers everywhere picked it up. This was a tremendous story, to have this type of thing happen in Las Vegas, the convention city of the United States. Our local politicians *had* to start doing something.

I was dumbfounded by what had happened. Who would ever have thought that our letter could cause this much trouble? I was just as happy as I could be, and most of the black community was happy, walking around talking about it on their jobs and what have you. But some people were frightened and some of the ministers were frightened, saying that if we went and started a disturbance on the Strip, our side of town could wind up being burned down. But I stayed forceful, and the common people didn't want to hear that crap even if their ministers were speaking it. The ministers were saying, "Go easy, Mac. Go slow," but they did work with us from the very beginning. We even had meetings in the churches to plan our tactics, and this went on for several weeks.

Shortly after the news broke I had a meeting with Oran Gragson and Reed Whipple in my office. They tried to convince me to call off the demonstration, saying that it wouldn't be good for the city and the county, and they promised to be much more responsive to the black community in the future with city jobs and so forth. Reed Whipple, who was with the First National Bank at that time, said he would see to it that blacks could get loans to buy houses and start businesses and this and that. But they claimed they didn't have the power to do anything about segregation in the hotels and casinos and elsewhere. I turned them down. The demonstration was still on.

After the mayor and Whipple met with me there was no other movement to solve this thing. I'm wondering what in the hell I'm going to do now. I was getting death threats, telephone calls, letters, Ku Klux Klan people . . . my kids would answer the phone and they would wake up screaming at night because people threatened to throw bombs in the house. Bob Bailey and a group of men in the black community walked and stood guard around my house for ten days to make sure that we didn't have any fire bombing or shooting or anything like that.

After I turned down Gragson and Whipple, I had just ten days left to organize the demonstration. I'm threatening to have people picket with signs, people walking on the strip, blocking traffic, going into hotels, being arrested precisely thirty days from the date I had sent the letter. It didn't look like we could pull it off. We were having pep rallies in the churches, and the press and television people would cover these—we would make inflammatory statements about what we were going to do and how bad it was going to be. But that was all I had going for me. I didn't have any plans made for the march; I didn't have any groups volunteering to go into the hotels and get arrested and maybe get hit over the head . . . I'm hanging. I'm about to be out there with nothing covering my naked ass. I'm thinking I might have to leave town, because I'm going to fall on my face: "This isn't going to happen. These people are *not* going to march, and we're going to be ruined forever in this town." The only thing that I had going for me was that the caucasians had not faced this type of thing before and they really didn't know what was going to happen. They were afraid.

Then we got a break. Oscar Crozier called me up. He'd been in touch with some of the underworld people that was involved in running the Strip hotels. He said, "I want to talk to you, man."

I said, "OK, come on by the house."

Oscar told me that the people who owned some of these hotels had flown in to Las Vegas and had a meeting: "They said they want to know what you're about—this boycott, this marching and all of this. They told me to tell you to cool it or you might be found floating face down in Lake Mead."

I said, "Oscar, they can't get off that easy. Tell these people that I'm not a gambler. I don't have any money. I'm not trying to cut into this business. All I'm trying to do is make this a cosmopolitan city, and that will make more money for them. You tell them that and let me know what they say." I was almost ready to throw in the towel. If he had come back to me and said, "Man, they said no. You better cut this crap out," I would have peeked at my hole card.

A couple of days later Oscar called again. "Mac," he said, "it's OK. They're going to make their people let blacks stay in the hotels. They're going to integrate this town. You can make the announcement that this thing has been settled and that there will be no more discrimination in public accommodations. Black people can go into restaurants and stay at hotels and gamble and eat and everything else." He told me that what I had to do was call the Desert Inn and ask for Mr. Taylor, who was running the place for Moe Dalitz at that time. "He will tell you that they have given you the final OK."

I said, "I'm not going to make any announcement until a couple of days before the deadline we gave the city."

Oscar said, "That's OK."

After I got the information from Crozier, three ministers came into the office and said, "Mac, we just can't support you any longer. You're going to get our town burned down. You have to call off this march."

I said, "You mean to tell me you're going to leave me hanging out here like that?"

They said, "We don't care, we don't want you to march. We can't support you."

These were prominent men in the community, but I had lost all respect for them. I told them, "Well, I want you guys to know that you don't have to worry about your town being burned down. It's all settled. Don't say anything about it until I tell you to."

Everything Oscar Crozier told me came true. I phoned Taylor and said, "I'm supposed to call you in regard to this march and demonstration that we're going to have. And you're supposed to tell me that I don't have to have the march, and that you have accepted all the terms that we have talked about."

Slowly he said, "Yes, that's correct. It's been settled. We have accepted your terms."

Hank Greenspun has been working behind the scenes with some hotel owners, and he and I called a meeting at the Moulin Rouge to announce the settlement. There were churches in West Las Vegas where we probably could have met, but I suggested that we should meet at a neutral site. The place wasn't fixed up or anything for it— chairs were all stacked up in the hall, and we just moved them around and pulled the table out and had the meeting. David Hoggard, Woodrow Wilson, Bob Bailey, Donald Clark and I were there for the NAACP. We had the justice of the peace, the sheriff, Governor Grant Sawyer, Oran Gragson . . . all of these people came, and the press was there. We announced that there would not be any demonstrations, because discrimination in hotels and public accommodations on the Strip had ended. The following day we formed teams of NAACP men and women to go out to the hotels to test them. And all the hotels accepted them. They could go to the tables to gamble; they could go to the restaurants and eat; they could make reservations for rooms.

Years later the Moulin Rouge was named a historic site because that's where we supposedly met to sign the agreement that segregation would be ended in the city of Las Vegas. But there was nothing signed, and politicians had nothing to do with it. Governor Grant Sawyer was in Washington talking with the Kennedys or whatever when this damn thing busted in the papers. He got on a plane and flew back here quick, and I met with him and told him it had all been settled. Other politicians were at our meeting to announce the agreement, but they had done nothing. All of their hand wringing and all of their rhetoric didn't mean anything: they didn't own the hotels; they didn't own the gaming joints; they didn't own the restaurants. This thing was settled by Oscar Crozier and a handful of powerful hotel owners, and politicians played almost no role in it.

The hotels had settled because it was good business to settle. They knew that some southerners wouldn't want to gamble at an integrated casino, but they also knew that they needed to make sure that the convention business stayed, and that white people would not boycott Las Vegas. Money moves the world. When these fellows realized that they weren't going to lose any money, that they might even make more, they were suddenly colorblind.

*   *   *

I'VE LONG WONDERED whether I did the right thing by turning down the offer Mayor Gragson and Reed Whipple made when we were threatening to demonstrate on the Strip in 1960. We had momentum, but the mood of the country at that time would have given us integration anyway in three or four years. By insisting that it happen *now*, I lost a great opportunity to get red lining stopped, and to be given loans and mortgages and jobs to placate us. That could have been the right way to go . . . opening up the city eliminating segregation, didn't do anything but help the white establishment make more money. No economic benefit, nothing for black people. I thought that with a desegregated city, blacks would still go to black businesses and spend their money; but I soon saw how mistaken I was.

You can have all the civil rights you want, you know. You can get a job sweeping the floor downtown in a hotel or be a cocktail waitress, but if you don't have capital in your community . . . I hate to say this, but in Las Vegas, through the success of the civil rights movement and our NAACP actions, we actually hurt the black population. When blacks were confined to the Westside, that's where their money stayed: we had five black gaming joints and two Chinese joints in our community that would hire black people, put them to work. All the money was going into black hands where we could develop the community— restaurants, stores, gaming, and things. Then when we got civil rights, and we could eat, shop and gamble anywhere, all this business moved to the white man. Before desegregation Jerry's Nugget was just a slot joint on the fringe of the black community, and now it's . . . Jerry's Nugget didn't give us a damn thing. They got a lot of black business, but they only hired two or three black dealers for the whole operation. Here's how we lost all our money, all our capital; we were OK (sad to say this) as white people forced us to stay in our community, but when we solved that problem and tore the barrier down and could take our money and go, that's what we did. I'm saying that black businesses went under when we got our civil rights.

When desegregation finally came, and blacks began taking their money elsewhere, white businesses on the Westside were hurt too. The Westside had two clubs that were owned by Orientals, and it really didn't hurt my conscience at all that they lost all of their black business. In fact I was happy. They hadn't been doing anything to help blacks anyway except hiring a few, and they were taking the money and sending it to San Francisco or wherever it was. They weren't putting anything back in the black community. The black clubs were the ones that I felt sorry for, and the grocery stores and little shops. I thought that desegregation would make the town different, and the atmosphere would be better if we could go anywhere we pleased. But for thirty years after we won our battle I didn't see any construction going on in west Las Vegas. So there's a downside to integration.

"States' Rights Enterprise," from *Nevada: The Great Rotten Borough* (1966)

Gilman Ostrander

When evangelist Billy Graham brought his "Crusade for Christ" to Las Vegas in 1978, the New York Times *noted the irony of "the foremost spokesman for Christian virtue" preaching to the masses in the nation's "Citadel of Sin." Las Vegans failed to see the irony, but rather expressed pleasure that yet another superstar was bringing his "headliner excitement" to the city. The famed evangelist was quick to point out that Las Vegas contained far more churches than casinos and it was not the "greatest center for gambling in the United States." That distinction, he said, belonged to Wall Street. "I would not condemn Wall Street," he intoned, "and I did not come here to condemn gambling." Although no precise moment can be identified when Las Vegas shed its image as a "Citadel of Sin" and became a widely-admired metropolis, Graham's 1978 visit provides as good a turning point as any. Between 1931 and 1970, the national media routinely emphasized Nevada's unique ambience, most often in negative terms. During the early 1960s, the* New York Times *ran a series of hypercritical investigative articles by Wallace Turner that argued gambling in Nevada was "a force for evil." Like other critics, Turner viewed the efforts by Governors Charles Russell and Grant Sawyer to establish effective regulations over gambling as too little, much too late. In 1963, two well-established investigative reporters, Ed Reid and Ovid Demaris, published* The Green Felt Jungle *(1963) that denounced Las Vegas as a "grotesque Disneyland" that "fleeced" tourists, and in 1966, historian Gilman Ostrander unleashed a hyperbolic attack upon the entire state of Nevada. From its earliest days, he said, Nevada's history revealed a "rotten borough" in which there was little, if anything, of redeeming value.*

James Madison was aware that "possible mischiefs" might arise from the quality of representation in the Senate. He hazarded the further opinion in *The Federalist* that greater troubles were likely to occur as a result of the powers which had been retained by the states than as a result of those which has been conferred upon the national government. "A local spirit," he wrote, "will infallibly prevail much more in the members of Congress, than a national spirit will prevail in the legislatures of the particular states."[1]

By 1787 there already had been abundant evidence to support this view in the irresponsible fiscal policies of states such as Rhode Island and the selfishly anti-national tariff programs of states such as New York. To guard against such manifestations of "local spirit" the Constitutional Convention had been called, and the founding fathers had struck down these specific practices without dissent. What neither Madison nor the other founders foresaw, living in the relatively Arcadian world of eighteenth-century America, was the increased range of mischiefs which would result from the industrial and transportation revolutions. Among the states of the nation, Nevada has been the busiest in availing itself of the advantages of legal mischiefs made possible by the federal system.

Although the greatest profits to Nevada from states'-rights enterprise proved to be mainly in the areas of marriage, divorce, and legalized gambling, other lines of activity were not neglected. At the turn of the twentieth century, the Sagebrush State decided to do what it could to establish the little town of Reno as the national capital for corporate enterprise, and there was nothing especially presumptuous about it. Little Delaware, as well as New Jersey, had already pioneered in this area of states' rights economics with lax incorporation laws, and such Western states as Arizona had quickly followed suit.

According to the Delaware law, corporations, no matter where they were physically located, could make Delaware their legal residence by paying a fee and sharing an office and a resident agent in the state with other similarly inclined companies. Conveniently located for Eastern businesses which wished to avoid restrictions imposed upon corporations by states such as New York or Pennsylvania, Delaware in the twentieth century became the home of more than 28,000 corporations, paying taxes of more than $5 million a year.[2]

An observer of the American political system who was unfamiliar with the oddities of American federalism, might be surprised that one state could legally usurp authority, as well as tax money, from another state in this manner. He might find it equally surprising that a nationwide monopoly such as the Standard Oil Company could incorporate on a state-wide basis and then could move its legal place of residence arbitrarily from Ohio to New Jersey without having to move any of the business itself. To tell the truth, a good many Americans themselves were surprised by the ease with which Standard Oil accomplished this transformation at the end of the nineteenth century, making itself magically invulnerable to the supreme court of Ohio, which had ordered its dissolution. It was shortly after this much publicized escape from peril by Standard Oil that Nevada, along with other states, hopefully developed its own legal sanctuary.

Amid so much competition, Nevada was obliged to content itself with battening mainly on California, which was the only nearby state with enough business life to make it worthwhile. It is true that a Boston corporation would have suffered little disadvantage in incorporating in Nevada rather than in New Jersey, but it appears that, with few legal advantages to choose between, the corporations usually made their mythical settlements close to home.

Nevada passed its cut-rate general incorporation law in 1903, and the incorporation agents, who immediately sprang into being, were at once deluged with inquiries from corporate enterprises all over the country, existing corporations as well as contemplated ones. There was, of course, a great deal of comparison shopping, "I have just completed an examination of your general incorporation law," an enterpriser wrote from Indianapolis, ". . . and believe it a better law than New Jersey or Arizona, although it is somewhat cheaper in the latter. . . ."[3] The trouble for Nevada was that there were other states, such as Arizona, that wanted to get in on a good thing.

One of the leading agencies in Nevada for incorporating businesses from other states was the State Agent and Transfer Syndicate, Inc. This firm was troubled during the early years of the incorporation law because it did not know what the law meant; nor did its customers. The main points of the law were understood, however, for they were simple. As a company official explained to an inquirer:

"There is no annual tax on corporations nor is there any supervision over the conduct of the business other than a general compliance with the corporation law. The principal requirements are that a principal office must be established and maintained, in which office there must be an appointed agent to receive any legal service; in said principal office there shall be filed a copy of the articles, a copy of the ByLaws and also be kept on file a duplicate stock ledger; which said ledger is a confidential service as the ledger is not open for inspection save as set forth in the General Corporation Law."[4]

As for costs, the state required twenty cents per $1,000 of capitalization and a minimum of $50; additional fees included $2.50 for notarization and twenty-five cents for filing.[5]

Many of the companies incorporated in Nevada under the new act were fly-by-night operations, much like the promotional mining companies with which Nevada was long familiar. At the same time, the state registered blue-chip organizations, such as the California Standard Oil Company, a customer of the State Agent and Transfer Syndicate, organized to operate in South America as a subsidiary of the Standard Oil Company of California. How a business went about sending its sword to the marriage in such cases is to be seen in the instructions form Standard Oil to the State Agent and Transfer Syndicate:

> We will appreciate it if you will organize with persons from your office, and upon completing the organization, have the board of your directors resign, and call a stockholders' meeting, at which the following directors should be elected . . .[6]

A board was elected and then persuaded to resign, and a stockholders' meeting was held to elect the officers suggested by the legal firm which was handling the affairs of the California Standard Oil Company.[7]

Nevada's old enemy, California, passed a law in 1917 which virtually prohibited the sale in California of stocks of Nevada corporations which did not meet California's legal requirements for incorporation.[8] That Blue Sky Law knocked the bottom out of a growing business, but Nevada continued to operate a modest incorporation activity. However, after the passage of that law, the Nevada legislature began, more and more to employ the lure of tax benefits, rather than that of corporate benefits, in its effort to siphon off some of the growing wealth of the Golden State.

The obvious key to Nevada's program of tax reform was the fact that the resident population was small and the tourist population growing. The shift of the tax burden from the former to the latter was most successfully accomplished through the gasoline tax. By this means the highways returned the largest share of Nevada's taxes just as the railroads had been obliged to do a generation earlier. In 1955 the income from state and county gasoline taxes was more than $7.3 million; whereas the income from gambling taxes was only $4.75 million.[9]

It might be argued that this tax was justified by the fact that there were more miles of highway per capita in Nevada than elsewhere and that out-of-state users could reasonably be expected to bear their share in the costs of construction and upkeep. They were, however, already doing so. According to the terms of the Oddie-Colton Act of 1927, the federal government was given the authority to increase the federal highway funds available to states that include a large share of the public domain. Consequently, the federal government has put up about eighty per cent of the money to finance Nevada's highways. During the year ending June 30, 1952, Nevada received approximately $6 million of federal money for highway construction.[10]

By the mid-thirties, the Nevada legislature had eliminated all taxes which would seriously affect residents. There was no income tax, no inheritance or death taxes, and no transfer, sales, or gift taxes.[11] The removal of sales and gift taxes was designed to encourage Californians to buy expensive items in Nevada to escape the sales tax levied in their own state. To facilitate further the development of Nevada into a busy distribution center, its cities were maintained as free ports. Manufacturers were allowed to ship goods into the state and store them indefinitely in warehouses without being taxed; only a few other states permitted this.[12] California retaliated, however, with a use tax on goods imported into the state, and Nevada had to reintroduce the sales tax.[13]

To attract wealthy men to the state, the inheritance tax, instituted in the Progressive reform year of 1913, was repealed in 1925. Consequently, when a wealthy Los Angeles business man died in 1928, his estate was exempt from the California inheritance tax because he had established his legal residence in Nevada through owning a summer cottage on the Nevada side of Lake Tahoe. The publicity which greeted this novel aspect of his death brought other millionaires legally to Nevada and encouraged the legislature to make further tax reforms in their behalf. In 1936 it limited taxes on personal property and real estate to five cents on the dollar, and in 1939 it reduced real and personal property taxes still further. At the same time, it launched a nationwide campaign to lure rich men and businesses to a state that had few taxes and no labor problems.[14]

The campaign has been at least modestly successful in bringing into the state a wealthy class known contemptuously to the old Nevadans as "the tax dodgers." A key figure in this affluent immigration has been Norman Biltz, a Los Angeles salesman who became a Nevada real estate promoter in the 1920s, concentrating especially on the Tahoe region.[15]

In the search for methods of public finance which would not involve taxation of its citizens, the Nevada legislature, returned every now and then to the idea of a state lottery, for which hundreds of thousands of tickets would be sold illegally at great profit in other states. Such a scheme finally passed the legislature in 1937. It required a constitutional amendment, however, which in turn required the affirmative vote of the people, and it was voted down. The opposition to it had been effectively organized by the gambling interests in the state, who, naturally, opposed any proposal in which the state competed with what was rapidly becoming its leading private industry.[16] (The gambling interests were also successful in outlawing bank night in the motion-picture theaters of Reno.[17])

II

Nevadans can hardly deny that their taxes have been structured for the purpose of obtaining money from foreigners and especially Californians; nor, probably would they wish to deny it. From the time of the Comstock Lode to the period of the partially successful attacks by Progressives on railroad-rate discrimination, Nevada was economically a California colony, ruthlessly plundered to enrich San Francisco's entrepreneurs. Every good Nevadan believes that his state has a lot coming to it from California, and this attitude is undoubtedly responsible for much of the support given to the gambling interests by Nevadans who otherwise disapprove of them.

Nevadans are apt to take umbrage when accused of enacting easy divorce laws and legalized gambling only for the purpose of milking strangers. They will argue that this legal laxity in the Sagebrush State is simply an honest expression of that Western individualism which leaves every man free to go to the devil any way he wishes. Unquestionably there is a good deal to this argument. Nevada obviously is not economically motivated in allowing everybody to drive as fast as he likes on its highways, with never a thought of a state speed limit. The absence of a speed limit is in harmony with the generally libertarian outlook of a state devoted almost exclusively to mining and cattle-raising during most of its history.

Legalized prostitution is a more colorful example of Nevada's adherence to the moral code of the old West for sentimental, rather than economic, reasons. Moral forces succeeded in outlawing prostitution in 1923, but it soon returned, by public demand, under police supervision and with mandatory registration and medical inspection. The red-light areas were severely limited, and no soliciting was permitted on the streets. In Las Vegas there was Block 16, a row of shacks just a few blocks from the main thoroughfare. In Reno the "Stockade" or "Bull Pen" was somewhat more removed from the center of town but still accessible. It operated more as a public convenience than as a vested interest: a girl rented one of eighty cribs for two dollars per day and pocketed all of her take.[18]

With the coming of World War II, the Armed Forces brought pressure on the communities of western Nevada to close up their brothels, and open prostitution came to an end in Reno and Las Vegas, as it had a generation earlier during World War I in New Orleans. Since the second world war, prostitution has been, in practice, subject to local option, legally suppressed in the two main centers of population, but somewhat covertly permitted in other towns of the state. (State law, however, prohibits the establishment of a bordello within 400 yards of a church or school house.)[19] It is not likely that prostitution is looked upon with favor by the gambling interests, for it diverts customers from the tables and is out of harmony with the note of innocent good fun to which the gambling casinos are profitably keyed. That it continues to exist openly in some areas is testimony to an existing public opinion opposed to all sumptuary legislation as a matter of principle.

The easy divorce law, like prostitution and gambling, was inherited from Nevada's frontier past long before it came to be exploited to lure foreign dollars into the state. In 1861 the territorial government established a six-months'-residence divorce law, and this law was retained when Nevada became a state. The period of six months corresponded to the six-month period required for state citizenship. Throughout the nineteenth century, only Nevadans availed themselves of their law, and there were few divorces in the state, because few women lived in it."[20]

The new era opened in 1906 with the lavishly publicized Reno divorce of Laura Corey. Laura's husband William was president of U.S. Steel and, at the age of forty, a leading Eastern financial figure. Corey lost his heart to a singing actress, Mabelle Gilman, and deserted his wife in 1905. A year later, the sorrowing Laura arrived in Reno, amid a prodigious fanfare of national public indignation, and took up residence to receive the most avidly followed divorce of the day. Corey waited nine months and then married his Mabelle, and Reno became almost overnight the divorce capital of the nation.

Because California had passed a law in 1903 requiring a year's wait after a divorce before issuance of the final decree, it soon became the chief source of Reno's new prosperity. However, Nevada's lawyers advertised widely in the East and drew many cases from that area also. By 1910 the number of Nevada divorces had risen to about 300 a year. Nevada's lapse into moral order followed in 1913, during the climax of Progressivism, when it prohibited gambling and instituted an inheritance tax. That year the legislature passed a law requiring a year of residence for at least one of the parties in any divorce suit. Consequently, Reno suffered a severe business slump accompanied by a sharp falling off in church attendance, so in 1915 the state returned to the six-month residence period.

In 1920 Mary Pickfold divorced the movie actor Owen Moore to marry Douglas Fairbanks, and this aided the resurgence of the divorce business. Then, in 1927, faced with growing competition from Mexico and France, and threatened by the possibility that Wyoming might adopt a three-month's residence divorce law, Nevada lowered the period from six months to three. The year 1930 saw the granting of 3,000 divorces in Reno, which then had a permanent population of only 18,000; the estimated profit to the town was $3 million. In 1931 Nevada lowered the residence period to six weeks, and Reno divorces rose to 4,745. That, however, proved to be the high water mark. Idaho and Florida also reduced residence requirements to six weeks, but the Nevada legislature was dissuaded from lowering its requirements from thirty days by lawyers who feared that such divorces might be invalidated by the courts in other states. Divorces then dropped to 2,854 in 1934 and to about 2,000 in 1940. By the latter date, however, the business was still providing the main support for 180 lawyers in Reno, with the side result that Nevada politics has been dominated by bench and bar to an unusual extent.

The marriage business in Nevada also moved briskly, and California provided even greater profits from this than from divorces after it passed a law, in 1940, requiring a blood test and a three-day waiting period after issuance of a marriage certificate. Nevada offered instant marriage, around the clock, at a cost of only two dollars for a marriage license and a small donation to the justice of the peace or minister. Richard Lillard, the historian of Nevada noted that the competition for the office of justice of the peace in Reno during the 1930s was every bit as furious as the competition for sheriff had been during prohibition. In 1932 in Nevada, 7,088 marriages were performed, compared with 3,989 divorces.

III

Legalized gambling, like easy divorce in Nevada, was the consequence of the old libertarian Western tradition and the new states' rights avarice. A prohibitionary gambling law of 1909 was unsatisfactory from the beginning. Underworld figures infiltrated the state, and police bribery became scandal. Then in 1912 the law was liberalized to permit "social games" such as poker and whist, provided that winnings were paid off in merchandise instead of in money. In 1913 gambling was again prohibited, but two years later the resulting discontent and corruption again forced the state to moderate the prohibition.

Gambling operators were licensed, and card games legalized, so long as the game was not banked by the operator. This law was observed mainly in the breach until its repeal in 1931.[21]

The Great Depression hit Nevada hard, perhaps harder than it did most other states, and at the same time the prosperity of the divorce mills of Reno was being threatened by the passage of easy-divorce legislation in competing states. The liquor prohibition law had placed Reno under gangster rule—although apparently a rather easy-going one—and the gambling casinos were operating almost as openly as the speakeasies.[22] Most Nevadans probably had as little respect for the one law as for the other, and it would have been quite natural for the state legislature to have repealed the anti-gambling law, solely in response to the wishes of the constituents. At the same time, the 1931 act that completely legalized gambling again was looked upon as a recovery measure, for it was designed to bring outside money into the state.

Nevada gambling establishments celebrated the passage of the law, but they were remarkably slow in adjusting to the new order of things. Professional gamblers, like saloonkeepers, are essentially a deeply conservative class of people. Their rituals have long been prescribed and, quite aside from economic benefits deriving from their observance, tend to remain controlling factors. An extreme version of this conservatism may by seen today in almost any of the "horse parlors" in Nevada. The Turf Club in Reno, for instance, famous for its Chicago-style kosher pastrami sandwiches, maintains the dignified, studious, atmosphere of a Christian Science reading room. Elderly gentlemen peruse the racing forms and follow the results of races as they are marked up on the blackboard in quiet surroundings, undisturbed by the clatter of slot machines and the jingle of juke boxes which assail the ear in the coffee shops and drug stores throughout the Biggest Little City in the World.

Most Nevada gamblers continued the dear old ways throughout the thirties. They operated in darkened and secluded halls, the dealers in shirtsleeves and green eyeshades, dealing to the same customers as in former days. The idea of advertising their places of business apparently occurred to them no more than it did, at that time, to banking establishments. Their business, no doubt, increased, especially with out-of-state customers, as a consequence of their newly won legality, In Reno, the Bank Club, especially, became more prosperous. The real revolution in modern gambling, however, did not begin until the arrival of an ex-carnival man, Raymond Smith, and his sons, Harold and Raymond, Jr., who, with no professional gambling experience behind them, introduced the basic innovations in the business which characterize it today.[23]

Smith left the West Coast in the middle of the depression with a little capital and opened a small gambling casino on Virginia Street in Reno, which he named Harolds Club after his son. From the first, Smith advertised as widely as his resources permitted, and by the end of the decade his billboard advertisements were scattered across half the nation. To attract customers from among those whose incomes had been reduced by the depression, he introduced penny roulette, and to gain publicity, he introduced such gimmicks as mouse roulette, where the winning number was selected by a live mouse. Smith prospered and expanded rapidly.

Smith's basic purpose was to democratize gambling as Henry Ford had democratized the automobile. The older casinos not only catered chiefly to experienced male gamblers, but, so far as possible, they concentrated their efforts on the "high rollers"—fellow professionals whose big bets during an hour or so determined a casino's profit of loss for the evening. Smith always remained true to his penny-roulette beginnings, catering to the common man, with the result that his profits increased over that of his competitors, while his risk was reduced to the vanishing point.

Smith sought the patronage of the common woman even more assiduously than he pursued that of the common man, and with even greater success. Harolds Club was located on the main street of Reno, its row of glass doors opening twenty-four hours a day onto its brightly lighted bars and gambling tables. He substituted female dealers for men at the twenty-one tables, and also employed female shills, inexpensively acquired and quickly trained from the floating population of divorcees. The female dealers operated according to a fixed set of rules, without choice as to whether they would hit or stick, so that they never pitted themselves against the players. To the contrary, they were instructed to help the customers out by giving them counsel, if requested, on the best possible lines of play. Under this kind of friendly tutelage, women warmed to twenty-one, as well as to craps and roulette, so that they now probably contribute at least as much, and perhaps more, to Nevada's profits from gambling, than men do.

In other ways as well, Smith brought an atmosphere of respectability to his gaming place. He instituted a baby-sitting service, so that children would not be left alone in motels, while their mothers were cranking the handles on the slot machines. He installed a museum of western Americana for the edification as well as the entertainment of his customers, and he contributed many large scholarships to deserving students attending the University of Nevada, which is a little more than a mile up the street. Everywhere there were signs reminding customers that they should not spend more than they could afford. If, as sometimes happened, these admonitions were ignored in the heat of play, Harolds Club readily lent funds for the trip home.

When they finally became convinced that they could not beat Smith, the professional operators in the other casinos grudgingly adopted some of his ways. After the war, new casinos were situated as close as possible to Harolds Club, and they copied it as faithfully as they could. The ex-Detroit gambler Lincoln Fitzgerald built the Nevada Club, departing from the model of Harolds Club by building into his casino a private apartment, from which he seldom emerged onto the street.

The Nevada Club has become, probably, the second most successful of the half-dozen of so direct imitations of Harolds Club in Reno. The most successful has been Harrahs Club, located next door to Smith's establishment, which it resembles in almost all respects. Luckily for the proprietor of the new casino, his name was William Harrah; so nothing could be done about his name cashing in on the all but transcontinental billboard advertising of his rival. Like Smith, Harrah came from California with no experience as a professional gambler but with that of an operator of legal games of chance—in his case, bingo—carried on in a carnival atmosphere. These two men, with this common experience, did better than any of the professional gamblers, who operated virtually all of the other large casinos in the state.

IV

At the time that gambling was legalized once again in 1931, Reno was the nearest thing to a center of population which Nevada contained, and the only town in the state which was nationally known. Las Vegas was only a dot on the map, a railroad division point on the line from Los Angeles to Chicago. At the time gambling was legalized, Las Vegas was just beginning to show life, with the construction of neighboring Hoover Dam, authorized by Congress in 1928. It is typical of Nevada statesmanship that this vast project, crucially important to the development of southern Nevada, was sponsored by two Californians, in the Swing-Johnson Bill, while Nevada's Senators were mainly busying themselves on behalf of the silver interests.

Boulder City was created as a government-owned community near Las Vegas, bringing a permanent population to the area, as well as a transient group of construction workers. Because Boulder City was absolutely dry, Las Vegas received the custom of the construction workers, whose historic mission proved to be not only to create Lake Mead and to irrigate the Southwest but to prime the pump for the subsequent torrent of gambling and allied tourist business in Las Vegas, which has increased continually since then.

Except for legalized gambling, Las Vegas has less economic reason for being than Reno, which remains an important distribution point for a large area. Las Vegas, however, draws its customers from the metropolitan areas of Los Angeles and San Diego, more populous and more rapidly growing than the San Francisco Bay region. Consequently, Las Vegas has far outdistanced the rest of the state in its rate of growth. In 1959 the population of Clark County, where Las Vegas is situated, was 122,000, while that of Washoe County was 83,000. Total population of the state stood at 280,000.[24] Nevada prides itself on being the most rapidly growing state in the nation, but outside these two gambling centers, the population has made only modest gains over the past generation.

Initially Las Vegas developed its gambling activities after the pattern established in Reno, but on a smaller scale, its casinos concentrated within a few blocks on Fremont Street in the center of town. Until the close of World War II it was distinctly small-time, compared with the older city to the north. Its first big casino, the Golden Nugget, was built in 1946, under the direction of Guy McAfee, a retired captain of police, and it repaid its original investment in nine months.[25] The Golden Nugget remains the main downtown casino, but it was rapidly overshadowed by developments outside the town along what came to be known as "the Strip."

In 1947 Marion Hicks, a local construction and hotel man, in cooperation with Lieutenant Governor Clifford Jones, built the Thunderbird, which was to be a model for the more lavish hotel-resort-casinos to follow on the Strip. In 1950 Wilbur Clark built the Desert Inn for $4.5 million. The Sahara was completed in 1952 for $5.5 million, followed by the Sands, Showboat, Royal Nevada, Riviera, Moulin Rouge, Dunes, Stardust, Martinique (at a cost of $15 million), Tropicana, Continental, Trade Winds, Vegas Plasa, Casa Blanca, San Soucis, Horizon, and others.[26]

With the development of the Strip, Las Vegas asserted its independence of Reno and enthusiastically submitted to the influence of Hollywood. The Desert Inn was a typical Strip operation, employing a manager and two assistants, eighty-five dealers, eighteen pit bosses and box men, seven change girls, and three slot machine supervisors in its casino. In the mid-fifties it kept $2 million on hand for an average day and up to $3 million on weekends.[27] Where the Desert Inn and its more luxurious counterparts departed from Reno hotel casinos—the Riverside, the Mapes and the Holiday—was in its lavishness of décor and of free entertainment. In 1954 the Strip hotels paid $8 million for entertainment, in 1955 the outlay rose to $20 million and it has increased continually since then.[28] The Reno and Lake Tahoe casinos began, then, to imitate those of the Strip, but they have not kept pace.

The palaces on the Strip are calculated to attract the big spenders, leaving the dollar-ante crowd to the downtown casinos. The high rollers from Texas and Los Angeles continue to be an important part of the play on the Strip. However, the big shows are as attractive to the small spenders as to the high rollers, so that the little man and his wife have begun to leave downtown for the Strip, as evidenced by boarded-up casinos on Fremont Street. As in the case of Reno, gambling is de-emphasized in the promotional literature of Paradise, as the unincorporated area which includes the Strip is named. The advertisements instead proclaim the wealth of free entertainment and "fun in the sun." Special airline and hotel rates put a vacation in Las Vegas within the reach of families of modest means throughout the nation, providing the casinos are avoided. However, the promoters expect that the casinos will not be avoided either by these vacationers or by the highly paid entertainers.

In the mid-fifties, at a time when there were only ten resort hotels on the Strip, the Las Vegas area supported thirty-five commercial hotels and 250 motels. The total money left in Las Vegas by tourists in 1955 was computed to be $164,325,992.50, a little more than $3,650 for every living man, woman and child in the town.[29] Since then the number of resort hotels has more than doubled, outrunning the rapidly increasing population, and it may be supposed that the profits from "tourism" have at least kept pace with the expansion of the community. Reno has been cut off from such expansion by the booming Lake Tahoe development, and it therefore retains a good deal of its original natural beauty, which one may find only a few blocks away from the "Alley," where Harolds, Harrahs, and the other clubs keep up the action around the clock every day in the week.

Nevadans, who welcomed legal gambling in the midst of the depression, have mixed emotions about the current state of affairs. One old Nevadan commented recently that "The Nevadans don't like it, and one day they may vote it out. But in the meantime, they have it under control. The Nevadans don't go to these places, and they don't associate with divorcees. And many people coming into the state don't like this either." Some Nevadans evidently continue to look upon themselves as belonging to a mining and cattle state which permits gambling because cattlemen and miners have always engaged in it, but it has long been obvious that this is no longer the case.

In 1958 the personal income derived from ranching comprised 1.2 per cent of the total state income; that from mining, 2.5 per cent. Wholesale and retail trade were more important, at 12.1 per cent; while the income of government workers was increasing and stood at 15.6 per cent. The biggest share, however, came from amusement, recreation, and services, which contributed 29.1 per cent of the state's payroll. In terms of percentage of the work force employed in 1959, mining and agriculture accounted for 10 per cent, as compared with 29 per cent for "services and miscellany" largely gambling and attendant activities. Government accounted for 17.7 per cent and wholesale and retail, for 19.3.[30] The state is dependent upon gambling as upon no other line of business. Since gambling does much to support Nevada's retail trade, its nearest competitors as employers of Nevadans are the federal, state, and local governments. In the area of free enterprise, the gamblers control the economy: they know it and the politicians know it.

V

Down to World War II, gambling in Nevada, centered in Reno, was regarded as a home-operated industry. Raymond Smith, of Harolds Club, the leading operator in the field, was, to be sure, an outsider, but he was devoid of out-of-state gambling connections, and he was making Nevada his home. Following the war, however, only the most guileless of Nevadans could fail to observe that professional gamblers had moved in from out of state to take over the casinos. They were, after all, the people most qualified for the positions. Raymond Smith was unusual in having succeeded in the field without prior experience. He commented once, however, that it had cost him about a million dollars in losses through cheating before he had ironed out the wrinkles.[31]

In 1946, Benjamin "Bugsy" Siegel built the Flamingo Hotel—one of the first on the Strip—with $1 million of his own and $6 million of borrowed money.[32] It has been said that Siegel, as a notorious underworld figure, was not welcomed in the community. At the time he went into business, however, all that was required to receive a gambling license was the making of an application to the city or country commissioners, and no investigation was made of the criminal record of the applicant. Even after 1949, when such investigations began to be made, imprisonment for a gambling offense elsewhere was not counted against the applicant, because gambling was legal in Nevada.[33] Siegel, moreover, held the whip hand over other gambling houses in the area by his control of the racing wire service of the Al Capone mob which was used in all of the larger casinos.

In 1947 Siegel was the spectacular victim of a gangland murder in his home in Los Angeles, and his assassination drew national attention to the possibility of gangster control of Nevada gambling. Then Harry Sherwood was shot in his Lake Tahoe resort, Louis Strauss was arrested and identified as "Russian Louis" of the Eastern underworld, and Benny Binion, indicted in Texas for operating a numbers racket, was questioned concerning the murder of Herbert "the Cat" Noble.[34] The likelihood that these happenings indicated widespread criminal infiltration of Nevada was widely discussed, but the official line in Nevada appears to have been that only Siegel, among the nation's gang leaders, had been seriously involved in Nevada affairs, and that the slate had been wiped clean by his death.[35]

However, in 1950–1 the Senate investigating committee, headed by Estes Kefauver of Tennessee, put an entirely different face on the matter. Siegel, the committee found, had carried on gaming operations in California and elsewhere before coming to Nevada and had been associated with Charles "Lucky" Luciano, Frank Costello, Joe Adonis, Meyer Lansky, and other Eastern mob leaders. Among them, Lansky had become an important Las Vegas operator. Siegel had controlled the Las Vegas racing wire service since 1942, through Moe Sedway, a convicted gambler and former Eastern mobster. After Siegel's death, the Flamingo had been taken over by another gambler with a long record of arrests, Sanford Adler, and his associates. Adler had later sold out his interests to other hoodlums and had removed to the Reno and Lake Tahoe areas to continue his operations there.[36]

The committee found the Desert Inn to be operated by Wilbur Clark, an old-time gambler who had once worked the gambling boats off California, and whose business associates were identified as gamblers and bootleggers from the Middle West and elsewhere.[37] It also learned that the Bank Club in Reno

> . . . is owned and operated by William Graham and James McKay, who were convicted of mail fraud in New York, but who returned to Nevada after the expiration of their prison terms. . . . Also operating in Reno are Mert Wertheimer, a big-time Michigan gambler who has been in partnership in Florida with such notorious gangsters as Joe Adonis, the Lanskys, and Frank Erickson, and with Lincoln Fitzgerald and Daniel Sullivan, members of the Michigan gambling syndicate.[38]

Kefauver elicited from Lieutenant Governor Clifford Jones and State Tax Commissioner William J. Moore the fact that prior to 1949 little or no effort had been made to screen the applicants for gambling licenses. After that time some effort was made to deny them to undesirables, but those already holding licenses were not disturbed, and gambling convictions were not held against new applicants. It was the conclusion of the Kefauver Committee that,

> ... too many of the men running gambling operations in Nevada are either members of existing out-of-state gambling syndicates or have had histories of close association with the underworld characters who operate those syndicates. The licensing system which is in effect in the state has not resulted in excluding the undesirables from the State but has merely served to give their activities a seeming cloak of respectability.[39]

The committee concluded that two major national crime syndicates existed, and that both of them were operating in Nevada, or at least had associates operating there.

Jones and Moore, despite their responsible positions in the state with respect to controlling gambling, were financially involved in the gaming business. Moore, who was on the commission directly responsible for gaining control, was part owner of the Last Frontier, and he had recently received a wire service deal which, in the opinion of the committee, gave him a considerable financial advantage over his competitors. Jones was part owner of the Thunderbird and holder of a small share in the Pioneer Club, which had been sold to him for $5000 and had regularly returned $14,000 annually to him thereafter. Jones's law partner, the committee further pointed out, was the district attorney of Clark County.[40]

It was not until 1955 that the first real efforts were made to bring Nevada gambling under actual governmental control. In that year the Thunderbird's gambling license was suspended until Marion Hicks and former Lieutenant Governor Jones divested themselves of their interests. The New Frontier's license was delayed pending an investigation, and the motion picture actor George Raft was denied the right to purchase two per cent of the Flamingo because of his long association with such mobsters as Mickey Cohen and "Bugsy" Siegel. Tony Cornero Stralla was denied a license for his $6.5 million Stardust, because he had been convicted as a rum-runner and had operated gambling ships off the coast of California.[41]

Governor Charles H. Russell, in the course of his efforts to reform Nevada gambling in 1955, conceded that the state's leading industry had been infiltrated by elements of Murder, Incorporated, and by hoodlums from New York, Chicago, St. Louis, Miami, and Detroit. He declared, however: "I am determined that Nevada's licensed gambling shall not be invaded by hoodlums or organized crime."[42] To this end, a ninety-day moratorium was imposed on new gambling licenses, except those which were already pending. A three-man commission was organized with authority over gambling throughout the state and with the power to impound casino records and to compel the attendance of witnesses at hearings. Their control over state gambling is subject to request by the tax commission for the reopening of any licensing case.

The Gaming Commission has listed men believed to be leading figures in the national crime syndicates, and has told state gambling interests not to associate with them in any way. In October 1963 the commission revoked the gambling license of Frank Sinatra because he had permitted a black-listed hoodlum to stay at the Cal-Neva Lodge at Lake Tahoe. The effect of this was to force Sinatra to sell his 50 per cent interest in the Cal-Neva and his 9 per cent interest in the Sands Hotel in Las Vegas, holdings valued at an estimated $3.5 million.[43] These efforts to assert governmental authority over Nevada gambling were begun only after a decade of virtually unopposed infiltration by gangsters, and it does not appear that anything is seriously contemplated that would divorce gambling from those gangsters who are already entrenched in the business.

VI

"Among the many unlooked-for treasures that are bound up and hidden away in the depths of Sierra solitudes," wrote the naturalist John Muir, "none more surely charm and surprise all kinds of travelers than the glacier lakes." Muir supposed that there were not less than 1,500 of these, but the undoubted queen among them was Lake Tahoe.

> Lake Tahoe, 22 miles long by 10 wide, and from 500 to over 1600 feet in depth, is the largest of all the Sierra lakes. . . . Its forested shores go curving in and out around many an emerald bay and pinecrowned promontory, and its waters are everywhere as keenly pure as any to be found among the highest mountains.[44]

Mark Twain walked up from Carson City to Lake Tahoe in the early sixties and camped there for several weeks, and like Muir, he was most struck by the lake's "keenly pure" waters:

The forest above us was dense and cool, the sky above us was cloudless and brilliant with sunshine, the broad lake before us was glassy and clear, or rippled and breezy, or black and storm-tossed, according to Nature's mood. . . . The view was always fascinating, bewitching, entrancing. . . . So singularly clear was the water that where it was only twenty or thirty feet deep the bottom was so perfectly distinct that the boat seemed floating in the air! Yes, where it was even *eighty* feet deep. Every little pebble was distinct, every speckled trout, every hand's-breadth of sand. . . . Down through the transparency of these great depths the water was not *merely* transparent, but dazzlingly, brilliantly so. All objects seen through it had bright, strong vividness, not only of outline, but of very minute detail, which they would not have had when seen simply through the same depth of atmosphere.[45]

Today travelers coming upon Lake Tahoe from the south side by Highway 50 may well be surprised at what they see, but they will not be charmed. They will come, first of all, upon a dirty beach, one of several around that great, high lake, which are maintained for the public, complete with life guard and hot-dog stand. The lake will be there to see, but it will take several more miles of driving before it is framed for them above by the dense, cool forests. They must, of course, drive past Stateline; past Harrahs and Harolds and Harveys and so on, and after that they must find a place, between the private cottages and smaller casinos, where they can go down to the water.

Some might wonder why Lake Tahoe was not set aside as a national park long before the real-estate promoters came and cut it into private lots. It might be supposed that Francis G. Newlands, Nevada's most distinguished senator and the leading conservationist in Congress, might have made some effort to preserve this part of his state. That was not the kind of conservationist that Newlands was, however, nor was this the kind of conservation which appealed especially to his Progressive colleagues. He and they looked upon conservation less as the preserving of nature than as the putting of nature to intelligent use for the benefit of society. Newlands, as he wrote the Nevada *State Journal* in 1909,[46] saw Lake Tahoe as source of water power and as a navigable water way, even though, from a navigational point of view, it is difficult to see that Lake Tahoe had much to offer. The Progressive movement was good but not beautiful.

Lake Tahoe was left mainly to the real-estate promoters, and on the Nevada side they appealed to the well-to-do summer-cottage crowd, to the winter-sports enthusiasts, and, in ever greater numbers, to the "tax dodgers." There were also coffee shops and bars which had slot machines, but the real potential of Lake Tahoe was not understood until William Harrah moved in, in the 1950s.

It appears that during the fifties, Harrah took up where the Smiths had left off in the development of gambling operational methods in Reno. During the late forties and early fifties, Harolds Club suffered from the fact that one of the owners, Harold himself, went on a ten-year drinking bout, consuming according to his own accounts, as much as four quarts of whiskey in a day. During that period, he gambled away his money in rival casinos to the point where it was feared that other operators might gain influence in the Smith organization. Harold Smith finally got a grip on himself and made a vow to the "Big Gent Upstairs," as he puts it, and he became president of the organization.[47] In the meantime, the gaunt, gray, austere, efficient William Harrah moved methodically ahead to become the state's leading operator of gambling establishments.

Incredible as it may seem, Harrah was the first big-time Nevada operator to reason that the state line at Lake Tahoe, as the closest point to the California customers, was strategically located for a gambling casino. It was urged against this idea, that a casino in that area would have to close during the winter and that in other seasons there would be no place for customers to stay overnight. Nevertheless, Harrah bought up the acres adjoining the California border and built two large casinos and a spacious parking lot. Since it was an inconvenient trip for San Franciscans to make in one day—almost five hours each way— Harrah started bus lines.

Characteristically scientific in his business operations, Harrah paid the non-profit, tax-exempt Stanford Research Institute $16,000 to tell him how he could get customers around the clock by bus. The resulting monograph, entitled *An Investigation of Factors Influencing Bus Scheduling*, concluded that his typical client would be "elderly, in low occupational status, unmarried, a renter rather than home owner, and without a car," and that such persons comprised "an unusual segment of the total population."[48] It was also a segment of the population which had relatively little money, but what money it did have Harrah went after. Accepting the conclusions of the monograph, he advertised for this segment in Stockton, Manteca, Oakland, and elsewhere.

Following the advice of the Stanford Research Institute, Harrah wrung such a fortune from these marginal economic groups that similar operations were set up by rivals. The number of motels in the area increased from ten to 375, and customers began driving in as well as coming by bus. The casinos vied with one another for big-time, million-dollar entertainment, the highway became an all-weather route, and Lake Tahoe was well on its way toward eclipsing its parent town, Reno, as the gambling center of northern Nevada.

The new development posed new problems, and one of them was sewage. Lake Tahoe is in a great basin surrounded by forested mountains. Its one outlet is the Truckee River, which serves Reno. With thousands of people coming into the area, an effluvium problem arose which was temporarily solved by treating the sewage and then spraying it on the surrounding forests. This was the least expansive method possible, except for dumping the sewage directly into the lake or into the Truckee River. In the opinion of experts, however, this spraying of forests, if continued, would pollute the lake irrevocably. Meanwhile, the gambling center at Stateline continued to develop, and a number of new building applications were approved, including a twenty-nine story addition to Harrahs, (estimated to produce an additional 200,000 gallons of effluvium daily) and Del Webb's Sahara-Tahoe casino-restaurant-hotel (estimated to produce an additional 240,000 gallons daily). Smaller approved projects were, of course, expected to produce lesser amounts of additional effluvium.[49]

As an interstate lake, Tahoe is clearly a concern of the national government. Accordingly, the President's Water Pollution Control Advisory Board convened with representatives from California and Nevada in September 1963. Experts testified at the meeting that Lake Tahoe would be ruined by a continuance of the existing sewage-disposal system, which would cause algae to develop in it, eventually turning it from its crystal purity to a scummy, murky green; and that such algae had already been found in the lake, which showed that its ruination had begun. The experts concluded that the sewage would have to be removed from the area altogether and that the best method would be to purify it and send it down the Truckee River.

Presumably this could have been done hygienically, or the experts would not have recommended the method, but politically it was out of the question. Governor Grant Sawyer of Nevada turned it down. The spraying of sewage would therefore continue, unless Governor Edmund G. Brown of California called upon the federal government to intervene, which he was clearly invited to do. Brown had a good deal to say against the gambling developments on the Nevada shore of Lake Tahoe, but he refrained from asking the national government to intercede.

Nevada has a Bureau of Environmental Health. The director of this bureau,W. W. White, attended the Water Pollution Control meeting, and in connection with the spraying of sewage he confessed that "there isn't much land left. I don't believe we have capacity for our sewage here more than three or four years." He had no positive solution to the problem, but he said that he would at least halt construction in the area "until we find some answers or it gets too hot."[50] It got too hot immediately. White's statement was made on September 27, 1963. On October 3, White said that he was now ready to approve permits to put an additional 650,000 gallons of sewage a day into the Lake Tahoe treatment plant. Asked why he had changed his mind, he answered that permission for this additional sewage was necessary to the plans of the casino enterprisers—Harrah, Del Webb, and the smaller ones—who were planning to build in the area in the next six months.[51]

The Lake Tahoe sewage plant failed to function properly, for some reason, early in October, so signs had to be put up along streams in Eldorado County, California; they read: "Warning. Do Not Drink, Fish, Swim, or Wade in this Water. By Order of the Eldorado County Health Department."[52] There remained the problem of what to do with a putatively sovereign state, where, as Hugo Fisher, the administrator of the California Resources Agency, said: "powerful local interests appear to be stronger than the State jurisdictions in effect."[53]

A meeting between Governors Brown and Sawyer in November did nothing to clear problem, so, naturally, Governor Brown felt called upon to defend himself in a subsequent speech before a conference of the Resources Agency of California. He was certain, he said, that Nevada gamblers would turn their side of the lake into a "neon jungle of high-rise buildings." He saw that the consequence might well be the polluting of Lake Tahoe past redemption, "so that multimillionaire gambling interests can get a little fatter from the profits of the slot machines and crap tables." He then defended his own role in the controversy, by pointing out that one governor cannot tell another what to do.[54]

In 1787 the American Constitution provided for the first federal republic in the history of the world. None of the leagues or confederations of Europe, ancient or contemporary, constituted a true precedent for the design of the founders, and none exerted any significant influence as an example for the delegates to the Constitutional Convention, who discovered acceptable precedents only in their own state constitutions and in the Articles of Confederation. The government which resulted has provided the classic example of federalism from the time it was established to the present, and *The Federalist*, its best contemporary defense, is recognized to be the most authoritative treatise on federalism.

The Federalist presented the best arguments which the authors were able to make for a particular Constitution which none of them entirely endorsed privately. Of the three writers of the *Federalist* papers, Madison was perhaps the most favorably disposed toward toward the Constitution, for he, more truly than any other man, was the document's author. As has been seen, however, Madison had some private doubts, especially about the upper house of the legislature, while his co-author, Hamilton, basically disbelieved in the whole federal principle.

If these defenders of the system held such reservations, it is probable that reservations were common in the nation, even though its citizens agreed, after much bitter debate, to reconstitute it under the new federal system.

This spirit of suspicious and tentative acceptance continued through the first generation of the new government until the age of nationalism which abruptly followed the War of 1812. What resulted from that war was irrevocable acceptance of the Constitution by almost all Americans, who believed that it provided the most nearly perfect form of government devised by man.

During the early nineteenth century prominent New England Federalists felt free to denounce the Constitution, especially its provision for admitting new Western states into the Union, at a time when they could not even have conceived of such an outlandish state as Nevada. In the period following the War of 1812, however, even the impeccably orthodox Boston Federalist Edward Everett came to assert that "by the wise and happy partition between the national and the state governments, in virtue of which the national government is relieved from all the odium of internal administration, and the state governments are spared the conflicts of foreign policies,"[55] the limitless expansion of the nation was possible in full accordance with republican principles. The Civil War was, among other things, the result of a failure of the Constitution to work, but the war did not indicate that the Constitution was any less universally accepted, for both sides fought to uphold it as they understood it.

During the late nineteenth and early twentieth centuries, after the union was reconstituted, the American federal system came to be viewed by European liberals as the master plan for libertarian government, to a greater extent, probably, than in the pre-Civil War days of Alexis de Tocqueville's *Democracy in America*. Accordingly, the great historian Lord Acton chose to conclude his *Lectures on Modern History* with a historical account of the American Revolution and Constitution, as though the true course for his own generation had been revealed by these events.

He made this point explicit in his concluding paragraphs, observing that under the American system only certain powers are delegated to the federal government, whereas all other powers are reserved to the states. He further noted the Great Compromise, through which the lower house had been based upon the principle of representation proportional to population, and the upper house upon equality of representation among the states. In the last sentence of his final lecture, he concluded that the United States, "by the principle of Federalism . . . has produced a community more powerful, more prosperous, more intelligent, and more free than any other which the world has ever known."[56]

America today is much more powerful and prosperous than it was at the opening of the century, when Acton spoke those flattering lines, and—although this cannot be so readily demonstrated—it is possibly also more intelligent and free. To the extent that these attributes resulted from the federal system embodied in the Constitution, Madison, as the document's chief architect, stands vindicated today as never before. However, the gamblers' recent take-over of Nevada's economy provides strong evidence supporting his chief criticism of the Constitution: the "possible mischiefs" which small states might get into under its provisions.

By authority of the powers reserved to the states, Nevada was able to rebuild its economy on the foundations of the gambling industry and place that industry at the disposal of ex-convicts from other states. Then, through its spokesman in the United States Senate, it was able to protect its new basic industry from federal harassments, such as the prohibition of slot machines in interstate commerce or the crippling of the gambling industry by taxes.

What will result eventually from this burgeoning business may hardly be guessed at, because the industry, as a legitimate one, is new and developing rapidly, and because Congress would probably be able to suppress gambling, if it ever decided to do so. A lesser question, to all but nature lovers, is whether "keenly pure" Lake Tahoe will be turned a murky green by the effluents from the rising gambling city of Stateline. If that greatest of the glacier lakes *does* turn green through the seepage of Stateline sewage, it will become an appropriate symbol of twentieth-century Nevada states' rights enterprise, especially since most of the lake is on the California side.

"Musings of a Native Son"
(1989)

William A. Douglass

Publication of Gilman Ostrander's Nevada: The Great Rotten Borough *in 1966 capped two decades of blistering attacks upon Nevada. During the 1970s and 1980s, as the mobsters departed and casinos were taken over by prominent multi-national corporations whose stocks were traded on the New York Stock Exchange, the barrage of criticism declined rapidly. One state after another established lotteries and licensed casinos, and consequentially Nevada no longer stood alone as the nation's only gambling center. There was, however, one more blast to be fired, this one from a native son. James W. Hulse, born in 1930 and raised in the small southeastern Nevada mining town of Pioche, had enjoyed a long and productive career as a professor of history at the university in Reno. Modern-day Nevada, he charged, was "a parasite and a provincial backwater, contributing little of its social or material energy to the problems of war and peace, human rights, or protection of the environment. It has submerged its social conscience and sense of duty to the effort to keep the gambling business and the fantasy that surrounds it, 'healthy.'" Critiques such as this prompted another University of Nevada scholar, William A. Douglass, to respond. Born into a pioneering Nevada family, Douglass built an academic career as a distinguished anthropologist who played a major role in the development of the university's Basque Studies Program. Douglass had also pursued with equal energy and success his role as part owner and executive of several Reno casinos. As his introspective essay explains, he grew up in an environment where gambling was a normal and accepted part of everyday life. Writing in 1989, when the state's population was rapidly growing, Douglass took a broad and tolerant look at the state's history. Nevada, he emphasized, was founded by a small group of "self-reliant, independent entrepreneurs disposed to extraordinary risk-taking." Gambling, it seemed, was a normal part of life in a society where*

*speculation and risky investments were common. Like many
Nevadans, Douglass viewed gaming as the only viable option available to state leaders. "No one," Douglass concedes, "would argue that
gambling is a particularly noble enterprise, but neither is it the most
ignoble human activity." Considering the dearth of viable alterna-
tives, Douglass concludes, Nevadans should make peace with their
state's maverick history, however tarnished it might seem.*

Times Past

My grandfather died in 1929, ten years before I was born. According to
the headlined obituaries published on April 22 in the *Tonopah Daily
Bonanza* and on April 23 in the *Tonopah Daily Times*, William James Douglass was one of the key founders of the town. He was born in Virginia
City in 1867. His father was a mill operator from Vermont and his
mother a pioneer in the mining camp of Aurora. Billy Douglass, as he
was known, became an assayer in Candelaria in 1890s. With the collapse of silver prices in 1893, he and some associates went prospecting
for gold. They founded Douglass Camp in Esmeralda County, which
enjoyed some initial successes. In 1900, when news of the Tonopah
strike reached him, Billy immediately set out across the desert, becoming the thirteenth man to enter the fledgling camp. He secured a lease
from Jim Butler, and throughout the leasing period of Tonopah's history (or until late 1901 when the Butler groups sold out to eastern interests), Billy Douglass ran the local assay office. He then became a
principal owner and general manager of the Midway, West End, and
Tonopah Montana mines. In partnership with H. C. Brougher, he founded the Tonopah Banking Corporation and served as its vice-president.
He grubstaked Harry Stimler and William Marsh, discoverers of Goldfield, and was their partner in that district's Kendall, Sandstorm, May
Queen, Nevada Boy, and Gold Banner mines. He was subsequently
instrumental in development of the Tonopah Divide district and had
interests in several Nevada and California mining camps. With Billy's
passing the newspapers proclaimed the end of an era, the *Daily Times*
even going so far as to publish a short list of the "Surviving Pioneers."

I have two mementos of the grandfather I never knew. I bear his
name and I carry his gold pocket watch. The latter came to me along
with a story that I cherish more than the remarkable timepiece itself.
Its back is embossed with three figures—the intertwined initials WJD,
a spider, and a wasp. Inside its cover there is photograph of my grandmother, Kathleen McQuillan, herself a daughter of the Comstock, and
my Uncle Bud, one of the first children born in Tonopah. Bud's real

name was Belmont, which was my grandparents' way of honoring the community of Tonopah's discoverers and, not incidentally, Billy's business partners.

According to the story, the watch was a present from Philadelphia investors who, about 1907, sent their engineers to Nevada to look over potential properties. Billy Douglass had a reputation for grubstaking almost anyone in need, and in the process, he picked up interests in several hundred, mostly worthless, claims throughout the state. He was approached by the eastern engineers and provided them with maps and directions. About a month later, they returned from the desert to make him an offer. It seems that they were prepared to pay $100,000 for the group of claims called the Spider and the Wasp that he held in Wonder (between Fallon and Gabbs). According to Hugh A. Shamberger's recent book on that mining camp, the claims were indeed quite valuable and proved to be among Wonder's best. Billy said he wanted to think it over and would meet with them in the Tonopah Club that evening. There he opined that $100,000 was excessive but that he was willing to sell for $75,000! The deal was made and the buyers commissioned the watch in Switzerland as a token of their appreciation. Is the story true? Possibly.

I believe my grandfather's watch is an excellent example of both the wonderful quality and tenuous nature of Nevada history. It harkens back to an era long since past but which in so many ways still dominates Nevada thought. It is rather axiomatic that we must learn from history in order to avoid its errors; however, for Nevada's this task is made more difficult because our heritage is as much a creation as a chronicle. Indeed, in at least a psychological sense, one might argue that our historical baseline derives from such works as *Roughing It* and the colorful vignettes from newspapers like the *Territorial Enterprise* and its subsequent mining camp emulators. The image that emerges depicts a world of self-reliant, independent entrepreneurs disposed to extraordinary risk-taking—whether raising livestock in one of the nation's most arid and hostile settings or scratching holes in bleak mountainsides in pursuit of elusive, unlimited wealth. Rather than the product of pioneers seeking to sink roots permanently into virgin soil, the nineteenth-century Nevada settlement comes across as a collectivity more than a community, a group of sojourners of questionable character hoping to make their fortune without breaking too many rules before going elsewhere to spend it. Excepting a few Mormon colonies and the servicing centers that emerged along the transcontinental railway, most Nevada towns were as unstable as the tumbleweeds blowing down Main Street, subject to abandonment and dismantlement at the latest rumor that El Dorado exists and has just been discovered somewhere "over yonder." That the state developed permanent settlement was inevitable, yet viewed from the perspective of nineteenth-century Nevada reality it seems epiphenomenal.

There is a sense in which Nevadans still invoke a spirit of "rugged individualism" anchored in our past. Periodically, it is reaffirmed by our best contemporary writers, as in Robert Laxalt's *Nevada* and his *National Geographic* article "The Other Nevada" or James Hulse's *Forty Years in the Wilderness*. Perhaps this is necessary catharsis for a people who arguably share with Mississippi the dubious distinction of having the worst national image (albeit for different reasons). Yet might we not question whether this provides a viable charter and blueprint for forging our place in the contemporary and future worlds? We were both blessed and cursed by having Mark Twain, one of the consummate writers (and notorious tale spinners) of world literature, among our original interpreters. However, to my mind, Nevadans real challenge lies not in meriting his mastery but in transcending it.

Times Present

I attended Manogue High School when I was a boy growing up in the Reno area—not the present modern school next to the university but the "Old Manogue" quartered in a made-over ranch house situated along the Truckee River southeast of Sparks. Surrounded by miles of pasture, grazing livestock, fruit orchards and fields of vegetables cultivated by Italian truck gardeners, the tiny Catholic high school was truly out in the country. The rural atmosphere was not belied by an urban skyline hovering on the horizon—at least not until the Mapes Hotel was constructed, prompting our awestruck schoolboy imaginations to draw fanciful comparisons with the Empire State Building. Reno and Sparks remained separate communities, linked by old Highway 40, rather than arbitrary divisions on the map of a continuous metropolitan area.

As I reflect back on my high school days, I realize now that I did not so much attend class at the Old Manogue as in the surrounding countryside. A true believer in the anti-intellectualism characteristic of my classmates (pervasive at rival Reno and Sparks high school as well), I found little of interest within the confines of the curriculum. However, I soon discovered the wildlife inhabiting the Truckee River, the farmland sloughs, and the marshes of the nearby Nevada Game Farm. My interest and energy became focused upon the attractions of this magical world and its denizens.

The beginning of the school term meant fur prospecting within walking distance of the high school, as I staked out beaver colonies and muskrat slides and searched for signs of the elusive mink. Late autumn and early winter were devoted to running a trap line that ended at Vista. In the lowering dusk my partner and I would hitchhike back to Reno, entering the vehicles of our unsuspecting benefactors with a wet gunnysack filled with our gear and catch (few dared to ask). In springtime we pursued lizards and snakes, which we marketed by mail to biological supply houses and through our own auspicious sounding "Sierra Reptile Farm."

I gained my literacy during my Manogue years, but not through attentiveness to my teachers. Rather, I became an avid reader of works like Raymond Ditmars's *Reptiles of the World*, trapping and fur farming manuals, and the magazine *Fur-Fish-Game* (to which I contributed my first article—a description of trapping experiences in the Reno area).

Little remains of the world of Old Manogue. The Reno Cannon International Airport and a golf course now occupy the drained marshes of the Nevada Game Farm. A young boy's imagination could scarcely be fired by the asphalt and industrial parks that now cover most of the fields and sloughs that were once my kingdom.

While we were largely unaware of it at the time, the forces that were to convert Nevada into its present reality had already been unleashed. Between 1940 and 1950 the state's population had increased nearly 50 percent, or from 110,000 to 160,000 residents.[1] While northern Nevada experienced some of the growth (Reno gained a third of its 1950 population during the decade), the spectacular development was in Clark County. During the 1950s Washoe County was eclipsed demographically by the upstart to the south; however, for northern Nevadans there was still a qualitative difference between the two. Though only a third of Nevada's population resided in the Reno-Sparks-Carson area, our claim to political and, particularly, intellectual leadership remained unchallenged. Reno, with its 32,000 residents, was the largest city in the state and housed its only university. Carson was the seat of state government. Therefore, we *were* Nevada regardless of what some southern Nevada arrivistes might think. To the extent that we looked elsewhere for spiritual sustenance it was to northern California and "the City," and certainly not to our neighbors in the south with their obvious ties to southern California and "tinsel town." Our smugness might have allowed us alternately to patronize and to ignore the "cow counties" and southerners but, in retrospect, I believe that it was at our peril. For it precluded us from addressing meaningfully Nevada's real twentieth-century challenge—namely, growth and its prerogatives.

In the north, as the growth issue became more and more blatant, we turned against ourselves. Where once there was degree of harmony and community spirit, we divided over such issues as the routing of Interstate 80 and the siting of the convention center and airport. The battles lasted for years and left a legacy of acrimony and bitterness. Suburbanization of commerce, as retail services moved to the shopping centers to be replaced in the downtown area by casino expansion, created new divisions between periphery and core, "residents" and "tourists." In short, public debate in northern Nevada increasingly acquired schizophrenic overtones as we split into "growth" and "no-growth" factions. There was also an element of illogicality and hypocrisy as we became increasingly dependent on the very tourist dollar that we damned and blamed for our environmental problems.

Another source of ambiguity in the public debate was the changing nature of the collective pronoun. With each new census, it became increasingly obvious that "we" referred to a shifting reality. Despite the fumbling attempts to rein in growth, the population of Washoe County almost quadrupled in the three decades between 1950 and 1980 (from 50,000 to 193,000 inhabitants).

Ambivalence best describes my own feelings about the process. I was saddened to watch my old boyhood haunts disappear pell-mell into the irresistible and insatiable maw of development. At the same time, I was pleased to witness the flowering of the arts made possible only by increased population—creation of the Nevada Opera, the Nevada Repertory Theater, the Nevada Festival Ballet, and the Reno Philharmonic, the Sierra Art Museum, and the more than forty other arts organizations that now provide Reno with a variegated cultural landscape. This is in stark contrast with my youth when culture in Reno meant a ticket to the Community Concert Series, to the Reno Little Theater, and to San Francisco. I also cannot ignore the irony when I am exhorted by people who moved to northern Nevada, and thereby changed irreversibly "my" Reno, to make common cause with them against potential newcomers in defense of "our" way of life. How would they have viewed a similar campaign back in the 1950s, when it really might have been possible to opt for a future modeled after Monterey or Ashland? There are disturbing implications for such a process carried to its logical conclusion, for if I have the right to exclude people from Reno, I thereby confer upon someone else the right to exclude me from San Francisco or any other place that I might choose to live.

Meanwhile, the contrast between northern and southern Nevada could not be greater. The combination of disdain and myopia with which we northerners continue to view southerners allows us the delusion that we are still contenders in a contest over the state's economic and political hegemony. For the past four decades northern Nevadans have managed to consistently underestimate the south. For us it seemed axiomatic that the bleak and arid setting of Las Vegas would itself set natural limits upon its capacity for expansion. Who in their right mind would choose to settle permanently in the hottest corner of the continent? Each new Las Vegas project was greeted in the north with incredulity; each cyclical downturn in the southern Nevada economy was treated as a harbinger of imminent collapse. Yet Las Vegas, imbued with a "can do" spirit, not only survived but triumphed beyond the wildest dreams of its sanguine boosters. In the process Clark County acquired nearly 60 percent of the state's population, or approximately two and a half times that of Washoe County.

Consequently, it is no coincidence that today the governor, lieutenant governor, and both of Nevada's U.S. senators are from Clark County. The reapportionment after the 1990 census will further consolidate southern Nevada's political base. In short, the south will enjoy an absolute majority in every statewide political arena. Consequently, Clark County is in a position to dictate Nevada's future social, economic, educational, and political agendas. Indeed, within a democracy is this not as it should be?

At the same time there is a challenge implicit in the new contemporary reality, particularly for northern Nevadans. One questions whether we can afford any longer the luxury of Las Vegas-bashing. I believe that to date southern Nevadans have displayed remarkable restraint in their dealings with the rest of the state. They have yet to flex their political muscle in arbitrary or punitive fashion. There may yet be time to bridge the hundreds of miles, and the even wider conceptual gulf, between the north and the south. One can only conclude that ultimately northern Nevadans have a greater stake in doing so than do our southern Nevada fellow citizens.

Times Future

Mother had a sense of the historic and momentous. When the all but moribund V&T Railroad was about to expire, she took my brother John and me out of school in order to ride the train to Carson City. As the virtually empty car swayed precariously, she lectured two mildly hyper boys, energized by the thrill of sanctioned hooky, on the importance of remembering what struck us as a simple outing.

It was in this same spirit that she awakened us about 4:00 A.M. one brisk autumn morning and bundled us into the car. We drove out of town towards Washoe Valley to escape the lights of the city and parked on a rise facing to the south. Mother made small talk trying to prevent her less than enthusiastic audience from lapsing into slumber. As she voiced her concerns about possible cancellation, the entire horizon exploded in a cold, white flash that lingered momentarily like a fleeting smile on the lips of an oracle and then was gone.

This atomic dawn, telegraphed to us instantaneously from hundreds of miles to the south, left us sobered and speechless. We drove back to Reno through the comforting cloak of restored darkness and stopped for breakfast at an all-night diner. I cannot recall Mother's exact words, but I remember their spirit. Subsequently, I witnessed other detonations from the flanks of Mount Oddie while visiting my cousins in Tonopah. From there we could see the cloud and then feel the tremor. Yet the mood was frivolous and festive as we watched a show that seemingly was staged by the federal government for our benefit in order to countermand the boredom of everyday small-town life. That morning in the diner, however, Mother told us that we had seen the future. It was clear from her demeanor that she was far from pleased.

Father was a gambler in both the figurative and the literal senses of the term. During my youth he was part-owner of a coin-operated device distributorship. Its place of business was on East Second Street, or a short walk from St. Thomas Aquinas grammar school where for a portion of each day I was forced to listen to Dominican nuns naively lecture the *cognoscenti* on the sorrows of purgatory. Once released from daily confinement, however, I could dash down the street to the Nevada Novelty Company and its wonders. There were pinball machines that passed through the premises for repairs before going out "on location" to some bar, restaurant, or bowling alley. If luck was with you, and you managed to be inconspicuous enough not to annoy the adults, you could spend the entire afternoon in an orgy of free games. Of equal interest were the jukeboxes, or rather the used 45 RPM phonograph records that they disgorged. My record collection was never current but it was complete.

The mainstay of the business, of course, was the slot machines. I recall being mystified at the attraction to adults of a device that provided neither interesting sights nor sounds, but I was under no delusion regarding its importance in the grand scheme of things. Indeed, from time to time Father would take me on one of his regular trips to rural Nevada to service his "slot route." We would visit such metropolises as Fallon and Hawthorne, linked by asphalt ribbons, before bouncing over the dirt roads that ended in places like Gabbs and Flanigan. It was there in ramshackle bars or general stores that the Nevada Novelty Company had its three or four slot machines. Usually, at least one would be "out of order" and turned to the wall, awaiting Father's less than polished mechanical skills. As likely as not, it was destined to be our companion in the back of the pickup truck on the trip to the slot-machine hospital in Reno. We would then roll and count the money. With our hand-operated coin wrapper, it took an hour to process even the meager proceeds generated by most locations. When all was ready, the proprietor was first reimbursed for any jackpots paid, after which the remainder was credited to country, state, and federal license fees. Once these expenses were met, the profits were divided fifty-fifty with the proprietor.

As we traveled along the desert tracks, we never discussed his business. It was a time when there were a few small casinos in the north, no Las Vegas strip, Jackpot, or Laughlin. Father was not prone to philosophize. While we counted nickels in back rooms in remote corners of the Nevada desert, it never occurred to him to tell me that I was glimpsing the future, although, of course, I was.

A nation's decision to explode its bombs in Nevada, on the one hand, and counting slot machine proceeds in the heart of the state's mining and ranching district, on the other, encapsulate for me our dilemma as we contemplate the future. That is, for many Nevadans there is a feeling that we are somehow in the clutches of arbitrary outside forces—the federal government and gamblers, each sinister in its own fashion.

Germane to this view is the notion that the authentic Nevada lies somewhere east of Sparks and north of Las Vegas, is rural in character, and resulted when those rugged individualists referred to earlier gained a mining and ranching toehold in a hostile, frontier environment. As a boy I was taught that Nevada was the least populated of the forty-eight states, yet sixth largest in size. In 1940 our 110,000 inhabitants divided niftily into our 110,000 square miles, mathematics which seemed to give each Nevadan a privileged place on the planet, at least as measured in terms of elbow room. While the numbers have changed, the mind-set has not. Psychologically, the state's "wide-open spaces" still constitute for Nevadans a redoubtable refuge in which to escape the crassness of twentieth-century materialism and modernity.

More germane to the state's present and future reality, however, is another numerical coincidence. I refer to the fact that if 85 percent of our land, including most of the authentic Nevada, is under federal ownership, as of 1980 85 percent of our population resides in urban centers, largely outside the federal preserve. In terms of percentages, then, and despite our rural imagery, Nevada is the fourth most urbanized state in the nation!

I once lived for a year in Australia and was struck by the similarities between Aussies and Nevadans in this regard. Although a nation of coastal dwellers, of which the overwhelming majority live in five cities, the Australians' national images turn on kangaroos, koala bears, and the Outback. Few Sydney-siders have ever visited the Outback, or plan to, yet concur in the notion that somehow Australia's essence lingers there. As of 1980 approximately 650,000 of Nevada's 800,000 residents lived in the greater Reno and Las Vegas metropolitan areas. As those of us who do frequent Nevada's interior in near solitude can attest, few Renoites or Las Vegans have ever experienced the Black Rock Desert, the Jarbidge country, or Monitor Valley.

Insofar as our rural imagery provides us with psychological strength and satisfaction, it is benign or even positive. However, when it is allowed to assume a critical role in debates over our future, it becomes a legitimate cause for concern. Stripped of their mythic properties, Nevada's ranching and mining traditions seldom proved reliable foundations for the state's economy. In strict ecological terms Nevada has much more in common with Afghanistan than with Iowa and, consequently, its agriculture can be viewed as only marginal at best. Lack of moisture and a short growing season alone set insurmountable limits upon it. This can be contrasted with our mining successes. Indeed, Nevada is one of the most mineral-rich corners of the globe, and individual discoveries such as the Comstock in the mid-nineteenth century, Tonopah-Goldfield at the turn of the century and, more recently, the "invisible" gold operations in places like Carlin provide the state with some of the most spectacular mining booms in the annals of human history. At the same time mining strikes are predicated upon a nonrenewable resource and are, therefore, intrinsically ephemeral.

It is thought provoking to consider the demographics of the state when the economy was based almost exclusively upon ranching and mining. In 1880, or during the afterglow of the Comstock-Austin-Eureka mining discoveries and the homesteading that followed the Civil War, our population reached 62,00 persons. Twenty years later, with the mining industry in a deep depression and agriculture in the doldrums, it had declined by a third to 42,000, and the possibility of stripping Nevada of statehood was under serious consideration by the U.S. Congress. The Tonopah-Goldfield discoveries and their spin-offs essentially saved the day by doubling the state's population to 82,000 by 1910; however, the inevitable playing out of the mines and the vicissitudes of international markets for agricultural and mineral products conspired to reduce our population to 77,000 by the 1920 census.

The essential point is that Nevada's "traditional" economy was incapable of supporting a population of 100,000 inhabitants in the best of times and proved particularly vulnerable to periodic crisis. In its modern guises, it is even less capable of providing a livelihood to our citizenry. By this I mean that nineteenth-century Nevada agriculture and mining were labor intensive compared to their modern counterparts. Last century small family ranches dotted the landscape, multitudes of hard-rock miners worked the diggings, and hundreds of prospectors roamed the desert. Today's ranch incorporates three or four of yesterday's abandoned homesteads, gigantic mining operations employ a few men versed in running state-of-the-art equipment, and a handful of geologists use satellite photos to pinpoint future prospects. Nor, for the most part, are these resources vested in the hands of native rugged individualists. Rather, today's ranch is likely to be owned by a movie star or a physician seeking a tax shelter, and the mines are controlled by multinational corporations.

It is therefore noteworthy that by 1980 rural Nevada's population (defined as everybody outside Washoe and Clark counties) approximates 150,000 persons, or almost twice that of the entire state during the palmier days of ranching and mining. Here, in fact, we confront the real Achilles' heel of the rugged individualist myth, since the bulk of rural Nevadans are employees of either the tourist and gaming industries or the government. Indeed, eliminate the jobs provided by the casinos and motels in Winnemucca, Jackpot, Elko, Wells, Wendover, and Ely; abolish those within the federal, state, and county bureaucracies; and dismiss the civilian employees of Nellis Air Force Base, the Fallon Naval Station, the Hawthorne Munitions Depot, and the Atomic Test Site, as well as those of the civilian defense contractors, and rural Nevada would become a vast economic wasteland. Whimsical "Sagebrush Rebellions" notwithstanding, rural Nevada is one of the most heavily subsidized and economically dependent regions of the nation.

We need only remember the anguished protests of the residents of Austin faced with the transfer of the Lander County seat to Battle Mountain and closure of the local offices of the U.S. National Forest Service, or the decision by Nye County officials to send a lobbyist to

Washington, D.C., to argue *for* the national nuclear waste dump (thanks to urban Nevada they got Bullfrog County instead). Conversely, it is a bit ludicrous when Nevada ranchers ask to "get government off our backs." This appeal is by now a litany that is repeated with the same monotony of Tibetan monks spinning their prayer wheels. While it, too, invokes rugged individualism, it ignores the fact that through agricultural price supports and range use fees that are considerably lower than rates on similar private land, the average Nevada rancher is more heavily subsidized than a floor full of welfare mothers in a Detroit housing project.

Such, then, is the past and present reality of the authentic Nevada. By any stretch of the imagination can it inform our future, except by way of a warning? In short, can the approximately one million Nevadans who now call the state home find much that is relevant in this tradition, other than to esteem it for its historical quaintness?

This brings me to the question of Nevada's tourist and gaming economy, frantically promoted in the south while at best tolerated in the north. Many Nevadans view gambling as artificial, a hybrid phenomenon superimposed upon the state by outside interests ranging from the Mafia to Holiday Inns. There is a sense in which this is true, since it can in no way be contended that gaming's spectacular development is a homegrown product. On the other hand, I would argue that the concept is homegrown, and that it is but one manifestation of a broader survival strategy that was honed, beginning about the turn of this century, on the perception that ranching and mining were both fickle paramours. After riding the boom-to-bust roller coaster, which resulted in the demographic fluctuations considered earlier, Nevadans began to posture their state to take advantage of the laws of neighboring ones.

We were the first to legalize prizefighting, and our history as a divorce haven is legendary. When other states liberalized their divorce laws, we invented the quickie marriage, thereby substituting today's wedding chapels for the divorcée dude ranches of my youth. Legalized prostitution and gambling provided additional attractions to potential visitors. A more modern manifestation of the same mentality is the warehouses that banished my muskrats and that offer American industry a legal means of circumventing inventory taxes in California, Oregon, and Washington. Our most recent and possible crowning achievement in shifting our civic responsibilities to others was the tax reform, which essentially insulated us from most of the onus of property tax (we dare not even brook the subject of a state income tax except, as happened in the last election, to banish the possibility through referendum). Thus, we have made our state coffers almost totally reliant upon the tourist trade (through the gaming and sales taxes) and federal rebates. As a consequence, our state government finds it difficult to set any kind of social or educational agenda that requires long-term planning. Rather, state officials are forced to engage in legerdemain with the ledgers, since all budgetary projections remain asterisked, subject to future results in casino counting rooms and merchants' cash registers.

One response to our essential ambivalence regarding near total dependency upon a single industry and its ancillary effects is to heed the clarion call of "economic diversification." While a worthwhile objective, it is fair to question our prospects and, consequently, the role that such aspirations ought to play in planning for the future. Realistically, our new commitment places us squarely in the pack with the forty-nine other states aspiring to host the next Silicon Valley. Without abandoning such initiatives, is it wise to assume in some vague sense that they really will reduce our dependency upon tourism and gaming? At the same time, it may even be relevant to ask whether they should.

By this I mean that, viewed strictly in economic terms, tourism and gaming have provided Nevada with its one unequivocal success story. The state is sometimes referred to as the "Gaming Mecca of the World." Despite the pretentiousness of the statement, it is scarcely hyperbolic since it reflects a certain reality. However, this very fact is a source of considerable ambivalence for some Nevadans.

This is particularly true of northerners who have somehow never quite lived down their shame over the conclusions of the Kefauver Report, which underscored the underworld influence in the state. Each new *Green Felt Jungle*, sensational feature article, or film depicting Nevada in such stereotypic terms only serves to feed the private self-loathing that results from dependence upon a disreputable activity. There are, of course, available defense mechanisms. It is common in the north to draw a distinction between "clean" northern casino operations and "hood"-operated southern ones, an exercise which might have had a certain validity at one time but has now been largely undermined by the progressively corporate nature of casino ownership at both ends of the state. Another ploy is for those who are not involved directly in the industry to maintain the illusion that they are not benefited, and thereby tainted, by it. Hence, some Nevada store clerks, physicians, and professors like to believe that they are insulated from gaming and could continue to pursue their careers here were the industry to simply disappear. Meanwhile, we have produced a cadre of critics, ranging from

Cassandras to moralists, who decry the evils of gambling and the precariousness of a society built upon it. While this provides guidance for our self-flagellation and affords catharsis to the guilt-ridden, it also obfuscates many of the real issues as we chart our course.

To my mind, it is essential that we become at least resigned, indeed reconciled, to the future importance of tourism and gambling in the state's economy and image. No one would argue that gambling is a particularly noble enterprise, but neither is it the most ignoble human activity. The salient point is that it appeals to human nature and is therefore a fact of life. Having stated this, however, I would hasten to add that those who believe that Nevada gambling is merely a response to human greed are engaged in gross oversimplification. In such a view, unscrupulous gamblers load the dice against unsuspecting or reckless players blinded by avarice. This is at best a patronizing depiction of the millions of tourists who visit Nevada annually. Indeed, its plausibility is undermined by their sheer numbers. It is also akin to invoking sloth to explain the behavior of the same individuals should they choose to simply lie about on a beach instead.

In reality, Nevada gaming is no longer just about gambling. By this I mean that our resorts now have much more in common with Disneyland, Cannes, Maui, and Acapulco than they do with parlor poker or back-alley dice games. They offer an escape from the mundane by means of what Umberto Eco recently called *Travels in Hyperreality*. It is the Caesar's Palace that somehow eclipses rather than emulates the glories of Ancient Rome—the trip on the Mississippi riverboat without the mosquitoes.

There is a sense in which we have become so accustomed to our internal debate and self-doubts about the worth of the gambling industry that we have ignored its changing image. There was once a time in which virtually all the national press regarding Nevada gaming was negative. Actually, it ranged from voyeuristic to the denigratory. We were essentially regarded as a gambling den and bordello, an aberration within national life. Of late, however, there has been growing recognition that Nevada gambling is actually part of a broader American tradition and that, in terms of architecture and design, it is a path breaker and pacesetter within the world's recreational industry.[2]

Finally, it should be noted that Nevada gaming is no longer unique and, hence, a virtually unchallenged monopoly. There was a time when we were the sole national renegade, at least with respect to casino gambling. This is no longer the case. Legalization of casinos in New Jersey is but the tip of an iceberg. Below the waterline several other states are considering a similar move, and most now have wagering in one form or another. The reality, then, is that Nevada gambling remains preeminent but far from unchallenged. It operates in a national and, increasingly, global market. While we draw some of our visitors from abroad, it is also true that casino gambling has proliferated in the majority of countries on every inhabited continent. In a real sense, we presently compete not just with Atlantic City but with Sun City, not to mention Macao, Monte Carlo, and Montevideo.

The very magnitude of our success, with the attendant per capita income and lifestyle to which we have become accustomed, indeed makes us vulnerable. One need only note the shiver that runs through the body politic at the mention of legalized casino gambling in our prime California market. Such a prospect is by far a greater problem for the state than for Nevada's casinos. The New Jersey experience has demonstrated clearly that expertise within the industry is at a premium. Just as much of the ownership and management of Atlantic City casinos originated in Nevada, should California legalize gaming, it might even prove to be an opportunity for many Nevada gamblers— the same cannot be said of our state. If the casino business transcends Nevada's boundaries and is no longer captive to our enabling legislation, as a state we have entered upon a new era of dependency upon it, at least until such time as we develop a viable alternative. This dependency is increasingly like that of Youngstown upon the steel industry. Steel plants can be relocated, Youngstown cannot. Consequently, we might question the utility of incessant hand wringing over what may be our ineluctable economic destiny.

Mirrors and Masks

Despite the critical tone in much of this essay, it is not my purpose to be peevish or pontifical. Indeed, I declare unabashedly that I love Nevada. In addition to being a native son, I am a returned native, since I now reside here by choice after having lived in many other parts of America and the world. In criticizing that which is so much a part of me, I feel like the proud parent who seeks to appreciate the virtues without being blinded to the faults of his beautiful, yet troublesome child.

There is a sense in which the analogy is particularly appropriate, since Nevada may be regarded as an adolescent. By this I meant that our recent growth is like that of the teenager whose physical maturity suddenly begins to far outstrip his emotional development. As a state our appearance has assumed adult form, yet we continue to have private doubts and fears regarding our future career. Given the fact that we have increased our population tenfold in less than half a century, it is scarcely surprising that we suffer at this point in our history from what might be likened to raging hormonal imbalance.

The only "cure" for adolescent woes is the progressive development of a self-concept and hence self-confidence. In successfully forging an adult *persona*, the individual contemplates his childhood, largely in order to become reconciled with its passing, and assesses his present circumstances, in order to be realistic about his prospects. In this regard, both the past and present become the mirrors in which he learns about himself in order to shed the masks of youth in favor of assuming an adult role. Collectively, we Nevadans face a similar challenge. It is the purpose of this essay to suggest that it is only possible to transcend our adolescence if we are willing to remove our mask *before* gazing into our mirrors.

"A-Bombs in the Backyard: Southern Nevada Adapts to the Nuclear Age, 1951–1963" (1983)

A. Costandina Titus

When the Atomic Energy Commission (AEC) decided in 1949 to establish a nuclear test site in the United States, attention naturally focused upon the uninhabited expanse of federal lands in Nevada. Although locations in other states were considered, the AEC quickly decided upon a large tract on Frenchmen's Flat, eighty miles north of Las Vegas. This site had been used as a bombing and gunnery range by the military during the Second World War, and its proximity to railroad lines and Las Vegas provided practical reasons for its selection. As Dina Titus explains, Nevadans of all political persuasions welcomed the nuclear age to Nevada. Political and economic development leaders had learned a powerful lesson from the Second World War: the infusion of federal dollars had produced the greatest period of growth and prosperity in Nevada's history. Anticipated revenue from the establishment and operation of the Nevada Test Site (NTS) staggered the imagination. Not only would the construction of the base at Camp Mercury produce an initial outpouring of federal money, but the ongoing operation would continue the flow for decades to come. Nevada's leaders were also quick to support the site because of their unquestioned patriotism in the early stages of the Cold War. Republican Governor Charles Russell and the Nevada congressional delegation, led by the fiercely anti-Communist Democrat Patrick McCarran, were unified in welcoming the AEC to Nevada. Nevadans brushed away a few skeptics' concerns about the dangers of earthquakes resulting from explosions, of exposure of humans and livestock to dangerous radiation from the fallout from above ground testing, or

*of contamination of underground water supplies and the land itself.
The AEC's reassurances about safety were largely accepted at face
value. Such acquiescence was not the case, however, in the early
1980s, when military planners proposed to develop a massive mobile
nuclear launching system (MX) in which specially equipped trains
carrying operational missiles would continuously crisscross vast
stretches of Nevada and Utah desert. For the first time an informal
coalition of political and community leaders successfully opposed the
spending of federal dollars within the state. A decade later, when the
Department of Energy focused on the NTS area of Yucca Flat for a
national nuclear-waste repository, the reaction was even greater than
to the MX program.*

... There have been so many detonations of nuclear devices at the test
site in the past ten years that the community [of Las Vegas] is completely accustomed to, and unconcerned about, radiation hazards
from such operations.[1]

Nineteen eighty-three marks the twentieth year since mushroom
clouds last appeared above the Nevada desert. On August 5, 1963, the
Limited Test Ban Treaty was signed, moving atomic weapons testing
underground and ending an era of great significance in American and
Nevada history. This essay examines the years of atmospheric testing,
1951 to 1963, and two main themes are emphasized. First, it describes
the government's atomic testing policy with emphasis on activities at
the Nevada Test Site (NTS) and the Atomic Energy Committee's public relations program designed to win popular support for these "backyard" operations. Second, the essay analyzes Southern Nevada's
response to the atmospheric testing program by examining the politics,
the press, and the popular culture of the region during those years. The
inescapable conclusion of this inquiry is that throughout the dozen
years of above-ground testing, Nevadans enthusiastically supported
the atomic testing program and considered the NTS an asset to the
state's development.

Historical Background

At 5:30 A.M. on July 16, 1945, the United States exploded "Trinity," the
world's first atomic bomb, at White Sands near Alamogordo, New
Mexico. The secretive work of the Manhattan Project was declared a
success.[2] President Truman, conferring in Potsdam at the time with

Churchill and Stalin, was immediately notified that ". . . results seem satisfactory and already exceed expectations."[3] Within two weeks similar bombs were dropped on Japan, devastating two of its cities and bringing World War II to a close.

Although it was the first nation to develop the A-bomb, the United States had little understanding of the future potential force and effects of such a weapon. To acquire that knowledge, the Joint Chiefs of Staff, shortly after the end of the war, ordered a task force to select "a suitable site which [would] permit accomplishment of atomic tests with acceptable risks and minimum hazards."[4] Such a site had to meet several requirements: it had to be in an area under U.S. control and in a suitable climatic zone; it had to be uninhabited or sparsely populated; and, of course, it had to be far away from the United States.[5]

In January 1946, the government selected as the best site Bikini Atoll, a semicircular chain of some thirty small land dots located in the Marshall Islands region of Micronesia, 2,400 miles southwest of Hawaii.[6] On February 10, 1946, Commander Ben Wyatt, military governor of the Marshalls, addressed the residents of the atoll and told them they would have to move. He compared the Bikinians to the children of Israel whom the Lord had saved from their enemy and led into the Promised Land. "Would you be willing to sacrifice your island for the welfare of all men?" he asked.[7] The Bikinians agreed to move, and they were relocated that spring on Rongerik Atoll; the government promised to take care of them there until it was safe to return.[8]

"Operation Crossroads" began immediately. This first series of tests consisted of two shots, "Test Able," detonated on July 1 in the air over a target fleet including the venerable battleship *Nevada*, and "Test Baker" on July 25, an underwater explosion designed to test the effects of a nuclear blast on the hulls of ocean vessels and submarines. These shots received international press coverage; for the first time, reporters from every major American and European newspaper and magazine witnessed and described a nuclear explosion.[9] By 1958, when President Eisenhower ended the South Pacific testing program, twenty-three nuclear devices, including the hydrogen bomb, had been detonated on Bikini.[10]

Meanwhile, a second atomic testing site was established in the fall of 1947 at nearby Eniwetok Atoll, where forty-three tests were to be conducted over the next ten years.[11] Again people were relocated and the island was closed for security reasons. The first tests conducted at the new site were dubbed "Operation Sandstone," and they resembled the Bikini maneuvers in both the nature of the bombs detonated and the experiments conducted. One major difference existed, however: whereas "Crossroads" was witnessed by the international press, the "Sandstone" series occurred under a virtual news blackout. Secrecy was the order of the day; posters depicting a fish with his mouth open warned participants, "Don't be a sucker. Keep your mouth shut."[12]

Atomic Testing in Nevada

While tests were being conducted in the South Pacific, pressure was building for a site within the continental United States. The creation of such an installation would simplify the complex logistical problems and reduce the mounting costs of managing, supplying, and safeguarding a remote test area. Prompted by the Soviet detonation of an atomic bomb in August 1949[13] and U.S. involvement in the Korean conflict, the ARC[14] ignored persistent warnings from the scientific community about possible health hazards and appealed to President Truman to establish such a continental test site. Relying on a top secret feasibility study code-named "Nutmeg" conducted three years earlier by the Pentagon, the AEC further recommended that the site be located at the Las Vegas-Tonopah Bombing and Gunnery Range which was situated in the desert of Nye County some sixty-five miles northwest of Las Vegas.[15]

The southern Nevada site was selected from a list of five possibilities which included Alamogordo/White Sands, New Mexico; Dugway Proving Ground, Utah; Pamlico Sound/Camp Lejuene, North Carolina; and a fifty-mile-wide strip between Fallon and Eureka, Nevada. The AEC chose the site near Las Vegas for reasons similar to those used in the selection of Bikini and Eniwetok: it was the largest area; it was already under complete control of the federal government; it enjoyed little rainfall and predictable winds from the west; and it had a very low population density. Furthermore, it was a site whose security could not easily be impaired by an outside enemy force; and Camp Mercury, the temporary air base located at the tip of the 5,400 square mile gunnery range, could readily be converted into a testing center.[16]

On December 18, 1950, President Truman approved the opening of the Nevada site; and six weeks later, on January 27, 1951, the first atmospheric test was conducted over a section of the desert known as Frenchman's Flat. This initial series, "Operation Ranger," consisted of five bombs, dropped from the air, which ranged from one to twenty-two kilotons in yield. The shots were fairly uneventful with the exception of the fourth, an eight kiloton device detonated on February 2, which shattered several store windows in Las Vegas and prompted one scientist to report that "the factors controlling this are poorly understood."[17] Safety monitors detected no "significant levels" of radioactivity outside the testing area, and no one received any detectable injuries during the series. All in all, the operation was praised for its efficiency, safety, and speed.[18]

Plans were immediately made for the expansion of facilities at the test site. Eight million dollars were appropriated and construction was begun on utility and operational structures, including a communication system, a control area, several detonating towers, and additional personnel accommodations. As a safety measure, ground zero (the point of detonation) was moved twenty miles north from Frenchman's Flat to Yucca Flat, a huge expanse of desert surrounded on all sides by mountains.[19] And even more significantly, arrangements were made between the AEC and the military for soldiers to participate in atomic warfare maneuvers at ground zero, beginning with the next test series scheduled for October. These exercises were to provide tactical training for the troops and allow researchers to observe and evaluate the psychological impact of the bomb on participants. To accommodate these needs Camp Desert Rock was built to station troops near the test site.[20]

From 1951 through 1958, the NTS was the location of 119 atmospheric tests of nuclear devices. Thirty-one of those were safety experiments which produced very slight or no nuclear yield. Twelve of these 31 were conducted at the surface; six in tunnels; seven in uncased and unstemmed holes; five from the top of steel or wooden towers; and 1 suspended from a balloon. In addition, there were 88 weapons-related tests which did produce a nuclear explosion; these included one at the surface; one rocket; one airburst fired from a 280mm cannon; two cratering experiments; five in tunnels; 19 dropped from aircraft; 23 suspended from balloons; and 36 from the tops of steel or wooden towers.[21]

There was a short-lived, voluntary moratorium on nuclear testing, agreed to by the U.S. and the U.S.S.R., between October 1958 and August 1961. Upon its expiration, testing resumed and there were 102 American detonations occurring over the next two-year period. Of these, however, all but five were deep, underground shots; one of the five was a cratering test and the other four were at or near the surface.[22] When the Limited Test Ban Treaty (prohibiting testing in outer space, underwater, or in the atmosphere) was signed in Moscow on August 5, 1963, atomic testing moved underground, and some 400 shots have been fired to date.[23]

Selling the Bomb at Home

The 1950 decision to begin atomic testing within the continental United States was made in great secrecy and with extreme caution. In his memoirs, President Truman recalled the need to take special care not to frighten people about "shooting off bombs in their backyards."[24] From the start, every effort was made by the federal government to insure not only public acceptance but also support for the new "backyard" testing program.

First and foremost, the government took the position that the continued development of nuclear weapons was absolutely essential to the country's national security. In light of international developments after World War II,[25] it was not difficult to convince the public that the communists were a distinct threat to the American way of life. Loyalty oaths for government employees were required;[26] the House Un-American Activities Committee investigated dozens of people;[27] and the Rosenbergs were executed as atomic spies.[28] Such red-scare tactics were reinforced by the preparedness activities of the Federal Civil Defense Administration, an agency created by Congress in December 1950 to establish community bomb shelters and instruct the public on how to protect itself in the event of a nuclear attack.[29] The military also propagated the notion of a potential nuclear war with the Soviets; soldiers at Camp Desert Rock participated in mock battles against an enemy which was always portrayed as a communist force invading the U.S.[30]

The government's second strategy for gaining popular acceptance of the testing program was to constantly assure the people that the tests were safe. Numerous proclamations were issued by the AEC throughout the decade of the 1950s claiming that radioactive fallout posed no danger to human health.[31] In addition, 30,000 copies of a small green pamphlet entitled "Atomic Tests in Nevada" were distributed locally to convince the neighbors of the test site that the blasts were benign. The pamphlet began by apologizing to the residents in the case they had been "inconvenienced" by the operations, and went on to claim that ". . . findings have confirmed that Nevada test fallout has not caused illness or injured the health of anyone living near the test site."[32] It contained cartoons and rhetoric which made light of the potential danger of fallout from the tests; the precautionary measures which residents were advised to take suggested that the risks were minimal: "Your best action is not to be worried about fallout."[33]

Evidence contrary to this position was suppressed or discredited. In the spring of 1953 when some 3,400 sheep, grazing near the test site, died after being exposed to radioactive fallout, the AEC reported that "the highest radiation dosage to the thyroid [of the sheep] has been calculated to be far below the quantity necessary to produce detectable injury."[34] And on March 1, 1954, following the "Bravo" H-bomb shot, when the wind shifted and carried radioactive fallout over several inhabited islands[35] and a Japanese tuna fishing boat,[36] AEC Chairman Lewis Strauss reported to the press, "Today, a full month after the event, the medical staff . . . advised us that they antic- ipate no illness, barring of course disease which might be hereafter contracted."[37]

Third, the government argued that continued testing was vitally needed for the development of peaceful uses of atomic energy.[38] As early as 1948, the testing at Eniwetok was justified not only on grounds of national security, but also because it would "yield valuable informa- tion pertaining to the civilian employment of atomic energy."[39] This was to become a familiar rationalization in the years to come. For instance, when testing began to move underground in 1957, it was declared that such experiments would augment the development of mining and natural gas production.[40] And in 1962 the "Plowshare Pro- gram" was initiated; drawing its name from the Biblical verse in Isa- iah, "when men shall beat their swords into plowshares," the program involved testing of nuclear devices for such civilian uses as digging harbors or canals, developing underground water supplies, and open- ing new reserves of oil.[41]

Throughout this entire period the government was also involved in a general public relations campaign to promote a positive view of atomic power in all its forms. Various public relations techniques, including films, brochures, traveling exhibits, science fairs, public speakers, and classroom demonstrations, were employed.[42] The AEC even helped the Boy Scouts create an atomic energy merit badge;[43] and the American Museum of Atomic Energy was opened in Oak Ridge, Tennessee.[44] No stone was left unturned as the government sought to sell the bomb to the American people.

Public Response

These various propagandistic efforts by the U.S. government were overwhelmingly successful. Throughout the fifties and early sixties the vast majority of citizens strongly supported further development and stockpiling of nuclear weapons, and implicitly endorsed continued testing in Nevada. Those few who did not were routinely accused of ignorance, hysteria, or involvement in communist plots.[45]

The most vocal opponents of atmospheric testing during these years were scientists who expressed growing concern over cumulative fallout effects. Among their ranks were such noted researchers as Stan- ley Livingston, President of the Federation of American Scientists; Her- mann Muller, Nobel prize winner in genetics; George Beadle, President of the American Association for the Advancement of Science; and Linus Pauling, winner of Nobel prizes in chemistry and peace. For several years a scientific debate raged between these men and the AEC over the possible long-term effects of exposure to radioactive fallout.[46]

The press, however, gave only limited coverage to these scientists who challenged the wisdom of continued testing; consequently, the issue did not become a public one until the 1956 Presidential election. That summer the dangers of fallout were televised nationwide from the Democratic National Convention, and Adlai Stevenson began his campaign with a promise to halt H-bomb tests. Despite considerable evidence presented on the genetic and strontium 90 hazards from the tests, the country (including Nevada) went strongly for incumbent Eisenhower, a longtime proponent of the testing program.[47]

By the late 1950s, with red-baiting on the wane, the anti-testing movement picked up a little momentum. The National Committee for a Sane Nuclear Policy was founded in November 1957, and within one year had recruited 25,000 members.[48] Small scale "Ban the Bomb" protests took the form of sit-ins at missile bases and refusals to participate in air-raid drills.[49] More dramatic incidents involved several attempts by activists to sail into the Marshall Islands testing zone.[50] Nonetheless, the prevailing view remained steadfastly supportive of the government's position throughout the Cold War era.

Response in Nevada

Support for the atmospheric testing program exhibited by the majority of people in the United States was even greater among the citizens of Nevada.[51] When the government first announced the testing was to be conducted in Southern Nevada, the locals welcomed the infusion of funds that a testing facility would generate. Las Vegas had a limited economy and small population base, and the federal expenditure of millions of dollars and the establishment of a permanent payroll meant increased financial prosperity. Employment opportunities increased; real estate prices rose; and the construction industry boomed. Scores of professional scientists were attracted to the area; and Las Vegas suppliers of varied goods and services enjoyed a bonanza. Even the budding tourist business flourished as people flocked to Las Vegas not just to gamble but to see the mushroom clouds and watch history in the making. As a result, most Nevadans during the fifties seemed generally to believe that the economic advantages of the AEC operations in the state outweighed any potential dangers.[52]

This positive attitude toward the atomic testing program in Nevada was evident on three levels. First, the powerful politicians of the state supported the AEC's activities both in Washington and in Carson City. Second, local newspaper coverage of the test site operations during these years was consistently favorable. And finally, the mushroom cloud itself became a prevalent symbol of southern Nevada's popular culture.

In 1950 Nevada was represented in the U.S. Senate by a powerful Democrat, Patrick A. McCarran.[53] Realizing McCarran's potential influence as a member of the Senate Appropriations Committee, AEC Chairman Gordon Dean paid him a special, personal visit to inform him of plans to open the NTS before it was publicly announced. This "courting" continued to insure McCarran's support and smooth the way for AEC activities in his state.[54] It worked. McCarran consistently voted for increased funding for the AEC, praising the agency for its precision and care in making its tests: "The lead in development of this science is in the best interest of the United States, and we must maintain it. We have an avowed enemy who is developing atomic energy and we must keep ahead."[55]

Nevada's governor during the early fifties, Charles Russell, also publicly defended the NTS against any criticism which arose from leery constituents. His attitude toward the testing activities was captured by his comment to a *New Yorker* reporter in 1952: "We had long ago written off that terrain as wasteland and today it's blooming with atoms. . . ."[56]

This stand taken by the local papers was hardly surprising. From the start, news coverage of the testing program was presented in optimistic terms: "Baby A-Blast May Provide Facts on Defense Against Atomic Attack,"[63] "Use of Taller Towers . . . Introduces an Added Angle of Safety . . . ,"[64] and "Fallout on Las Vegas and Vicinity . . . Very Low and Without Any Effects on Health."[65] Editorials invariably took the AEC's side. On January 15, 1951, just prior to the first test blast conducted at the NTS, the *Review Journal* reassured its readers that the furor regarding A-bombs at Indian Springs was "entirely uncalled for."[66] Shortly thereafter, on January 30, 1951, the *Sun* stated "atomic experimentation must be carried on if we are to maintain our lead in the atomic and guided missiles field."[67] In the spring of 1953, following the "Dirty Harry" shot which sprinkled fallout on St. George, when Utah Representative Stringfellow called for an end to testing in Nevada, the *Review Journal* warned Stringfellow to stay out of Nevada's business and editorialized, "We like the AEC. We welcome them to Nevada for their tests because we, as patriotic Americans, believe we are contributing something in our small way, to the protection of the land we love."[68]

Local reporters frequently traveled the sixty-five miles to Camp Mercury to cover the announced test blasts. Perched on bleachers at News Nob ten miles from ground zero, they witnessed, photographed, and reported on the nuclear detonations. It was deemed a privilege to be a member of the Ancient and Honorable Society of Bomb Watchers, which included Walter Cronkite, Dave Galloway, John Cameron Swayze, and Bob Considine among its members.[69] Hardly a day passed during the fifties and early sixties when some story dealing with atomic weapons or a related topic did not appear on the front page.

One particularly noteworthy story revolved around the "Shamrock" shot on March 17, 1953. A typical American community was constructed near ground zero to determine what would happen if it were to become the target of an enemy's atomic bomb. Officially named "Survival City," it was soon dubbed "Doom Town" by troops and reporters. The houses were fully furnished and stocked with supplies, and late model cars were parked in garages; mannequins wearing the latest fashions represented inhabitants of all ages.[70]

Graphically describing the aftermath of a similar exercise, Archie Teague of the *Review Journal* wrote, "Potshot inspection tours were held to learn the odds of survival in the atomic age. People played by dummies lay dead and dying in basements, living rooms, kitchens, and bedrooms."[71] Such accounts were typical of the coverage during these shots; they focused on the descriptive, visual implications of the bomb and failed to question more serious potential hazards.

Not only did atomic news dominate the headlines, but the mushroom cloud also became the symbol of the generation, quickly permeating many aspects of the local culture. The "atomic hairdo," originally designed by GeeGee, hairstylist at the Flamingo, was a popular request for special occasions; the hair was pulled over a wire form shaped like a mushroom cloud and then sprinkled with silver glitter; the cost, $75.[72] The "atomic cocktail" was also a big seller in bars along the Strip; made from equal parts of vodka, brandy, and champagne with a dash of sherry, the potent drink was served at breakfast parties following the predawn shots.[73] Many of the hotels packed box lunches for bombwatchers to carry to picnics at Angel's Peak.[74] One establishment even called itself the Atomic View Motel because guests could witness the flash without ever leaving their lounge chairs.[75] In the Desert Inn Sky Room, pianist Ted Mossman first played his boogie woogie tune "Atomic Bomb Bounce," which soon had people dancing all over town.[76] Postcards were printed with the mushroom cloud rising in the background over "Glitter Gulch."

The Clark County official seal also displayed a large mushroom cloud, as did the 1953 yearbook cover for Las Vegas High School. The feature story for the June–December 1955 issue of *Nevada Highways and Parks* was about the NTS with a "typical, mushrooming cloud of fire, smoke, sand and radioactive particles" pictured on the cover.[77] Local merchants also played on the atomic theme; car salesman "Boob" Jones proudly advertised "Atom Drops on High Prices,"[78] and Allen and Hanson, Las Vegas haberdashers, placed a barrel full of broken plate glass window panes in front of their store with a sign, "Atomic Bomb Souvenirs—Free." Several casinos posted signs that warned if a tremor from a bomb blast caused the dice to turn or roulette balls to jump to another slot, the house man's ruling was final.[79] In Southern Nevada evidence of this atomic "mania" was widespread, and reflected the public's interest in the testing program, and belief in its necessity.

Epilogue

When atomic testing was moved underground late in 1963, the danger of fallout lessened as a matter of concern; many believed that radioactivity was now being contained far below the earth's surface where it could do no harm.[80] New issues drew the attention of the public and press away from the arms race; napalm, pickax handles, and love beads replaced the mushroom cloud as the star attraction on the 6 o'clock news. As the proliferation of nuclear weapons accelerated during the sixties and seventies, the public focus on atomic warfare and its dangers declined. Convinced of the necessity of first-strike power, and anesthetized by constant reassurances from the government that they could be safe in the event of nuclear attack, considerable segments of the American people had long since become accustomed to living with the bomb. As a result, the operations at the NTS slipped quietly into comparative obscurity.

Only one major local critic of the NTS arose during the late sixties: Howard Hughes, eccentric billionaire, big-time investor in Las Vegas, and ironically, the nation's largest prime defense contractor. Politically conservative, Hughes was not philosophically opposed to nuclear weapons; he only objected to their being tested near him or his hotels. He began a low-key campaign against the AEC in 1967, which escalated to a virtual war by the spring of 1968. Hughes contributed campaign funds to presidential candidates, lobbied the AEC, threatened to withdraw his investments from Las Vegas, and offered to pay any expenses which would result from delaying tests; he even wrote personally to President Johnson urging him to stop the testing program.[81] Interestingly, although Hughes had had little difficulty lining up press support for most of his Nevada resort projects, he was unable to convince the local papers to side with him against the AEC.[82] Shortly thereafter, Hughes' mental and physical health further deteriorated, and his interests turned elsewhere.

The NTS made the news again in a big way on December 18, 1970, when the "Baneberry" underground shot vented and sent a cloud of radioactive particles into the air.[83] The wind carried the cloud over area 12 where some 600 NTS employees were working and had to be evacuated. Three hundred of the workers were found to be contaminated and 20 were sent to the AEC laboratory for further observation and testing. Nominal precautions, such as showering, changing clothes, and washing their vehicles, were taken, but no one was found to need medical treatment.[84] The AEC reported that "the radiation presented no danger to human health or life and only the most minute traces of fallout were deposited on the ground."[85] Area 12 remained closed until after the New Year's holiday, but throughout the rest of the test site it was back to business as usual. No Nevada newspaper editorials or "letters to the editor" appeared criticizing the NTS and no official action was taken to interfere with its operations.

In the late seventies the issue of atmospheric testing hazards was revived. Medical findings indicated a higher than normal rate of leukemia among veterans who had participated in maneuvers at Camp Desert Rock and among residents who had lived "downwind" from the test site during the fifties.[86] Several Congressional hearings were convened;[87] President Carter named a task force to investigate the long-term effects of low level radiation;[88] and the Pentagon initiated a follow-up study of "atomic veterans."[89] Interest groups, including the Nevada Test Site Radiation Victims Association, the National Association of Atomic Veterans, Citizens Call, and the Committee of Survivors, were formed and began pressuring the federal government to admit negligence and compensate the alleged victims of atomic testing. Several court cases were also filed,[90] and legislation was introduced which would provide benefits to help pay medical expenses of those harmed by radioactive fallout.[91]

The reaction to these events in Nevada has been less than enthusiastic. The local papers covered the proceedings of the Salt Lake City case filed by "downwind residents" and the Baneberry case filed by two test site workers exposed during the 1970 venting, but there had been no public outcry about the validity of these claims. Although Nevada's representatives in Congress were cosponsors of the legislation to compensate "atomic victims," no mention was made of the bills by any of the parties during Nevada's heated political campaigns in 1982. Relatedly, no nuclear freeze question appeared on the ballot in Clark County, although it was a major issue in many areas.[92] And on January 27, 1983, the thirty-second anniversary of the first atmospheric shot at the NTS, a protest in front of the Federal Building drew only thirty marchers.[93] Though no official polls have been conducted, one is led to believe that, despite increasing evidence that activities at the NTS have caused damages in the past, the majority of southern Nevadans still support the test site and favor its continued operation in the state.[94]

"Nevada Red Blues" (1992)
Adrian Louis

"Nevada No Longer" and "Hawthorne" (1999)
Shaun Griffin

"Tidings" (1996)
Gary Short

Given its unique frontier experience and fluctuating population, it is understandable that Nevada has inspired a relatively modest body of creative writing. To be certain, over the years several novelists and essayists published localized works of high quality (such as Ada Meacham Strobridge's stories and essays written early in the twentieth century about family life on the Nevada frontier), but only three writers with strong Nevada connections can be said to have become part of the national literary scene: visitor Mark Twain; Walter Van Tilburg Clark; and between 1957 and his death in 2001, Carson City native Robert Laxalt, most of whose 17 books of fiction and nonfiction described life in Nevada. His second book detailed the emotional visit to the Basque homeland by his aging father, Dominique Laxalt, who had herded sheep in the Sierra for decades. Sweet Promised Land *(1957), which received a Pulitzer Prize nomination for its evocation of America as a land of opportunity and cultural asssimilation, is generally considered Laxalt's best work. Several of Laxalt's other novels received critical acclaim, including* The Basque Hotel *(1989), a coming-of-age story about growing up in Carson City, where Laxalt's mother, Theresa, operated a traditional Basque hotel. Nevada has yet to produce a poet of the national stature of these three writers, but those who take western literature seriously recognize the work of three contemporary poets who have explored Nevada themes. All have published collections with the University of Nevada Press, and their reputations have grown as they have matured as writers. The poems reprinted here are illustrative of their work. All have expressed concerns about the environmental impact of corporate mining operations and the United States military, especially nuclear testing. Shaun T. Griffin lives in Virginia City, Nevada, where he writes, translates, and edits while operating an educational program for homeless children. Adrian C. Louis, a member of Lovelock Paiute Tribe born and raised in rural Nevada, has published nine collections of poetry and a series of short stories, and teaches at Southwest Minnesota State University. Gary Short, who also lives in Virginia City, has published three collections of poetry. He received the Western States Book Award for Poetry (1996) and was named a Wallace Stegner Fellow by the Stanford Creative Writing Program.*

Nevada Red Blues

by Adrian C. Louis

"Where live fire began to inhabit you."
—Pablo Neruda

We live under
slot machine
stars
that jackpot
into the black
velvet
backdrop
and
mirror the greed
of the creatures who soiled our land.

Numa,
it was
not
enough
for
Taibo
to make
our sacred land

a living
though
pustulous
whore.

He
had
to drop
hydrogen bombs
where
thousands
of years
of our blood
spirits lie.

Nevada No Longer

by Shaun T. Griffin

This is a case in which the public has to trust the scientists.
> —Tony Buono, USGS Hydrologist,
> Nevada Test Site

Nevada is never on the map, not now,
not ever.
        If only
I could finger a word
for the few who live
                by the sun,
what would it be: itinerant,
sparse dragon people
                who fly
in the sand and spin before the books
that name a cactus to clothe
the loins of uranium down deep?

No, it would not be harsh; rather
we live here.
We raise family, split wood,
shovel snow, and read of our absence.

Nevada is never on the map,
not now, not ever,
                    save the day
a green lung percolates
from two miles below volcanic tuff—
then you will recognize us
as the place that kills
or was killed, but for now
I cannot find a way down Alternate 95—
not scholarly, not radical, not
known. And still, faces cling
to the taverns of Beatty,
Tonopah, and Yerington.

Where do I go to lie with the yucca? California?
No, it is many things but quiet.
Oregon? No, it is wet and
dry there, so I remain
home
with states before and aft
coming like insects
to the Test Site, coming
with something to read.

Today, I tell my son
of a desert with no name. He remarks
"Why?" I do not know—Nevada is
never on the map, not now,
not ever.

Hawthorne

by Shaun T. Griffin

for Gary Short

In a town where bombs
buy a day's work and bunkers
blight the desert like bones,
how happy can you be
straddling a stool at El Capitán

with the windows coiled in smoke
and the jukebox jarring K-9
through the reeds of country soul?

The casino fades to lavender
shoulders on Highway 95.
Tourists brake to read "Danger—
Low Flying Aircraft, Do Not Stop,"
and the hangars climb to the sky
and detours swallow transport trucks
bound for Reno or beyond.

And still the bunkers lie, mouths open
like barrels in the rain.

The Cliff House Saloon, quiet as fog,
boasts "Armed Forces Day—
Proud to Serve You," and the old ones
wait for the second Tuesday in July
when the hydroplanes
light up Walker Lake.
Even it looks flatter than it should.

The children play on decommissioned
three-inch, fifty-caliber anti-aircraft guns
as if they were powder-blue
dinosaurs in Ladybird Park,
thinking, how much better can it get?
In a once-mighty high school,
seniors graduate to thieve from Mormon sky.

And bunkers die in peacetime.

The barracks are nearly closed now.
The moon rises in sills of solitude
and the last drunk shuffles from
Joe's Tavern like a cloud
come to rescue this swollen town.
And the wind moves like a skirt
through the clapboard siding
beached in stones at her feet.

Tidings

by Gary Short

Bitterness will flow
The earth will burn

—from a Mayan prophecy

The bloated carcass of a wild horse
is not abstraction
but a specific example—

the cyanide that seeps into the creek
from heaps of dirt leached for microscopic gold,
its residue. The death of a mustang,
wind bristling a fetlock's stiff hair,
is a political statement.

Bitterness will flow

There are well-funded scientists
in a lab in California who breed weapons
delivered & unleashed at the Test Site
near cloud-shadowed Yucca Mountain.
A clacking train shakes the dreams
Of a child in Fernley, Nevada.

Walking, she looks out the window. Her breath,
a quivering cell on the cold glass,
grows & then shrinks.
The bow on her white-sheep nightgown
is tied to sign for infinity.
She hears the lurching

boxcars full of harm
now past her. She cannot see
the steel tracks glint on & off in moonlight,
silvery rills of a stream
that runs to the vanishing point . . .

the earth will burn

from *Earthtones: A Nevada Album* (1995)

Ann Ronald

Ann Ronald has written extensively on the literature of the American West, including an examination of the writings of the maverick defender of the desert lands of the Southwest, Edward Abbey. Ronald's writings reveal a deep and sensitive appreciation of the environment of the Great Basin. During her career as a college professor and administrator, she has found time to explore the vast expanses of uninhabited Nevada. A native of the state of Washington, where the green forests of the Cascade Mountains are prominent, she admits that Nevada's landscape took some getting used to. "Since moving to Nevada," she writes, "I've adopted an aesthetic that embraces horizons unencumbered by the niceties most tourists enjoy, that unabashedly appreciates this special earthtone landscape. Accustomed now to remoteness and rattlers, I've taught myself to get over the color green. Along the way I've fallen in love, I confess, with Nevada's well-wrought terrain." Ronald's writings reflect an ongoing conflict that stretches back many decades, pitting environmentalists and various federal agencies against Nevada ranching interests that historically enjoyed easy access to open rangeland for the purpose of grazing cattle. During the 1970s, throughout the West, enforcement of Environmental Protection Agency policies produced an outcry from spokesmen for ranchers, loggers, and land developers. In the 1970s, rural Nevada became a center of the Sagebrush Rebellion that spread across western states. This movement attempted to persuade Congress to transfer federal lands to state governments or to permit their sale at low prices to private interests. Federal court decisions and the lack of sympathy in urban areas caused the rebellion to lose much of its momentum, but not before it produced some sensational headlines about testy confrontations between federal agents and Nevada ranchers.

Too many people picture Nevada landscape the way eastern newspaper reporters and urban advertising agencies imagine it. High-Rise Casinos and High-Tech Theme Parks. Frank Sinatra and Barbra Streisand. Liberal Slots, Computerized Poker, Craps. A Get-Rich-Quick Mentality. Glamour, High Rollers, Spectacle. Holiday neon punctuating empty terrain. The previous generation's Nuclear Test Site. The next century's Hazardous Waste Dump. Mile after mile after mile of America's Loneliest Roads.

Few tourists, few essayists, few photographers bother with the sparse horizons beyond the neon, the lonely wilderness spaces of California's less comely neighbor to the east. Writing five short essays now collected in *Steep Trails* John Muir set what I consider an unfortunate aesthetic tone. He described Nevada scenery as "a singularly barren aspect, appearing gray and forbidding and shadeless." Even though Muir admired some isolated peaks and valleys, he generally treated the Nevada landscape harshly. Calling the Silver State "this thirsty land," he imagined it "like heaps of ashes dumped from the blazing sky" and summarized his feelings by envisioning "one vast desert, all sage and sand, hopelessly irredeemable now and forever."

Someone blankly staring through a car window might well agree with Muir's dry assessment. Rivers are few and far between. Interstate 80 stretches across a lot of sand and sage, with only an occasional glimpse of the evaporating Humboldt that weary pioneers trailed 150 years ago. Highways 50 and 93 and 95 alternate sinewy mountain passes with flats of alkali and dust, relieved only by winter snow or summer cloudbursts. None of these major routes is scenic in any conventional way.

Nor are the views from an airplane window any more obviously picturesque. While a casual traveler might glance once or twice at the striations of brown, chocolate, and beige, might briefly puzzle over the shadowed ridgelines, might even shake his or her head at the vacant horizons below, most find more pleasure in the refreshments being served. My seatmate last October, making idle conversation, echoed the Illinois couple overheard at an interstate rest stop two months before: 'What is there to see out there?" "It's so empty." "It's so drab." "It's so depressing."

One of Wallace Stegner's essays, "Thoughts in a Dry Land," touches briefly on why we are unable to change our aesthetic minds about what is scenic and what is not. He insists that we have to get over the color green. Stegner is right, of course. Almost all of us have been taught a worldview that prefers green and blue to ocher and beige, that values redwoods and oceans more than rabbitbrush and sinks. Stegner concludes by saying that we inherently lack appreciation for such things as sagebrush and raw earth and alkali flats. These, he suggests, are acquired tastes, ones not easily adopted by conventional sensibilities.

Empty space, and the concomitant exposure of geologic time, are acquired tastes too. As someone who grew up in the forested Pacific Northwest, I not only was indoctrinated by the beauty of green but I also was comforted by vine maple, maidenhair ferns, and shin tangle. The near view—perhaps a high meadow filled with purple gentian, perhaps the riffle of a stream—was pleasingly, narrowly defined. Any long view was supposed to be grandiose in a European kind of way, punctuated by two-hundred-foot Douglas fir and glaciated peaks with romantic-sounding names. I possessed no imaginative comprehension for the shapes and shades of basin and rockbound range in a "'land of little rain."

Now that I've spent nearly twenty-five years tracking such desert distances, however, I've developed a very different aesthetic eye. From the air, I ignore my seatmate's imprecations and look down on a Jackson Pollock oil. Framed by the plane's window, the colors stipple from black-topped ridges to creamy basins with pale cuts muted red, like dried blood. Curved washes narrow, then widen, then narrow again. The trace of a river twists into tight coils, a series of oxbows unwilling to dry themselves out. The shadows that follow the oxbows are metallic tints from a desiccated palette. Sere green—not emerald hues, but tones befitting the jaded contours of the land below.

Closer to the ground, heading east to west across a lonely highway, I picture not a gallery hung with postmodern paintings but a film unrolling before my eyes. Rounded hills fold into wrinkled cavities, amber curves sharpen against a darker sky. An evening raincloud spills from its top a Niagara that will never reach the earth. Three mustangs browse silently through the yellowed grasses. At the sound of my truck approaching, two golden eagles erupt from the pavement. One, clutching a roadkill rabbit, flies off; the other, settling on a nearby fencepost, glares at the highway. I stop the truck, grab my binoculars, and stare back at the huge bird.

That's what the man and woman from Illinois might have seen, had they known that scenery need not be green, that shapes and shadows may segue into figures and forms, and that seductive details can be spotted when one goes slow. If they had strolled out into the sage, they might have discovered how much a single lens can reveal. In springtime the brown hills turn lime velvet for a week or maybe a month. Even after a dry winter, showy phlox the size of my little fingernail cluster underfoot and alongside abandoned dirt roads, while a wet winter brings forth a patchwork of purple lupine. Blizzard white transforms lumpish limestone blocks into peaks reminiscent of the Alps, while cloud shadows in any season writhe the distance into a close-up kaleidoscope of colored motion.

Too many visitors to the Silver State never see my Great Basin. Or, if they do see it, they don't know how to describe it. Their Nevada is a preconceived one, a product of instinct, intuition, and intellects unwilling to look favorably at dry desert scenery. Their Nevada, I'm afraid, is an unfortunate cliché. *Earthtones: A Nevada Album* presumes to refute this point of view. Neither "a singularly barren aspect" nor a landscape "hopelessly irredeemable, now and forever," our Nevada is one seen through sympathetic eyes.

Teal sky and a sea of purple sage. Mountain mahogany, white fir, a crimson mass of claret cup cactus. Rawhide Springs and Green Monster Canyon. A bobcat tiptoeing along Corn Creek. Desert tortoise, a marmot whistling for his mate, a nesting long-eared owl. The Black Rock playa, Lake Lahontan. Currant Mountain and Duckwater Peak, Rainbow Canyon and Calico Hills. Limestone, sandstone, and tuff. One stone wall, a few broken bricks; dry alfalfa, an empty irrigation ditch. A dust-blown sunset, vermilion and orange and gold. "One vast desert?" Not exactly. One vast deserted landscape of color and shadow and aesthetic dimension.

"Las Vegas on the Eve of the New Millennium," from *Neon Metropolis* (2002)

Hal Rothman

In 1940, Look *magazine published an article about Las Vegas entitled "Wild, Wooly, and Wide-Open," and in the years that followed more than a thousand additional feature newspaper and magazine articles attempted to describe and define Las Vegas. One of the more memorable was Tom Wolfe's controversial 1965 book,* The Kandy Kolored Tangerine-Flake Streamline Baby, *an early example of the "new journalism" that broke with accepted writing standards and with the rules of journalistic "objectivity." Wolfe's zany book captured the rebellious times of the 1960s. In one chapter—entitled "Las Vegas (What?) Las Vegas (Can't Hear You! Too Noisy). Las Vegas!!!"—he explored the city's drug scene and the aura of sexuality that underpinned the city's tourist appeal. Wolfe was also stunned by the sights and sounds of the city—the visual impact of an enormous array of lights and the cacophonous sound produced by whirring slot machines, clanging bells, lounge musicians, and thousands of voices that rise from crowded casino floors. By the time Wolfe visited Las Vegas, the population of Las Vegas and Clark County approached 200,000. Although skeptics routinely predicted that the bubble would burst, Las Vegas continued to grow at a record-setting pace and the city's distinct new architectural forms and frenetic lifestyle attracted attention and comment. Scholars of urban life proclaimed Las Vegas to be the harbinger of the emerging postmodern American city of the twenty-first century. As the last hours of 1999 ticked away and the new millennium lurked beyond midnight, University of Nevada, Las Vegas historian Hal Rothman took a close look at America's maverick city, a place that he identified as a "spectacle of postmodernism."*

A look down Las Vegas Boulevard, more widely known as the "World Famous Las Vegas Strip," on New Year's Eve 1999, revealed the triumph of postindustrial capitalism, information and experience, over its industrial predecessor. Billions of dollars from the world financial markets had been fashioned into the long line of multicolored casinos that lit the night sky. This spectacle of postmodernism, a combination of space and form in light and dark that owes nothing to its surroundings and leaves meaning in the eye of the beholder, is one of the largest private investments in public art anywhere. It produces no tangible goods of any significance, yet generates billions of dollars annually in revenue. Here is the first city of the twenty-first century, the place where desire meets capital, where instinct replaces restraint, where the future of a society, for better and worse, takes a form that had been inconceivable even a generation before. In the 1990s, Las Vegas came into its own, became a city on par with other American metropolises in its significance, but one that generates its sustence in a different way than any other city on earth.

In the twelve years since the opening of the Mirage on New Year's Eve, 1988, the Strip has become a world-class center of entertainment encased in a fantasyland portrayal of time and space. The golden Mandalay Bay at the southern tip, the pyramid-shaped Luxor, and the faux medieval castles of the Excalibur melds fake history with an illusion of the exotic. The green glow of the MGM Grand and the raucous architecture of New York, New York, graced by the Statute of Liberty, arm thrust in the air somehow more aggressively than in the original, offers American life recast on a scale and in a style that reminds one of Disney but promises something entirely more fantastic. Paris Las Vegas, complete with Eiffel Tower, and the Bellagio, a little Lake Como with its orchestrated fountains presents Europe and its cultures as Americans wish they were. The Mirage's volcano and Treasure Island's hourly battle between a pirate ship and the British Navy offers imaginative fantasies of adventure in the South Seas and the stories of Robert Louis Stevenson. Caesars Palace, gaming's most recognizable brand, with its tacit promise to make every man and woman a Caesar, gives the public gladiators and Cleopatras, and the Venetian's gondolas mark the newest claimant to the throne of preeminence in the war for the heart of the visiting public. These little city-states, interrelated little kingdoms, entirely self-contained and at war for customers, run by their own logic. They share a purpose, making money by providing pleasure, but they pursue this objective in varying ways. Against a backdrop reminiscent of commercial competition during the first great age of exploration, the Strip offers the past, the present, high, low, and Nobrow culture, all in the space of one long city street. It offers a world fantastic and unreal, yet simultaneously tangible and available for purchase. Here is the unbelievable made temporal, held in your hands. Here is America in the new millennium.

As it does every night, Las Vegas offers much more than a visual spectacle during the New Year celebrations in 1999. For pleasure that millennial weekend, the city presented Barbra Streisand, a Tina Turner and Elton John co-bill, Bette Midler, the Eagles, Celine Dion, Carlos Santana, Rod Stewart, Gladys Knight, Hall and Oates, and a host of other headliners; for experience, the sheer thought of hundreds of thousands of people in the same place celebrating was enough to make anyone who craved that sort of thing giddy. The national television networks covered Las Vegas; NBC, Fox, and CNN could be found at Caesars Palace. Connie Chung and ABC 2000 broadcast live from a floating platform in the Bellagio's artificial lake. Some wondered if she'd need an umbrella when the fountains did their dance, sending water as high as 240 feet in the air.

The media and the 300,000 people who flocked to Las Vegas that night had come to participate in an orgy of the unruly combination of experience, self, and commodity that is what culture has become in the United States. We crave experience as affirmation of ourselves; the packages of experience we buy in all its forms set us apart from one another and grant us our claim that we're unique. In an age when goods alone no longer offer true distinction, we use experience to prove that we're special, to set ourselves apart from others, to win the ultimate battle of the cocktail party by having the most interesting story to tell. Through its own bizarre alchemy, its chameleonlike ability to imitate so well that the copy it creates is more enticing than the original, Las Vegas accomplishes a neat trick: it lets any visitor believe that they are at the center of the experience the Desert City offers. Las Vegas intuited the needs of the baby boomers, the group who look like the elephant a boa constrictor swallowed if you chart their progress through American society, and the changing national and global culture they created; the city replicated that culture's DNA and made it more palatable, more satisfying, and strangely more meaningful than the places, events, and concepts it mimicked. Like Disneyland, Las Vegas encapsulates what we are. Every year millions come to bask in its reflection. No one thinks Las Vegas is real; it is illusion, but visitors willingly suspend disbelief and pretend. Only snobs look down on Las

Vegas these days, for its magic is green and gold, the colors of power and status in the postindustrial world.

Las Vegas blends entertainment, experience, and opportunity for a broad swath of the American and the world public. It fulfills the desires of the baby boomers, reflects the abundance that they take for granted and the selfish indulgence, the hedonistic libertarianism, that is the legacy of the American cultural revolution of the 1960s. Las Vegas is the therapeutic ethos of our time run amok, our sociopsychological promise to ourselves to be eternally young writ large on the landscape of aging self-indulgence. In its promise of a luxury experience for a middle-class price, Las Vegas pretends to encourage social mobility; it guarantees escape from the mundane—with you at the center of the story. It is the freedom to experience to which the baby boomers feel entitled, and every dimension of their impact on American society reflects this desire. Postmodern, postindustrial capitalism is about consuming experience, not goods, about creating insatiable desire that must be fulfilled in front of an approving audience. Las Vegas is geared to meet this challenge, to provide the audience, to deliver more than anywhere else and hold out the possibility of still more. The ability to quench desire brings people; the chance to dream of more brings them back again and again.

Two generations ago, modern Las Vegas was born with a sophisticated cachet that quickly degenerated. Only a generation ago, in the late 1970s and early 1980s, Las Vegas retained its stigma as the sleazy home of tawdry sex and mobsters. Its face then was different, more twisted to the mainstream, yet alluring in powerful ways. Cleaned up, Las Vegas was what we wanted to become. It was the epitome of American deviance, and as such, it seemed headed toward a dismal end as visitation totals dropped in the late 1970s and early 1980s. Las Vegas seemed played out, passe, soon to be cast aside as a flimsy relic of a laced-up pseudomorality.

From that nadir, the merging of a constellation of forces, the liberalization of American culture, the growing premium on the self, and the normalization of Las Vegas prominent among them, has made Las Vegas the place to be and be seen as the new century begins. The former capital of deviance has become the linchpin not only of national obsessions—Las Vegas has long been a canvas on which Americans paint their neuroses—but of individual aspirations as well. Las Vegas simultaneously looks backward and forward, attracts and repels. Reflection demands both affection and dismay. Only the baby boomers could demand Las Vegas and the Strip. Only capitalism, with its peculiar genius for catering to desires it creates, could build it.

Topped by an enormous thirty-five-foot-high Coca-Cola bottle but still overshadowed by the billion-dollar behemoths around it, Showcase on the Las Vegas Strip offered something new when it opened in 1997. Next to the MGM Grand and sporting SKG Gameworks with Surge Rock, named for Coca-Cola's latest soft drink, in the middle, and the All-Star Café, this cutting-edge entertainment power center had not a single slot machine. No twenty-one tables, no buffet, none of the customary enticements of Strip properties could be found there. Instead, Showcase presented mainstream entertainment, wholesome and for the kids, packaged for the young of today and their plaint parents. From the All-Star Café, huge pictures of Joe Montana, Tiger Woods, Martina Navratilova, Andre Agassi, and Wayne Gretzky looked down on the new Las Vegas. Their images—all sports stars, all in sports on which you can legally wager in Nevada—gave the new Strip, the haven of leisure and entertainment for a society that has become more visual than textual, the figurative thumbs-up.

The brainchild of two young entrepreneurs, Barry Fieldman and Robert Unger, Showcase anticipated a future that was already here and pointed to changes not only in Las Vegas but in national culture as well. Showcase wasn't a casino and it wasn't a hotel. The development was a symbol, a project that could occur only in the context of growth around it. Its $160 million price tag made it minuscule compared to the nearby hotels, a number of which topped $1 billion in cost. No one came to the city specifically to see Showcase, but, joined to the visual and psychic transformation of the Strip, the property brought the future another step closer. Showcase articulated important links between what had once been the nation's capital of deviance and the core of the liberal consumerism that now passes for culture and has become American faith.

The enormous Coke bottle affirmed the new Las Vegas in a way that no other brand could. No better representative of transnational capitalism than Coca-Cola existed, and few companies were more conscious of their image and their place in the global economy. Robert Goizueta, Coke's chairman from 1981 until 1997, piloted the company to preeminence in the emerging global economy. From Turner Field in Atlanta to Fenway Park in Boston, Coca-Cola picked its spots. Coke's red-and-white logo was ubiquitous, but only a few chosen places received its symbolic anointment. In 1990 World of Coca-Cola, a prototype for Showcase, opened in Coke's hometown of Atlanta. It stood as a testimony to a future that no one thought would ever grace the Las Vegas Strip.

The sponsorship of the symbol of global capitalism—service, quality, and refreshment melded together—was a major coup for the American desert city. The participation of Forrest City, the Cleveland-based developer and a critical player in downtown redevelopment across the country, further enunciated the new significance. Las Vegas offered a development opportunity like no other, a reprise of other booms in a new and different shape. The home of the lounge singer had become safe and profitable. The new Las Vegas could stimulate, titillate, and be clean and fun at the very same instant.

Showcase was a small piece of a much larger transformation. One year later, in October 1998, Steve Wynn opened the Bellagio. The $2.1 billion hotel included Wynn's $350 million collection of masterpiece art, Rubens, Picasso, Degas, Monet, Gaugin, Van Gogh, and Warhol among them. Within eighteen months, Sheldon Adelson at the Venetian had entered into an agreement with the Guggenheim and Hermitage museums and hired renowned architect Rem Koolhaas to design a 35,000-square-foot satellite gallery. When Wynn sold his empire to meta-financier and impresario Kirk Kerkorian and MGM Grand in May 2000, he kept much of his art collection, and the MGM offered the rest for sale. High art seemed to reach a dead end in Las Vegas, but to the surprise of many, the gallery did not disappear. Instead, MGM negotiated with the Phillips Collection of Washington, D.C., for a traveling exhibit that recorded more than 200,000 visitors in its first five months of display. Wynn planned to display his collection in the property he intended to build at the Desert Inn, and Koolhaas's Guggenheim opened in fall 2001. After the purchase of the Mirage group, Las Vegas ended up with more masterpiece art, a counterintuitive result that reflected the city's new status. Mainstream commercial culture arrived, and so had the tattered remains of highbrow culture, the very cultural elitism that had long led its adherents to disdain Las Vegas. In the clearest reflection of the rise of Nobrow culture, high art seemed likely to become permanent in the desert.

The combination accelerated the transition of Las Vegas. The town had once been a risqué aberration in a society persuaded of its own morality. Las Vegas was excluded from the main patterns of post-World War II American prosperity in industrial America. The corridors of growth and development bypassed it, and the city had to forge its own divergent, idiosyncratic way. Until 1970, the centers of power in American society did not invest in the desert oasis. The idea of an initial public offering of stock in a casino was ludicrous. The rare attempt fell flat, victim of a marketplace that disdained casinos and looked down on places that condoned vice. The wealthy and the powerful wanted no connection to gambling and corruption. Gambling had been a pastime for the lazy, those who wanted a shortcut. The neo-

Victorian culture scorned it as a vice and more: not only sinful, but demeaning to individuals and their society as well. Even those who are tempted by dollar signs feared disapproving friends at the country clubs or scathing editorials in the newspapers. The financial markets would not touch gambling. With money to be made elsewhere and the gambling industry marred by the stigma of the hoodlums, Wall Street saw no percentage in backing deviance. Gambling was illegal everywhere else. American society grappled with the transition from deferred gratification to immediate self-indulgence, and Las Vegas's idea of fun as excess was too much. In a society in which Ward and June Cleaver were the iconography of normal, how could staid bankers, pillars of the community and first pew at church, finance casinos—with half-naked showgirls—run by guys with accents?

As late as 1980, as the baby boomers began to reach positions of power, this stigma remained powerful. Even though American morality had loosened considerably, Las Vegas was not yet truly legitimate. In 1983, CitiCorp located a service center in Las Vegas. This financial giant so worried that its credit-card clients would balk at mailing payments to a Las Vegas address that it invented a fictitious town, "The Lakes, Nevada," to soothe its customers. No one in Las Vegas minded. "We would have let them call it Citibank City then if they'd wanted to," recalled Somer Hollingsworth, then a leading banker and president of the Nevada Development Authority in 2000. The tarnished image of Las Vegas stood, solid and visible, almost twenty-five years after the Del E. Webb Corporation simultaneously owned by the New York Yankees and the Sahara on the Strip; seventeen years after Howard Hughes departed from his train car and pulled up to the Desert Inn in his combination ambulance-luxury vehicle; seven years after Atlantic City legalized casino gaming; four years after Chemical Bank determined that the Sahara needed $25 million more than it had asked for to renovate its property on the northern edge of the Strip; and as Circus Circus secured almost $500 million in bank loans near the prime rate to support its growth. CitiCorp recognized the economic advantages of a Las Vegas location. Wall Street already knew. But in the view of corporate executives, the American public—at least those who held credit cards at the onset of the great spasm of loosening credit—was still dubious of even a primary American corporation's ability to be responsible in the face of endlessly encouraged excess.

The opening of the Mirage began a new era, grander than any in the city's past. The Mirage Phase started with impresario Steve Wynn, the hard-edged but smooth former liquor distributor who morphed into the progenitor of a Las Vegas that blended gaming and entertainment, and his Mirage Hotel and Casino. The Mirage cost $630 million, $500 million more than any previous casino, and needed to clear $1 million a day to meet its overhead. The new hotels completed since then—Excalibur (1990), Luxor (1993), Treasure Island (1993), MGM Grand (1993) a few blocks off-Strip, the Hard Rock Hotel (1995), the Stratosphere Tower (1996), Monte Carlo (1996), New York, New York (1996), Bellagio (1998), Mandalay Bay (1999), the Venetian (1999), Paris (1999), and the new Aladdin (2000)—turned the city into a 125,000-room paradise of enormous properties, a metropolitan area of a mere 1.4 million people with twice the number of hotel rooms of New York or Los Angeles. Wynn's Bellagio was the capstone, a $2.1 billion casino, easily the most well appointed casino anywhere and a candidate for the most gracious public-private space as well. Wynn envisioned the Bellagio as a casino-hotel in which women would be comfortable, a different framing in a town known for pandering to male pleasure. The Bellagio enjoyed the "best assortment of shopping on the planet," Wynn proclaimed, and with amenities like the $350 million art collection, remarkable restaurants, and superior drinks—women swear that the Bellagio makes the best Cosmopolitan anyone's ever tasted—the attraction was obvious. Wynn made his reputation on service, and there was simply no place anywhere like the Bellagio. The ante in the Las Vegas poker game had become astronomical. Only the boldest of the bold could afford a seat at the table. In the space of a decade, Las Vegas had gone from gambling to gaming to tourism to entertainment—the culture of the future.

At the same time, American society underwent a remarkable shift. The old rules and standards were tossed out, and new ones, defined through media, evolved in a world without clear cultural distinctions. In this new world, experience has become currency and entertainment has become culture. Experience is what Americans trade, how they define themselves. Entertainment is the storehouse of national values. Authentic and inauthentic have blurred. It's not that people can't tell the difference—they can. But in a culture without a dominant set of premises or common values, topped by a strange twist of relativism, it's hard to communicate why conventional authenticity is better. "Better" becomes preference, and people do as they please, encouraged by talk shows, self-help books, and twelve-step programs. When the value is on the self, when people rationalize their pleasure as socially useful, when it's all "me, me, me, now, now, now," what they seek is Las Vegas.

To generations of Americans, Las Vegas is a code for self-indulgence and sanctioned deviance. It is a town of fun, of excess, where anything and everything is possible and for sale. It is Bugsy Siegel and the Rat Pack, Shecky Greene and Wayne Newton, Tom Jones, the Lido de Paris, the Folies Bergere, and countless bump-and-grind joints. Las Vegas is the place that you promise your mother you'll never go, then break that promise with a wink and a leer. No place in the United States gives permission like the Las Vegas of myth.

But there is another Las Vegas, a real place found now on the business pages of the *Wall Street Journal* instead of the police blotters or the scandal sheets. To date, the money people best grasped the city's recent change. For almost fifteen years, this Las Vegas has been the fastest-growing place in the nation. In the process, Las Vegas's population doubled and then nearly doubled again as its physical expanse exploded all over the desert. Rapid growth obliterated the old company town and replaced it with the postmodern metropolis, the leading tourist destination in the world and the only city in the world devoted to the consumption of entertainment. In 1999, Las Vegas surpassed Mecca as the most visited place on earth. This Las Vegas is featured in *Worth* magazine and is considered by entrepreneurs the best city in America to start a business, where despite sexual exploitation in the core of the economy, a phenomenal number of women open their own businesses and succeed. People are born by the thousands in this Las Vegas, a lot more in the 1990s than in the 1950s, and they live, go to school, work, start businesses, marry and raise families, and attend church, synagogue, and mosque here.

The new Las Vegas is a fast-moving place, through which billions of dollars travel—for land acquisitions, for infrastructure development, be it roads, sewer pipes, water and waste water projects, airports, and a plethora of related structures and systems, for hotels, casinos, homes, and the like. New strip malls and doctors' offices spring up daily, serving the never-ending stream of newcomers. Orange cones dot the roads, always under construction, ever longer and wider. Growth came so quickly in southern Nevada that when Senator Harry Reid ran for reelection in 1998, incumbency was neither advantage nor disadvantage; it was meaningless, a cipher. His constituency had no history with the senator. More than half the state's registered voters—almost all of them in Clark County, home to greater Las Vegas—had not been Nevadans during his 1992 campaign.

Out of this outburst of people, ideas, and money came something remarkable: an index of the economy, social mores, and culture of a changing society. As *Time* magazine announced in 1994, the nation had become more like Las Vegas. At the same time, Las Vegas became a lot more like the rest of America—in where its financial capital came from and who lent it, in the distribution of its demography, in who lived there and what they did, in its residents' levels of education, in the businesses that catered to the community, and in countless other ways. The flimsy aberration became more than a reflection of the salacious desire of the underside of American life. It offered a primary outlet in a self-indulgent and fast-changing society, the ability to reinvent the self to the applause of a paid audience. When roller coasters were good clean fun, Las Vegas was risqué. Now that casinos are a legitimate recreation and entertainment choice, Sin City is mainstream, nowhere near as shocking as pierced privates, gangsta rap, or the admissions fourteen-year-olds routinely make on the *The Jerry Springer Show*. Las Vegas is still socially sanctioned deviance. Its brand is just more comfortable to more Americans than it used to be.

Las Vegas is different from much of the nation precisely because it is a part of the future that never shared in the prosperity of the past. It is a rare human who has eaten an apple grown in an orchard in the Las Vegas Valley or worn a sweater from the wool of sheep that grazed in the valley. Few machine tools have ever been ground to a fine edge in Las Vegas. Even fewer people have made their living in its automotive plants. Las Vegas's past is on the margins of American society, in the places now abandoned, forgotten, overlooked, or just hanging on. Its history shares more with Carlsbad, New Mexico, whose city officials were ecstatic to receive the nation's first low-level transuranic nuclear waste dump, than it does with New York or Los Angeles or even Omaha. Las Vegas doesn't have traditions unless they're staged for visitors. It recognizes the past for what it is, an ephemeral and malleable story line, and remakes it not for the present but for the future. Among the places that never found their way in the industrial world, Las Vegas is unique: it forged a divergent future at which the good people at the center of American culture turned up their noses, and made it into a remarkable success. While small towns around the nation withered after 1945, Las Vegas became a city—at odds with the rest of the nation to be sure, but a real city nonetheless—and then the rest of the nation caught up, tried it out, and found that it had a lot more in common with Las Vegas than most would care to admit.

Las Vegas has pieces of the puzzle of the future, ways to solve its problems, but not in a form that may translate to other places. The rhythms of Las Vegas are different from those of the rest of the country. They spring from different sources and lead to different results. Wearing lens of industrial America, the constellation of premises and expectations that shaped the first eighty years of the twentieth century, only fogs the Las Vegas landscape. The convergence so central to the future is obscured, cropped from the picture.

"This is America," the narrator in Neal Stephenson's 1992 futuristic classic *Snow Crash* asserts. "People do whatever the fuck they feel like doing . . . because they have a right to." In Stephenson's world, there are four things his "we"—the people who live in North America—do better than anyone else: they make music, movies, and microcode (software), and they deliver pizza. One of those, microcode, belongs to Silicone Valley and its offspring. The rest—service and entertainment—belong to the new Las Vegas.

From its twentieth-century inception, Las Vegas was ripe to become anything that paid. In the desert, away from the systems that sustained American cities, Las Vegas had to forge its own destiny. When middle-class America subscribed to a largely uniform set of values derived from the Victorian era, there were clear lines of conduct outside of which people strayed only at great risk. This created a culture of confinement, of proscribed values and behaviors, and a world in which a minor deviant turn at the wrong time or place could put someone entirely beyond respectable society. If you stepped over the line, you couldn't come back. "They hung a sign up in this town," Tom Waits writes of that world in "Hold On," "if you live it up you won't live it down." Everything went on your "permanent record," as the vision of venal authority, Dean Vernon Wermer, trumpeted in 1978's *Animal House*.

Such a controlled society desperately craved a release, a place to blow off its internalized steam, and to the post-1945 world, that outlet was Las Vegas. In the desert, you could indulge yourself, even sin for a fee without paying the social price. Slot machines and gaming tables were everywhere. Food and drink were abundant and free. Nevada even had legalized brothels and casinos engaged in a furtive sex trade. In Las Vegas, you could exercise your fantasies. Everything, it seemed, was for sale. In the 1930s Las Vegas offered an image of the mythology of the nineteenth-century West, where an individual could thrive and institutions could not impinge upon personal desire. This persisted beyond Bugsy Siegel's Flamingo in 1946 and continued for a generation. Las Vegas was first chic deviance, a place to sin with impunity, where actions that at home would certainly bring disgrace and might even land a person in jail were perfectly acceptable. This scapegoat of a town, a place to cast off sins in a morally and socially constricted society, was an absolute necessity for both its devotees and its detractors.

Its patrons needed its freedom, the glitz and glitter it promised, while its opponents needed its image to contrast good and evil. In this, Las Vegas served a clear, necessary, and widely accepted role. Occasionally there were scandals—the Kefauver hearings investigating organized crime in the early 1950s were a prominent example—but Las Vegas survived with a sense of humor and a bawdy irreverence. And why not? Its people had, to an individual, chosen a life at variance with the norms of their society.

Las Vegas changed before the rest of American society did. Its limitations forced Las Vegas to bend to the will of whatever would generate its revenues. This dependence gave Las Vegas a fluidity, a way around the rules of midcentury America, that locals learned to treasure. The city learned that its shape was always transitory, always flexible, not only because it responded to the emotions of a larger culture, but also because the forces that were behind the city were on the borders of legality. Even in moments of great success, Las Vegas had a powerful sense of impermanence, a strong intuition that whatever ruled today might well not tomorrow.

Malleability served Las Vegas well when both American society and the world economy were reinvented as American industrial preeminence came to an end. OPEC and the oil shortages it caused, inflation, and the end of postwar prosperity all hit at once, epitomized by the long lines to pay for even more expensive gasoline in 1974. In an instant, the pillars of postwar prosperity, cheap energy, the rising value of wages, and low inflation came crashing down. Gerald Ford, with his WIN–Whip Inflation Now–button, was the best response politics could muster. In 1974 the United States entered a twenty-three-year period that represented a regression to the American economic mean. The catalyst was the annual drop for each of those years in the real value of hourly wages. Simply put, people worked longer hours to stay where they were on the socioeconomic ladder. One-income families became more scarce. It took more hours to make the grade in each successive year, and middle-class women entered the workforce in greater numbers than ever before in American history. The reasons for this transformation of the so-called pink ghetto of teaching and nursing were as much social as economic, but the change in economic direction of the nation spoke of a harder, more competitive workplace with fewer opportunities to rise.

The global economic realignment that began with the OPEC oil embargo and the post-Vietnam War inflation masked larger considerations. The fundamental basis of the world economy shifted away from natural resources—of which Las Vegas had few—and toward a combination of information and entertainment that took advantage of an array of new technologies, from the VCR to the Internet. This transformation was as comprehensive as the industrial revolution. The global economy moved from its basis in industry to an information and service configuration. Knowledge and the ability to manipulate it became genuine power. When you could get anything you wanted in virtual time and space, a new premium was added to real experience. In an age when anyone with $399 a month to spend could lease a BMW, when you could ski the Alps virtually from your computer terminal, actual experience, the commodity that Las Vegas specialized in, gained rather than lost significance. The microchip spawned a new world with a new set of rules. Against all odds, Las Vegas became one of the winners.

At the same time, changes in the nature of American society made Las Vegas part of a broader American mainstream. The United States had been a place where Baptist preachers threw rock 'n' roll records onto Friday-night bonfires and Elvis Presley could be shown on television only from the waist up. The change to the individual-oriented culture of personal choice on the cusp of the new century created the context for the rise of leisure and the transformation of socially unacceptable "gambling" into the recreational "gaming." Las Vegas had perfected the service economy long before the rest of the nation encountered it. The rise of entertainment as a commodity increased the cachet of the city. With Frank Sinatra and Sammy Davis Jr. in the 1950s and 1960s and the Hard Rock Hotel thirty-five years later, Las Vegas captured high-status, commercial, cutting-edge culture. In the process, the town became more sophisticated at reflecting the desires of the public back onto it, at creating a script for visitors that placed them at the dead center of all that swirled around them.

Las Vegas's ability to change itself into the newest fashion is the root of its success as a purveyor of the low-skill, high-wage service economy. With more than a half-century's head start in offering people what they demand and in a culture that insists that the act of buying turns the purchaser into the focus of a story, Las Vegas has more to export than mere gaming. In the transformation to entertainment as the basis of culture, Las Vegas leads all others. Perfecting the art of putting a smile on every face, creating a city that implodes its past, pursuing theming that has replaced the desert of the Sands and the Dunes with the Italy of the Venetian and the Bellagio as well as the tinytowns of the Orleans, Paris, and New York, New York, Las Vegas has reached an astonishing maturity. At any time of the day or night, any day of the week, month, or year, the corners of Tropicana and the Strip and

Flamingo and the Strip are jammed. Hundreds of thousands walk the Strip to see the sights, from the Statue of Liberty at New York, New York, to the fountains at Bellagio, the Eiffel Tower, the volcano at the Mirage, and the pirate battle at Treasure Island. Locals muse that some-day a hotel on the Strip will surely accommodate those who stroll the Strip to marvel at its faux wonders; called "Las Vegas, Las Vegas," it will be a cutdown version of the Strip with all its hotels inside a Strip hotel. People will be able to see the Strip—at five-eighths scale—with-out ever going outside and they won't get sunburned in the process!

Las Vegas remains different, harder, tougher, and a little bit stranger than most places. It is a true desert city, built on a small oasis rather than a flowing source of water. *Las Vegas* means "the meadows," and underground artesian wells created the lush wide spot in the desert that became the genesis of the community. Now that ground is a wild patch in the city, a part of the Las Vegas Valley Water District's hold-ings. The underground water is diverted before it reaches the surface and the land is managed to be as natural as it can be in the middle of a metropolitan area. Las Vegas is the largest American city that truly began in the twentieth century. Its nineteenth-century incarnation as a Mormon outpost was an isolated moment rather than a piece of conti-nuity with the present one. It is the only city that can claim that its very survival hinged on Americans' willingness to transcend the norms of their society.

As the twentieth century ended, Las Vegas became the court of last resort for displaced humanity from around the globe. If you couldn't make it somewhere else, if your factory closed and you didn't want to wait around the union hall or go through retraining, if your logging job disappeared, if a friend lost a finger at the plant and the risk seemed too real for you to go on working there, if the crops finally gave out, Las Vegas offered the same promise it made to visitors. You could rein-vent yourself there. For a generation, most came expecting to beat the odds. These "something-for-nothing suckers" genuinely believed that they would defy probability and strike it rich in the biggest way. This wasn't just thug-turned-local-philanthropist Moe Dalitz's town or later, Steve Wynn's—it was everyone's fantasy town. At first these migrants were foolish, desperate people living on the very edge. Many wised up and realized that the real opportunity in Las Vegas was unskilled blue-collar work at union scale plus tips in a town with a low cost of living and no taxes to speak of.

The transformation created a town that was like everywhere else and simultaneously apart. Las Vegas seemed equal parts Washington,

D.C., a transient place where everyone was on the make; Los Angeles or Miami, as more and more conversations were in Spanish and signs restaurant and grocery store advertised *pollo* and *carne asada*; Phoenix, as almost 20 percent of the population was retired and medical care became a huge industry; Detroit of the old days, with its vocal and powerful semiskilled unionized workforce; and New Orleans, the city that, as Etta James still sings, "care forgot, where everybody parties a lot." At the same time, Las Vegas was different, newer, less structured, more vital, with fewer rules and wider degrees of what constituted normal. Its mythic status made it into its own place.

Las Vegas was and is a hard town that will make you pay for your inability to restrain your desires. "It turns women into men," comedian Alan King quipped, "and men into asses." "You have no idea how many families have lost daughters to the strip clubs," a well-dressed middle-aged African American woman told me with real pain in her voice. Atop Binion's Horseshoe, the casino that his legendary father, Benny Binion, built, Jack Binion stood next to mob lawyer Oscar Goodman, who was elected mayor of Las Vegas in 1999, and surveyed the city he knew so well. The lights twinkled, the city shimmered, and Binion observed, "Las Vegas is a wonderful place if you don't have a weakness." It was a remark only a survivor could make. If you have a weakness, Las Vegas will punish you.

People come, desperate for a last chance or a new beginning, fall flat on their face, and then find, in Jimi Hendrix's lyrical description, "tire tracks all across [their] backs," run into the ground by a place that is clear about what it values: winning and money. In this, the Desert City is only more frank than the rest of the nation. The thin veneer of civilization is rarely applied and when it is, it cracks in the baking sun. Class and wealth won't protect you. Doctors as well as bartenders succumb to their own excesses. As many as three thousand people a month move from Las Vegas, often leaving no forwarding address and a mailbox stuffed with creditors' notices. Those who think that they're the lucky one who will hit Megabucks, the progressive slot machine game that offers a multimillion-dollar payoff, find an enormous gap between their expectations and their abilities, and usually end up headed out of town, ground to a nub, happy to see the dust rise behind them.

Las Vegas is also a frontier town, maybe the last in the United States. The better part of the twentieth century passed before the American nation came to grips with its margins. New Mexico, with its long-standing Hispano dominance, has submitted to Anglo America only since 1945. Technological transformation and the pipeline turned Alaska from a frozen federal province into an oil fiefdom and now into a dependent of the Princess Line. The desert was equally harsh. Las Vegas's growth was possible only with air-conditioning and the other mechanisms of industrial society. Only then could Americans turn the desert into something tolerable, could build the endless suburbs with their miniscule but neatly cropped lawns, rolled out like a kid's play-mat and tended by armies of Spanish-speaking gardeners. Where the technologies of an industrial society are applied, communities like Las Vegas can flourish. Where they aren't, as around the Salton Sink in southern California or in nearby Pahrump, Nevada, Mad Max's world takes hold and anarchy is rampant. But in Las Vegas, the road from an older American society of industry is being paved to one version of a new, postindustrial world of service and information.

Almost by accident, Las Vegas has become the place where the twenty-first century begins, a center of the postindustrial world. It has become the first spectacle of the postmodern world. In this transformation, the old pariah has become a paradigm, the colony of everywhere, the colo-nizer of its former masters. Old Nevada allowed people to come there to cast off their sins; when prizefighting was illegal in every state in the union but one, Nevada filled the void with title bouts. This once dubious trait has become a virtue in the postindustrial world, where the people who once made things at respectable wages now stock bottles in conven-ience stores. Las Vegas has a peculiar cachet. It was the first city of the consumption of entertainment, and to be first at anything in a fluid cul-ture guarantees significance. Las Vegas offers an economic model to which cities, states, and regions look to create their own economic panacea—even as they hold their nose. Its consistent reinvention, once scorned as flimsy and fraudulent, shaped its transformation from peripheral to paradigmatic and has become a much-envied trait. Las Vegas has become normal; even more important, it points to the twenty-first century. What people see in Las Vegas today, as in Los Angeles, New York, and Miami, is what they can expect everywhere in the near future.

Las Vegas now symbolizes the new America, the latest in Ameri-can dream capitals. As New York once defined the commercial econo-my and Chicago, the city of big shoulders, epitomized the industrial city, Las Vegas illustrates one of the pillars of the postindustrial, post-modern future. Not only in its economy, but in every other aspect of its development, Las Vegas has become an icon. It is the place to be as the new century takes shape, for in its ability to simultaneously attract and repel, it characterizes American hopes and fears. Las Vegas tells us what has happened to American society and what we now aspire to:

simple possession of the ethos of status. It articulates what we value: our freedom and legal restraint of others. Las Vegas is rewriting the relationship between law and power as it privatizes public space and splits the definition of the First Amendment along public-private lines. In a world where entertainment is culture, Las Vegas's version is magical. As the bonds of cultural continuity and transmission fray in the proliferation of visual youth culture at the expense of text-bound literacy, Las Vegas's position improves. As travel becomes more important, Las Vegas's position as the mecca of postliterate faith will become even more secure.

Las Vegas leads in other ways. It offers the most fully developed version of a low-skilled, high-wage service economy in the nation and possibly the world. The power of unions in southern Nevada has made Las Vegas the "Last Detroit," the last place in the world after NAFTA where unskilled workers can make a middle-class wage and claw their way toward the American dream. With one-quarter of its population retired, Las Vegas already grapples with the future of the nation, and almost perfectly represents one of the socially complicated features of the coming decades: an older, mostly white, affluent population being served by a younger, increasingly non-white, far less affluent population with fewer options. This typicality is stunning. Only in a world that crossed a divide equal to the industrial revolution could such a rapid transformation of a city so large be possible.

Understanding Las Vegas requires that the observer discard the notions of space, order, economy, and standards derived from the industrial economy and replace them with a new kind of intellectual organization that is still being formed. In recent years, Las Vegas has been dubbed the "new all-American city" by *Time* magazine; Robert Brustein pilloried the town in *The New Republic*; Paul Goldberger chided its architecture in *The New Yorker*; and it even graced the cover of the *The Nation*, the famous "Degas in Vegas" quip. Why do Angelenos fear the rise of entertainment in Las Vegas? Because Las Vegas has more concert venues and more sources of revenue from acts and promoters than the City of Angels? How can Los Angeles be the leading city of the future if so many of its residents move to Las Vegas each year? How did Nevada become the state that gave more to both political parties than any other during the 1996 elections?

Clearly, a significant transformation has occurred. A city without any claim to a past, one that purposefully markets the destruction of its history, has taken its place among powerful American metropolises. In the twenty-first century, Las Vegas will lead. Its models, already exported, will be more widely copied as the shifting of the global economy away from traditional economics makes the anomaly of Las Vegas more tempting. Other places already copy casinos. Soon they will mimic the structures of companies such as Mandalay Resort Group and Steve Wynn's Mirage Corporation, the second most widely admired American corporation in *Fortune*'s annual ranking in 1997, and the capital formation strategies of Las Vegas. They already covet the entertainment options and the malleability of identity that defines the town. With 20 percent of the population retired and 20 percent Latino in 2001, Las Vegas foreshadows the coming retirement of the baby boomers and the native non-whites and the immigrants who will likely provide the bulk of their care. In all of these ways and so many more, the future, for better and for worse, has already arrived in Las Vegas.

"Will History Repeat Itself? Nevada's Economy After the Crash"
(2012)

Elliott Parker

Throughout its history, Nevada has endured wide swings of the economic pendulum because its economy has never been widely diversified. For the first eighty years of statehood, its economic fortunes were tied directly to the mining industry and limited ranching outposts. A strong philosophy of limited government pervaded state and local politics, which resulted in low taxes and minimal state budgets. Without natural resources other than precious minerals and arid land ranching to provide an economic base, the state grew very slowly. In 1930, Nevada's population was just 91,000.

Legalizing of full-scale casino gambling in 1931 changed the face of Nevada, producing a dominant tourist industry. Although it had modest impact during the 1930s, gaming began a spectacular ascent after the Second World War. In 1940, Reno was the largest city in the state with a population of 21,000, followed by Las Vegas with 8,000. With the rapid development of large hotel-casinos in the two decades after the war, the population of Las Vegas and Clark County easily surpassed Reno and Washoe County by 1950 and continued to expand its margin over the next six decades. The Census of 2010 reported that 2.1 million persons lived in Clark County as opposed to 420,000 in Washoe County.

During the first decade of the twenty-first century, growth in casino revenues slowed. The opening of many casinos by Native American tribes in California had a major impact, as did establishment of gaming enterprises in other states. Statewide, the flattening out of gaming revenues was not offset by increased economic diversification efforts. The boom in construction, especially housing and commercial developments in Clark County, for a time offset the slowdown in casino revenues. The construction boom, however, became an enormous bubble that burst spectacularly in 2008, as the national economy collapsed in a near perfect financial storm.

No wise man, it seemed, had considered the possibility that housing prices, which had risen steadily since 1940, might actually fall . . . and fall a great deal. Within a year, housing prices across the state had dropped 50 percent, and Nevada soared to the top of the list of states with mortgage defaults and mortgages held by individuals that were "underwater": that is the amount of the mortgage exceeded the value of the underlying property. Tourism is driven by the willingness of individuals to spend discretionary money on travel and entertainment; thus Nevada's primary industry was among the most vulnerable. Many businesses were forced into bankruptcy. In Las Vegas large skeletons of structure steel stood abandoned years after construction was halted on planned upscale hotel-casinos. State budgets were slashed, and many city and county government employees joined the growing army of unemployed from the private sector. The dilemmas produced by this economic debacle are discussed by economist Elliott Parker. His argument—that the major resource available to rekindle a new economic revival lies in an educated population—did not seem to resonate with either taxpayers or their elected officials, who supported massive cuts in budgets decimated by plummeting tax revenues.

Introduction

Nevada is in the midst of what is, essentially, an existential crisis. Creating a viable economy in a state with few resources has always been a challenge, and the crash of the gaming/construction model will be difficult to recover from. A key issue for Nevada's decision makers to grapple with is the role of the State's government itself, for many Nevadans misunderstand the role government has played, and must play, in the State's economic development.

But this is not the first time the State is being forced to recreate itself. A brief review of the State's economic history shows that more than a century ago Nevada saw the effects of its major industry on the wane, in a state with few other productive resources. Nevada struggled for decades until it found a viable model in gaming. Now that gaming is in decline, only time will tell whether Nevada is able to create a new productive resource, or if it will once again enter a time of decline.

The Rise and Fall, and Rise and Fall, of Nevada's Economy

Nevada was created, both politically and economically, in the backflow from the rush to California. With the discovery of the Comstock silver lode in the late 1850s, its bank-financed expansion in the 1860s, and its connection to the rest of the country with the Central Pacific, Nevada entered its first big boom, and Virginia City came to think of itself one of the richest cities in the world, at least in per capita terms.

The boom was relatively short lived. By the late 1870s, silver had been effectively demonetized by the Fourth Coinage Act of 1873, though Nevada's legislators were able to delay the impact on Nevada mining through the demands of the Carson City mint for producing less-than-popular silver dollars. Soon after the completion of the Sutro tunnel, the silver mines were exhausted. Though the search for minerals continued elsewhere in the State, Nevada entered a period of long-term decline. By the turn of the century, the State would lose half of its population, as miners left for Bodie, Tombstone, and elsewhere. Thereafter, population in Nevada fluctuated for a couple decades, with only a few new mineral finds in Goldfield, Tonopah, and elsewhere.[1]

The effort to create a viable economy in the high and dry desert of Nevada did not end with mining.[2] The railroad town of Reno became the center of a divorce-driven tourist industry, as Nevada tried to take advantage of the fact that until 1969, other states required lengthy residency periods and were stringent about the grounds for divorce. Ranching and farming provided some economic stability, as a few small communities became dependent on the federally funded diversion of water once flowing to Pyramid and Walker lakes. Federal construction of the Hawthorne Naval Ammunition Depot in the 1920s helped the state economy, and the small town of Las Vegas became host to the depression-era federal workforce constructing Hoover Dam.

But the legalization of gambling in 1931 provided a means to help fend off the worst effects of the Great Depression,[3] and Nevada also promoted its lack of taxes to encourage millionaires to relocate. Nevada's effective monopoly over gaming was the primary cause of its post-war growth, though it attracted more than its fair share of unsavory characters. The proximity of Las Vegas to southern California, which grew rapidly in part due to the effects of a great influx of federal defense spending, started the economic shift from north to south. Federally funded interstate highways brought trucking, warehousing, and tourists to both northern and southern Nevada. After the mid-1980s, once the reputation of Nevada's gambling industry was cleaned up, Nevada became the fastest-growing economy in the country, with the fastest-growing population and a mean per capita income significantly above the national average.

But Nevada's success created the seeds of its own downfall. Other states and countries learned from it, legislating their own casinos as new sources of tax revenue. In California, new casinos on small Indian reservations intercepted the flow of gaming tourists headed over the mountains, eventually cutting gaming revenues in Reno and Tahoe by two-thirds. Las Vegas was able to keep the tourists coming, at least for a while, by continuously upping the ante, creating new and bigger properties as they destroyed the old ones. Even so, gaming declined from 17% of Gross State Product in the 1980s to 10% in 2007, and then 8% by 2009 during the Great Recession. This created serious revenue problems in a state that depended significantly on gaming and tourism to finance its government.

As gaming slowed, construction took up much of the slack instead of a more general economic diversification. Once again the backflow from California brought a boom to Nevada. The construction of new casinos was augmented by the construction of new homes for the casino and construction workers moving here, and when another housing bubble began in California, Nevada's construction sector became the largest in the nation, as a share of the economy, at twice the national average.

As Figure 1 shows, housing prices in Nevada roughly kept pace with inflation until 2000, several years after prices in California started rising rapidly. Many in California were able to sell their homes and relocate to Nevada, especially once they retired and lower taxes and home prices mattered more than their jobs.

When the bubble finally burst, Nevada went from the fastest-growing state in the nation to the fastest declining. As Figure 2 shows, real per capita personal income declined by 11.9% in Nevada, compared to a 4.2% average decline for the nation as a whole. Homeowners lost half the market value of their homes, and inflation-adjusted housing prices fell to their lowest levels in several decades. Two-thirds of mortgages in

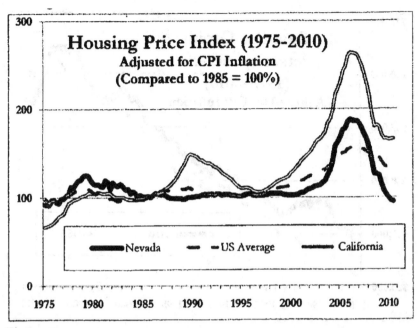

Figure 1
Housing Price Indices for Nevada, California, and the United States

Nevada exceeded the home's value, and Nevada had five times the national foreclosure rate. As Figure 3 shows, the loss of casino and construction jobs increased Nevada's unemployment rate to the highest in the country. By 2010, the rate held steady only because Nevada was losing population as fast as it lost jobs.[4]

The Pros and Cons of Government

In an interdependent and technologically driven economy, with external economies of scale, the unassisted free market offers little hope for Nevada's return to the good old days before the crash. While Nevada in 2008 was very different from Nevada in 1878, nonetheless the State remains relatively short of productive resources once the particular advantages of its geographic proximity and its gaming monopoly have ended.

Private investment, like water, tends to flow downhill. Firms tend to put their money where other firms are already investing, productive people prefer to live with other productive people, and firms follow suit to have access to the labor pool, the ready availability of suppliers, and the infrastructure that helps them all become more productive.[5] This is, essentially, why many firms in the computer industry are willing to pay higher rents and wages to locate in California's Silicon Valley.

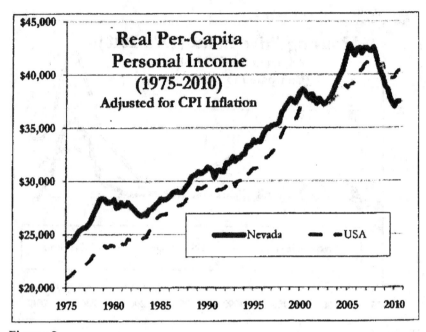

Figure 2
Real Per Capita Personal Income

Nevadans, however, have long had a mixed relationship with taxes and government. The first push for statehood in 1863 failed largely due to fears over taxes, but within a year a depression hit Nevada and voters changed their minds.[6] Once mining collapsed, Nevada's efforts to create a viable economy in the high and dry desert depended largely on federal spending projects and the excessive regulation of the other states.

During the Depression, Nevada's "one sound state" campaign tried to take advantage of the fiscal crisis other states were experiencing. Other states were implementing sales taxes and income taxes to replace their severely declining property taxes, but Nevada tried to rely primarily on the gaming tax, though after the war Nevada found this to be insufficient and implemented a sales tax anyway.[7] Nonetheless, Nevada continued to rely on its reputation as a no tax state as a good home for the wealthy, and Nevada attracted many people who preferred it that way.

In theory, the relationship between the size of government and economic growth is a complicated one. Free and private markets are efficient under certain conditions, but those conditions—perfect information, perfect competition, and complete markets in which sellers pay all the pro-

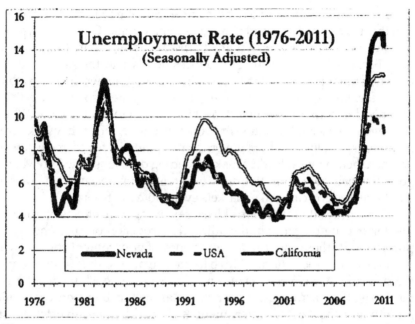

Figure 3
Unemployment in Nevada and in the United States

duction costs and buyers receive all the benefits—are often not met. When they aren't, governments may be able to address some of these market failures. In particular, government can provide or subsidize public goods, which are called that because they are things that benefit society but that can't or won't be adequately provided by the private sector. Police and fire protection, a justice system, national defense, financial regulation, highways, pollution control, sanitation, public health, and education are all good examples of public goods.

The taxes that pay for these public goods can distort incentives, however, because if we raise the cost of doing something, people will do less of it. Of course, there are times we want people to do less of something, which is why so-called "sin taxes" are popular, but in most cases economists think higher tax rates are inefficient. Taxes are less likely to distort incentives when rates are relatively low and collected from a wide range of activities, so that the relative prices of different goods are unaffected. And when taxes cannot be applied equally, taxes will have a higher ratio of revenue to inefficiency when we tax goods where buyers are not very price sensitive.

There are also other potential inefficiencies in government intervention that may sometimes lead to making things worse. Governments, like
private firms, are made up of human beings, and they share the same pit-
falls. Because the state usually produces goods that the private sector
does not, monopolies tend to become inefficient whether they are public
or private. All organizations require good management so that the actions
of individuals are made consistent with the interests of society. When
state agencies lack information or proper incentive, when they lack competition, especially in light of government's potential for coercive power,
or when their political leaders make spending decisions based on what is
good for their own reelection and fund-raising prospects, then government intervention can make markets even more inefficient.

Poot argues that there are at least seven separate effects of government spending on growth, including the provision of pure and quasi
public goods, the comparative inefficiency of government control over
resources and production, relative to the private sector it replaces, and
the distortionary effect of taxes on resource allocation.[8] In considering
the tradeoffs, Barro argues that the relationship between economic
growth and the size of government is shaped like an inverted-U, so
that there is potentially an optimal size.[9] Too little government, like too
much, leads to slower growth.

There are also short-term effects that have little to do with the
incentive problems of taxes or the relative value of public goods for the
economy. These effects have to do with the aggregate level of spending
in the economy. When the economy is near full employment, the public sector competes with the private sector for resources, and increases
in public spending are likely to crowd out the private sector by increasing prices, wages, interest rates, or—for the federal government at
least—an increase in the value of the dollar. In a recession, however,
high unemployment of labor combined with little investment demand
leads to a potential stabilizing role for the state.

In a severe downturn, states would be better off if their governments could cut taxes and increase spending, rather than the opposite.
Even the Hoover administration presided over a net increase in government expenditures and a reduction in tax revenues during the Great
Depression, but most of this was a natural outcome and not the result
of intentional policy. As Gross Domestic Product fell by 43% from 1929
to 1932, government expenditures rose a little overall due to an
increase in social benefits to the unemployed, while tax revenues
declined as the economy collapsed. As a share of GDP, however, total
tax revenues actually rose by a third. The Revenue Act of 1932 reflected President Hoover's primary concern with returning to a bal-

anced budget, and it raised tax rates significantly even as the economy continued to slide.

While the federal government has apparently learned its lesson too well, and often runs deficits even during good times, state governments are usually bound by balanced-budget rules that lead them to become "fifty Herbert Hoovers," in the phrase of Krugman.[10] They are prohibited from saving adequately, and find it difficult to borrow. Following booms they have an incentive to spend too much, while in recessions they are forced to cut spending or raise taxes, albeit with a lag. Since state and local governments together purchase more goods than the federal government, and employ far more people, cutbacks by states during a recession can overwhelm the efforts of the federal government to stave off a deeper recession. . . .

State and Local Government in Nevada

In deciding what should be done to recover from the crash, Nevadans will debate both the size and growth of their government. By most measures, Nevada has one of the smallest governments in the country. Whether measured by the average tax burden, or the size of the general fund relative to the overall state economy, Nevada's state government is the smallest in the nation even though the general fund includes spending on items that other states assign to local governments.

How does Nevada compare? First, while this measure of government size has not shown much directional trend on average, Nevada has trended downwards, relative to other states. Nevada's ratio ranked 31st out of 50 states for the first decade of the sample, but 46th out of 50 over the last ten years in spite of its smaller population and larger geographic size. In spite of concerns from some corners about unsustainable government spending, Nevada had a lower average share from 2003–2008 than it did from 1963–1972, even though there was a significant devolution of responsibility from the federal government to the states in the 1970s and 1980s.

An even better measure, however, is to consider the total number of government workers. According to the Census Bureau,[11] Nevada has the lowest number of state and local employees in the nation, as a share of population. Yet in per capita terms, state and local expenditures were only average, not the lowest in the nation. The only way to explain this inconsistency is that Nevada spent more on its average worker.

The *Statistical Abstract* reports that the average wage for Nevada's state employees was about 7% higher than the national average in 2008, while city and county employees earned 20% more. However,

Nevada's cost of living was about 10% higher than the national average, at least before the crash. These figures are further muddled by the fact that private sector workers have seen their benefits decline over time, by the fact that public employees tend to be much better educated than the workforce as a whole, and by what appears to be a much narrower wage gap between blue-collar and white-collar workers in the public sector, in that lower-paid workers earn more in the public sector while higher-paid workers earn less.

Averages disguise significant variation. State corrections officers made about 30% more in Nevada than they would have elsewhere, while local firefighters, especially in Las Vegas, made pretty high incomes compared to firefighters elsewhere. Salaries for K-12 teachers, however, were close to the national average. And before the crash, college professors were paid about the same average salary they would have earned at other similar universities in other states.

Similarly, aggregates also disguise variation. While the overall state budget may have grown faster than the economy in the decade before the crash, some parts grew faster than others. In the General Fund, the largest two components were K-12, which grew from 35% of 2000-01 budget to 40% of the 2010-11 budget, and human services, which grew from 25% to 31%. The remainder of the budget, including public safety, higher education, and everything else, fell from 40% of the budget to 29%. . . .

Higher Education in Nevada

With two public universities and no comparable private ones, Nevada still has the smallest higher educational system in the nation. Nevada ranked 49th in the country in the number of public higher education employees per person in 1999, with four employees per thousand people, ahead of only Massachusetts, which has a substantial number of large private universities. This was a third fewer employees per capita than the national average, and the gap between Nevada and the rest of the country has only widened over the last two decades.

For most of its first century, in fact, Nevada's system of higher education consisted of only one institution, which was originally located in Elko as the State University of Nevada before relocating to Reno. After the Second World War, as the State's population grew rapidly, new institutions were created. The University of Nevada, Las Vegas, began as an extension effort of the Reno campus in the 1950s. It became independent as Nevada Southern University in 1965, and in 1968 the Board of Regents granted it equal status with the University of Nevada, Reno.

The Desert Research Institute was created in 1959 to focus on specific areas of grant-funded research, becoming independent from the University of Nevada in 1969. Community colleges were created around this same time, beginning in 1967 with Nevada Community College in Elko, later Great Basin College. The Nevada System of Higher Education (NSHE) now consists of eight different institutions of higher education.

Under this system, Nevada has the lowest proportion of college students in the nation, and with an open admissions policy and a significant number of part-time working students, graduation rates were relatively low. While this proportion is affected by the small size of the higher education system in Nevada, it is also affected by the numbers of high school graduates ready for college. Graduation rates in public K-12 were among the lowest in the nation, and K-12 had 25% fewer employees than the national average, relative to population. But there was also a demand side to the problem, since before the crash many young people without a degree could earn above-average wages working in casinos or construction, at least for a while. Many of those who did choose to get a college degree went out of state. . . .

Conclusion

Now that the State has lost its gambling monopoly and the California-driven housing bubble has burst, Nevada must find a way to begin the accumulation of productive resources if it is to return to growth. Free markets can do many things, but relying on the magic of the free market alone will not bring Nevada back to a path of economic growth. Low taxes notwithstanding, in a state with few resources, in the high and dry desert of the Great Basin, productive investments and productive people are likely to flow out of the state, not in.

But the budget crisis that the crash created is leading Nevada to do the wrong thing. In an economy in which productive people are the primary resource, Nevada is on the verge of significant cuts to education that could lead to a brain drain and an economic downward spiral. The proposed cuts to higher education are only likely to worsen the crisis, leading to a decline in the attractiveness of an in-state college education for Nevadans, and pushing firms out instead of pulling them in. If we don't rethink our approach, Nevada's economic path of the future may be uncomfortably similar to the last time its main industry withered, with a decade or more of depopulation ahead.

Excerpts from the Nevada Constitution

The Nevada Constitution runs some 18,000 words in length, fully three times as long as the United States Constitution. On March 21, 1864, Congress approved a bill enabling Nevada to become the 36th state to join the Union. Delegates at a state convention in Carson City ratified the new Constitution on July 28 of the same year, and early in September voters approved it overwhelmingly. That was surprising, because, just nine months earlier, the same voters had soundly rejected an earlier draft by a 4–1 majority. The approved Constitution differed only in a few places from the original version, but the changes were significant. Much of the original opposition to statehood had grown out of opposition by small mine operators fearful of potential taxes, and widespread perceptions that powerful owners of the large mining operations were wielding too much influence upon the constitution-writing process. The reversal in sentiment by voters apparently stemmed from several factors, including new wording that greatly pleased the small mine owners; the new Constitution explicitly exempted mines from property taxes, taxing only their proceeds. Most likely, reports from the war that indicated Union forces were on the cusp of final victory had a significant impact on voters. The substantial majority of pro-Unionists wanted an opportunity to help assure Lincoln's reelection, and some perceived that unless they accepted statehood at this propitious time, it might be difficult to achieve for decades to come. With the referendum tally in hand, President Abraham Lincoln officially proclaimed Nevada a state with full legal standing on October 31, 1864. The fact that the Silver State was accepted into the Union during the Civil War explains the constitutional provisions prohibiting slavery and asserting "paramount allegiance" to the Federal Government. The timing of statehood also explains the state motto: "Battle Born."

Preliminary Action

Whereas, The Act of Congress Approved March Twenty First A.D. Eighteen Hundred and Sixty Four "To enable the People of the Territory of Nevada to form a Constitution and State Government and for the admission of such State into the Union on an equal footing with the Original States," requires that the Members of the Convention for framing said Constitution shall, after Organization, on behalf of the people of said Territory, adopt the Constitution of the United States.— Therefore, Be it Resolved, That the Members of this Convention, elected by the Authority of the aforesaid enabling Act of Congress, Assembled in Carson City the Capital of said Territory of Nevada, and immediately subsequent to its Organization, do adopt, on behalf of the people of said territory the Constitution of the United States[.]

Ordinance

Slavery prohibited; freedom of religious worship; disclaimer of public lands. In obedience to the requirements of an act of the Congress of the United States, approved March twenty-first, A.D. eighteen hundred and sixty-four, to enable the people of Nevada to form a constitution and state government, this convention, elected and convened in obedience to said enabling act, do ordain as follows, and this ordinance shall be irrevocable, without the consent of the United States and the people of the State of Nevada:

First. That there shall be in this state neither slavery nor involuntary servitude, otherwise than in the punishment for crimes, whereof the party shall have been duly convicted.

Second. That perfect toleration of religious sentiment shall be secured, and no inhabitant of said state shall ever be molested, in person or property, on account of his or her mode of religious worship.

Third. That the people inhabiting said territory do agree and declare, that they forever disclaim all right and title to the unappropriated public lands lying within said territory, and that the same shall be and remain at the sole and entire disposition of the United States; and that lands belonging to citizens of the United States, residing without the said state, shall never be taxed higher than the Land belonging to the residents thereof; and that no taxes shall be imposed by said state on lands or property therein belonging to, or which may hereafter be purchased by, the United States, unless otherwise provided by the congress of the United States. . . .

Preamble

We the people of the State of Nevada, Grateful to Almighty God for our freedom in order to secure its blessings, insure domestic tranquillity, and form a more perfect Government, do establish this Constitution.

Article 1, Sec. 1. Inalienable rights. All men are by Nature free and equal and have certain inalienable rights among which are those of enjoying and defending life and liberty; Acquiring, Possessing and Protecting property and pursuing and obtaining safety and happiness[.]

Article 1, Sec. 2. Purpose of government; paramount allegiance to United States. All political power is inherent in the people[.] Government is instituted for the protection, security and benefit of the people; and they have the right to alter or reform the same whenever the public good may require it. But the Paramount Allegiance of every citizen is due to the Federal Government in the exercise of all its Constitutional powers as the same have been or may be defined by the Supreme Court of the United States; and no power exists in the people of this or any other State of the Federal Union to dissolve their connection therewith or perform any act tending to impair[,] subvert, or resist the Supreme Authority of the government of the United States. The Constitution of the United States confers full power on the Federal Government to maintain and Perpetuate its existance [existence], and whensoever any portion of the States, or people thereof attempt to secede from the Federal Union, or forcibly resist the Execution of its laws, the Federal Government may, by warrant of the Constitution, employ armed force in compelling obedience to its Authority. . . .

Article 10, Sec. 5. Tax on proceeds of minerals; appropriation to counties; apportionment; assessment and taxation of mines. (Added in 1989.)

1. The legislature shall provide by law for a tax upon the net proceeds of all minerals, including oil, gas and other hydrocarbons, extracted in this state, at a rate not to exceed 5 percent of the net proceeds. No other tax may be imposed upon a mineral or its proceeds until the identity of the proceeds as such is lost. . . .

3. Each patented mine or mining claim must be assessed and taxed as other real property is assessed and taxed, except that no value may be attributed to any mineral known or believed to underlie it, and no value may be attributed to the surface of a mine or claim if one hundred dollars' worth of labor has been actually performed on the mine or claim during the year preceding the assessment. . . .

Article 11, Sec. 4. Establishment of state university; control by board of regents. The Legislature shall provide for the establishment of a State University which shall embrace departments for Agriculture, Mechanic Arts, and Mining to be controlled by a Board of Regents whose duties shall be prescribed by Law.

Article 11, Sec. 5. Establishment of normal schools and grades of schools; oath of teachers and professors. The Legislature shall have power to establish Normal schools, and such different grades of schools, from the primary department to the University, as in their discretion they may deem necessary, and all Professors in said University, or Teachers in said Schools of whatever grade, shall be required to take and subscribe to the oath as prescribed in Article Fifteenth of this Constitution. No Professor or Teacher who fails to comply with the provisions of any law framed in accordance with the provisions of this Section, shall be entitled to receive any portion of the public monies set apart for school purposes. . . .

Article 11, Sec. 8. Immediate organization and maintenance of state university. The Board of Regents shall, from the interest accruing from the first funds which come under their control, immediately organize and maintain the said Mining department in such manner as to make it most effective and useful, Provided, that all the proceeds of the public lands donated by Act of Congress approved July second A.D. eighteen hundred and sixty two, for a college for the benefit of Agriculture[,] the Mechanics Arts, and including Military tactics shall be invested by the said Board of Regents in a separate fund to be appropriated exclusively for the benefit of the first named departments to the University as set forth in Section Four above; And the Legislature shall provide that if through neglect or any other contingency, any portion of the fund so set apart, shall be lost or misappropriated, the State of Nevada shall replace said amount so lost or misappropriated in said fund so that the principal of said fund shall remain forever undiminished[.] . . .

Notes

Nevada: Beautiful Desert of Buried Hopes

1. Reproduction forbidden. Quotation limited to 800 words. Copyright, 1922. The Nation, Inc.

   This is the eighth article in the series entitled These United States. The first was on the State of Kansas by William Allen White (April 19), the second on Maryland by H. L. Mencken (May 8), the third on Mississippi by Beula Amidon Ratliff (May 17), the fourth on Vermont by Dorothy Canfield Fisher (May 31), the fifth on New Jersey by Edmund Wilson, Jr. (June 14), the sixth on Utah by Murray E. King (June 28), and the seventh on South Carolina by Ludwig Lewisohn (July 12).

2. Public Range Lands—A New Policy Needed; by Romanzo Adams. *American Journal of Sociology*, November, 1915.

3. *Ibid.*

Mining Illusions: The Case of Rawhide, Nevada

1. The headline is from the *Rawhide Press-Times,* March 12, 1908. For an insightful discussion of the promoter's role in creating mines, see Lewis Atherton, "Structure and Balance in Western Mining History," *Huntington Library Quarterly* 30 (November 1966): 55–85. News of the company's plans to begin shutting down its operation at Rawhide in August of 2002 was announced in the *Reno Gazette Journal*, January 22, 2002 ("Kennecott Rawhide Mine Set to Downsize in August").

2. For figures on mining's economic impact, including Nevada, see Thomas Michael Power, *Lost Landscapes and Failed Economies: The Search for a Value of Place* (Washington, DC: Island Press, 1996), 98–99.

3. See Jon Christensen, "After the Gold Rush," *High Country News*, April 13, 1995, 19–20; Bill Epler, "Joint Venture Led by Kennecott Nearing Capacity." *Rocky Mountain Pay Dirt*, January 1991, 4A–7A. Figures on rock processing are from Kennecott Rawhide Mining Company.

4. Richard Francaviglia, *Hard Places: Reading the Landscape of America's Historic Mining Districts*, (Iowa City: University of Iowa Press, 1991), 173.

5. P.R. Whytock, "The Rawhide District, Nevada," *The Mining World* 31 (July 31, 1909): 12.

6. Duane Smith, *Mining America: The Industry and the Environment, 1899–1980* (Lawrence: University Press of Kansas, 1987): 31–32. Smith observes that nonminers molded the industry's perception of itself as they toured, watched, and "created the glamorous image of mining." Peter Bacon Hales explores the history of American photographic booster books in "American Views and the Romance of Modernization," in Martha Sandweiss, ed., *Photography in Nineteenth-Century America* (Fort Worth: Amon Carter Museum; New York: Harry N. Abrams, 1991), 205–57.

7. George Graham Rice, *My Adventures With Your Money* (New York, 1913; reprint Las Vegas: Nevada Publications, 1986). Tantalizingly little is known of Rice's career. According to Russell R. Elliott, Rice was born as Jacob S. Herzig in 1870 and had been imprisoned before he arrived in Goldfield. The failure of his L.M. Sullivan Trust Company in Goldfield in 1906 was in large part responsible for the bank closures associated with the Panic of 1907 there. In Rawhide he teamed with popular New York comic actor Nat C. Goodwin to form a stock brokerage in the latter's name. Goodwin apparently financed Rice's main publicity vehicle, the *Nevada Mining News*. After exposure as a swindler in Rawhide, Rice left the state for New York City where he founded another brokerage house that promoted Nevada stocks. He was convicted in 1910 of using the mails to defraud and was sentenced to federal prison. It was there that he wrote *My Adventures With Your Money*. See Elliott, *History of Nevada* (Reno: University of Nevada Press, 1973), 220–221; Hugh A. Shamberger, *Historic Mining Camps of Nevada: Rawhide* (Carson City: Nevada Historic Press, 1970), 38.

8. The story of the boulder was repeated endlessly in accounts of Rawhide, always as a story overheard or reported by others. See *1908–1909 Rawhide Fallon and Vicinity City Business Mining Directory* (Reno: P&C Nevada Directory Co.), at the Nevada Historical Society; Emmett L. Arnold, *Gold Camp Drifter 1906–1910* (Reno: University of Nevada Press, 1973), 97–99; Nanelia S. Doughty, "Jim Moffatt's Recollections of Rawhide," *Nevadan*, March 19, 1972, 28–29; C. B. Glasscock, *Gold in Them Hills: The Story of the West's Last Wild Mining Days* (Indianapolis: Bobbs-Merrill Co., 1932), 287–89. Rice, *My Adventures*, 230.

9. Reginald Meaker, *Nevada Desert Sheepman* (Western Printing & Publishing, 1981), 70–71. For Rickard, see also Glasscock, *op. cit.*; Shamberger, *Rawhide*, 31–34.

10. Glyn's visit is described at length in Shamberger, *Rawhide*, 33–35. The contemporary witness was Jim Moffatt, as quoted by Doughty, *op. cit.*

11. Elinor Glyn, *Elizabeth Visits America* (London: Duckworth & Co., 1909), 213; Rice, *My Adventures*, 235. Rice's comment was reported in a 1920s reminiscence by Rawhide resident Joe McDonald, printed in Shamberger, *Rawhide* 34.

12. *My Adventures*, 260.

13. The song can be located in the Special Collections Department of the Getchell Library, University of Nevada, Reno. The poem is in the collections of the Nevada Historical Society, Reno. According to Shamberger, Knickerbocker's oration was the reason that Rawhide "has never been forgotten," (*Rawhide*, 2). The funeral, and the absence of notetakers, is reported on p. 27. Emmett Arnold reports the Rickard connection in *Gold Camp Driver*, 121, along with the fact that Knickerbocker was imported from Los Angeles for the occasion.

14. The use of photography as a promotional tool for non-mining western landscape is discussed by Peter B. Hales in *William Henry Jackson and the Transformation of American Landscape* (Philadelphia: Temple University Press, 1988) and Anne Farrar Hyde, *An American Vision: Far Western Landscape and National Culture, 1820–1920* (New York: New York University Press, 1990). For mining photography see Joel Snyder, "Territorial Photography," in W.J.T. Mitchell, ed., *Landscape and Power* (Chicago: University of Chicago Press, 1994), 175–201. See Francaviglia, "Victorian Bonanzas: Lessons from the Cultural Landscape of Western Hard Rock Mining Towns," *Journal of the West* 35 (January 1994): 53–63, for the importance of the built environment in advertising a mining town's prosperity and stability.

15. F.W. Clark, introduction, N.E. Johnson, *Souvenir Views of Rawhide* (Los Angeles: F.W. Clark, 1908); Arley Barthlow Show, "The Truth About Rawhide," *Death Valley Magazine* (May 1908), 88; *1908–1909 Rawhide Fallon Directory, op. cit.*, 5.

16. The technological sublime is discussed in chapter 5. See David Nye, *American Technological Sublime* (Cambridge: MIT Press, 1994), 37. He describes it as "a peculiar double action of the imagination by which the land was appropriated as a natural symbol of the nation while, at the same time, it was being transformed into a man-made landscape."

17. *Mining and Scientific Press*, March 28, 1908, 424.

18. *Rawhide Rustler*, February 29, 1908.

19. "Notes on Rawhide Nevada," *Mining and Scientific Press*, March 18, 1908, 424.

20. Ibid.; *Goldfield Review*, February 8, 1908; Fred S. Cook, *Historic Legends of Mineral County* (Pahrump, NV: The Printery, n.d.), 21.

21. For the later years of Rawhide, see Shamberger, *Rawhide* and Sally Zanjani, *A Mine of Her Own* (Lincoln: University of Nebraska Press, 1997), 284–300. According to resident Russ Tyler, in Charles O. Ryan, *Nine Miles from Dead Horse Wells* (New York: Exposition Press, 1959), many of the buildings in Rawhide were moved to Yerington. Both Ryan and Shamberger have the story of the beer being used in the fire.

22. *Nevada State Journal*, June 4, 1950.

23. Francaviglia, *Hard Places*, 167.

24. *Reno Evening Gazette* September 4, 1941.

25. In this regard the carefully cultivated and mysteriously enduring public image of Rawhide defies the melancholy effects that Patricia Nelson Limerick finds in another failed Nevada mining town of roughly the same vintage. See "Haunted by Rhyolite: Learning from the Landscape of Failure," with photographs by Mark Klett, in Leonard Engel, ed., *The Big Empty: Essays on the Land as Narrative* (Albuquerque: University of New Mexico Press, 1994), 27–47.

26. Quoted in Epler, "Joint Venture," 7A.

27. Archeological Research Services, Inc., "Historic Context for the Mining District of Rawhide, Mineral County, Nevada," prepared for Kennecott Rawhide Mining Company, February 26, 1993, 34.

Twentieth-Century Marvel

1. *Las Vegas Evening Review-Journal*, September 30, 1935; *New York Times*, October 1, October 6, 1935.

2. David McCullough, *The Great Bridge*, pp. 533–536; Waters, *The Colorado*, p. 337.

3. *Las Vegas Evening Review-Journal*, September 30, 1935.

4. "Honorable Harold L. Ickes, Secretary of the Interior, Delivers Address at Dedication of Boulder Dam," *RE* 25 (November, 1935): 209–210.

5. *Las Vegas Evening Review-Journal*, September 20, 1935.

6. "President Roosevelt Dedicates Boulder Dam, September 30, 1935, Text of Dedicatory Address," *RE* 25 (October, 1935): 193–194, 196.

7. "The Earth Movers I," *Fortune*, p. 214.

8. Kleinsorge, *The Boulder Canyon Project*, pp. 214–19; U.S. Department of the Interior, Bureau of Land Reclamation, *Hoover Dam: 50 Years*, pp. 36–40.

9. See Gerald D. Nash, *The American West in the Twentieth Century*.

10. Lear, "Boulder Dam," pp. 88–92.

11. *Los Angeles Times*, September 22, 1985.

12. Eugene P. Moehring, "Public Works and the New Deal in Las Vegas 1933–1940," *Nevada Historical Society Quarterly* 24 (Summer, 1981): 107–29.

13. Eugene P. Moehring, "Las Vegas and the Second World War," *Nevada Historical Society Quarterly* 29 (Spring, 1986): 1–4.

14. *Hoover Dam: 50 Years*, p. 32.

15. *Hoover Dam: 50 Years*, pp. 36–40; Author interview with Julian Rhinehart, Regional Public Affairs Officer, Bureau of Reclamation Lower Colorado Region, Boulder City, July, 1986.

16. *Hoover Dam: 50 Years*, p. 30.

17. Author interview with Julian Rhinehart, Boulder City, July, 1986.

18. May Sarton, *The Lion and the Rose*, p. 22.

Reno's Big Gamble: Image and Reputation in the Biggest Little City

59. Rowley, *Reno: Hub of the Washoe Country*, 51–52.

60. Ibid.

61. "When Reno Began to Spread," *Reno Evening Gazette*, 30 April 1923, 5.

62. "Stewart in Race for Re-election," *Reno Evening Gazette*, 20 March 1923, 6.

63. "No Monte Carlo yet Awhile," *Nevada State Journal*, 6 May 1923, 4.

64. "Roberts Swamps Opponents in Municipal Contest," *Reno Evening Gazette*, 9 May 1923, 1; "'We Must Pull Together and Make Reno a Bigger City' Is Statement of Newest Mayor," *Nevada State Journal*, 10 May 1923, 8; "Reno Mayor Talks to Sparks' Lions," *Nevada State Journal*, 22 August 1923, 2.

65. Parkhurst, "In Reno," 2.

66. *Nevada State Journal*, 28 November 1923, 7.

67. Eric N. Moody and Guy Louis Rocha, "The Rise and Fall of the Reno Stockade," *Nevada*, April/May/June 1978, 29.

68. Bolin, *Reno, Nevada*, 11–12.

69. Alfred Holman, "Nevada Set Firmly against Prohibition," *New York Times*, 27 June 1926, sec. 2, 3; Alfred Holman, "Nevada Campaign Under Way," *New York Times*, 22 August 1926, sec. 2, 3.

70. Parkhurst, "In Reno," 71.

71. "Bar Association Head Assails Bill," *Reno Evening Gazette*, 18 March 1927, 1, 3; "Reno Divorces, 1927 Model," *Literary Digest*, 9 April 1927, 13.

72. "Trick of Lobby Leads Nevada Legislators to Cut Divorce Residence Time in Half," *New York Times*, 19 March 1927, 1; "Divorce Suit Every Hour," *New York Times*, 24 March 1927, 12; "Cornelius Vanderbilt Jr. on Way to Reno; He is Reported to Be Seeking a Divorce," *New York Times*, 11 July 1927, 1; U.S. Department of Commerce, *Statistical Abstract of the United States, 1929* (Washington, D.C.: U.S. Government Printing Office, 1929), 92; U.S. Department of Commerce, *Statistical Abstract of the United States, 1931* (Washington, D.C.: U.S. Government Printing Office, 1931), 93.

73. Swift Paine, "As We See It in Reno," *North American Review*, June 1930, 726.

74. See Thorstein Veblen, *The Theory of the Leisure Class: An Economic Study of Institutions* (New York: Macmillan, 1905).

75. Stephen L. Hardesty, *The Site of Reno's Beginning: The Historical Mitigation of the Riverside Hotel/Casino* (Reno: City of Reno Redevelopment Agency, August 1997), 13–15; "Trick of Lobby," 1.

76. Winn, *Macadam Trail*, 74; Pringle, "Reno the Wicked," 395.

78. R. L. Polk & Co., *Polk's Reno City, Washoe County and Carson City Directory, 1925–26* (Oakland, Calif.: R. L. Polk & Co., 1925), 63, 64.

79. *R. L. Polk & Co.'s Reno City Directory, 1927–1928* (San Francisco: R. L. Polk & Co., 1927), 5.

80. W. M. David, "Ramblings through the Pines and Sage: A Series of One Day Tours out of Reno" (n.p.: Nevada State Automobile Association, ca. 1928), Autry Library, Autry National Center, Los Angeles.

82. Mary B. Mullett, "Mary B. Mullett Tells the Truth about Reno," *American Magazine*, October 1930, 26, 152.

83. "Slump Knocks Cupid Dizzy," *Los Angeles Times*, 27 June 1931, 3.

85. "Speakers Rap Proposed Law at Gathering," *Nevada State Journal*, 5 February 1931, 1.

86. Findlay, *People of Chance*, 119.

87. "Not So Very Different from the Old 'Wild West' Days," *San Antonio Light*, April 1931, 9.

88. Carol W. Cross, "Divorce Called 'Social Necessity,'" *Simpson's Daily Le Times* (Kittaning, Pa.), 11 May 1931, 5.

89. "'Old West' Returns in Nevada Gambling," *New York Times*, 21 March 1931

90. Ibid.

91. Daniel J. Boorstin, *The Americans: The Democratic Experience* (New York: tage Books, 1974), 64–77.

92. Schwartz, *Roll the Bones*, 355.

93. Kling, *Rise of the Biggest Little City*, 4, 123, 139.

94. "Streets Given Carnival Air; Rooms Needed," *Nevada State Journal*, 31 1931, 1.

98. "Nevada's New Scheme," *Portsmouth* (Ohio) *Times*, 23 March 1931, 6.

99. Pringle, "Reno the Wicked," 403.

100. Paul Hutchinson, "Reno—A Wide Open Town," *Christian Century*, 2 December 1931, 1519–1520.

104. "Reno Is Denounced to Endeavorers," *New York Times*, 14 July 1931, 2; Its Gambling Legalized, Reno Becomes Even More Like 'Sodom, Gomorrah and H *Kansas City Star*, 26 April 1931, 1C.

105. "Roberts Given Invitation as Defense Made," *Nevada State Journal*, 27 M 1931, 1–2.

106. "Reno Mayor Draws Throng to Church," *Nevada State Journal*, 30 March 1 1–2; "Reno Defender Goes It Alone," *Los Angeles Times*, 31 March 1931, 3.

107. "With Its Gambling Legalized," 2C.

108. "Why Laugh at Nevada?" *Helena* (Mont.) *Independent*, 29 March 1931, 14.

from *"Yes I Can"* and *"Fighting Back"*

1. On February 1, 1960, four African-American students from the North Carolina Agricultural and Technical College in Greensboro, N.C., protested segregation at the downtown Woolworth department store by taking seats at the lunch counter and refusing to move. This protest touched off similar demonstrations in nearly two hundred cities. On March 19 San Antonio, Texas, became the first major Southern city to desegregate its lunch counters.

"States' Rights Enterprise," from
Nevada: The Great Rotten Borough

1. *The Federalist*, #46.

2. Paul Dolan: *The Government and Administration of Delaware* (1956), p. 300.

3. P.B. Ellis: *Ms.*, The Bancroft Library. Lewis T. Coleman, Indianapolis, to J.D. Torreyson, Carson City, Nov. 28, 1903.

4. Ibid., Ellis to L.J. Clarke, Feb. 3, 1919.

5. Ibid., Ellis to W.B. Ames, May 31, 1917.

6. Ibid., Oscar Sutro, of Pillsbury, Madison & Sutro, to State Agent and Transfer Syndicate, Inc., Aug. 5, 1922.

7. Ibid., State Agent and Transfer Syndicate, Inc. to Pillsbury, Madison and Sutro, Aug. 8, 1922.

8. Ibid., from Automatic Electric Faucet Company, April 24, 1917.

9. Nevada Tax Commission *Report* (1955), p. 7.

10. Mack, et al.: *Nevada Government*, p. 218.

11. Lillard: *Desert Challenge*, p. 87.

12. Mack, et al.: *Nevada Government*, p. 122.

13. Lillard: *Desert Challenge*, p. 82.

14. Ibid., pp. 82, 86.

15. Moore: *Nevadans*, p. 98.

16. LIllard: *Desert Challenge*, p. 93.

17. Ibid., p. 86.

18. Ibid., pp. 327–9.

19. *Nevada Compiled Laws*, Section 10193.

20. The following discussion of Nevada divorce and marriage law is based on Lillard: *Desert Challenge* pp. 335–68.

21. Except where otherwise indicated, the discussion of Nevada gambling is based on Oscar Lewis: *Sagebrush Casinos* (1953).

22. Lillard: *Desert Challenge*, p. 320.

23. See Harold Smith: *I Want to Quit Winners* (1961).

24. R.A. Zubrov, R.L. Decker, E.H. Plank: *Financing State and Local Government in Nevada* (1960), p. 5.

25. Paul Ralli: *Viva Vegas* (1953), pp. 53–4.

26. Katharine Best and Katharine Hillyer: *Las Vegas* (1955), p. 65.

27. Ibid., p. 18.

28. Ibid., p. 98.

29. Alfred M. Smith: "A Study of the Natural and Industrial Resources of Clark County, Nevada," (mimeographed report, 1956), p. 17.

30. Zubrov, Decker, Plank: *Financing in Nevada*, p. 7.

31. Lewis: *Sagebrush Casinos*, p. 132.

32. Best and Hillyer, *Las Vegas*, p. 63.

33. U.S. Senate: *Hearings Before the Special Committee to Investigate Organized Crime in Interstate Commerce* (Kefauver Committee), (1951), Part 10, p. 24.

34. Best and Hillyer, *Las Vegas*, p. 79.

35. See Ralli: *Viva Vegas*, p. 2.

36. Kefauver Committee *Hearings*, Part 10, p. 91.

37. Ibid., Part 10, p. 92.

38. Ibid.

39. Ibid., Part 10, p. 93.

40. Ibid.

41. Best and Hillyer, *Las Vegas*, p. 83.

42. Ibid., p. 82.

43. S.F. *Chronicle*, Oct. 23, 1963.

44. *The Mountains of California* (1894), pp. 98, 100.

45. *Roughing It*, Ch. 23.

46. Darling (ed.): *Newlands Papers* I, 81–2.

47. Smith, *I Want to Quit Winners*, pp. 104, 18.

48. Keith Monroe, "The New Gambling King and the Social Sciences," *Harpers*, January 1962, is the source for this account of Harrah's Lake Tahoe enterprise.

49. S.F. *Chronicle*, Sept. 28, 1963.

50. Ibid.

51. Ibid., Oct. 4, 1963.

52. Ibid., Oct. 9, 1963.

53. Ibid.

54. Ibid., Nov. 16, 1963.

55. Quoted in Albert K. Weinberg: *Manifest Destiny* (1935), p. 106.

56. J.E.E. Dalbert, Lord Acton: *Lectures on Modern History* (1906), p. 314.

"Musings of a Native Son"

1. All the population figures cited in this essay were adapted by rounding off the statistics provided in *Population Abstract of the United States, Volume One, Tables*, ed. John L. Androit (McLean, Virginia: Androit Associates, 1983), 502–505.

2. Cf. John M. Findlay, *People of Chance: Gambling in American Society from Jamestown to Las Vegas* (New York: Oxford University Press, 1986) and Robert Venturi, Denise Scott Brown, and Steven Izenour, *Learning From Las Vegas* (Cambridge: The MIT Press, 1972).

"A-Bombs in the Backyard: Southern Nevada Adapts to the Nuclear Age, 1951–1963"

1. Edgerton, Germeshausen and Green, Inc., "The Nevada Test Site and Southern Nevada," Report No. L-512 (March 15, 1961) p. 12, Special Collections, University of Nevada, Las Vegas, Library.

2. For detailed accounts of the development of the atomic bomb, see: Barton Bernstein. *The Atomic Bomb: The Critical Issues* (Boston: Little, Brown and Company, 1976); Anthony C. Brown and Charles B. MacDonald, editors, *The Secret History of the Atomic Bomb* (New York: Dial Press, 1979); Arthur H. Compton, *Atomic Quest* (New York: Oxford University Press, 1956); Leslie R. Groves, *Now It Can Be Told* (New York: Harper and Row, 1962); Lansing Lamont, *Day of Trinity* (New York: Atheneum, 1965); and Henry D. Smyth, *Atomic Energy for Military Purposes* (Princeton: Princeton University Press, 1945).

3. Lamont, p. 255.

4. Jonathon M. Weisgall, "The Nuclear Nomads of Bikini," *Foreign Policy* 39 (Summer 1980) p. 76.

5. Ibid.

6. The Marshall Islands were seized from Japan during World War II by the

United States. They were placed under military control until July 1947, when the area became a U.N. strategic trust territory administered by the United States. See Robert C. Kiste, *The Bikinians* (Menlo Park, California: Cummings Publishers, 1974).

7. Ibid., pp. 86–90.

8. A 1967 AEC study found the area once again safe for human habitation and the Bikinians were returned to their homeland. It was a temporary arrangement, however. When subsequent radiological surveys indicated that Bikini was not safe, Secretary of Interior Rogers Morton interrupted the reconstruction and relocation process. He wrote to Secretary of Defense James Schlesinger in March 1975 requesting that a thorough survey of the area be undertaken. The Defense Department declined to take action because of the high costs of the proposed study. The Bikinians, frustrated and confused by the contradictory information they were receiving, filed suit in federal court in October 1975 to force the government to stop the resettlement program until such a survey was taken. The U.S. readily agreed to do so; but it was not until early 1978, after much internal bureaucratic squabbling, that the study was conducted. By March of that year, the atoll had been declared off limits and the inhabitants once again moved to nearby islands. The most recent reports indicate that the atoll may remain uninhabitable for at least another hundred years.

9. David Bradley, *No Place to Hide* (Boston: Little, Brown and Company, 1948); Stephen Hilgartner, Richard C. Bell, and Rory O'Connor, *Nukespeak* (New York: Penguin Books, 1983) pp. 72–74; William A. Shurcliff, *Bombs at Bikini: The Official Report of Operation Crossroads* (New York: William G. Wise, 1947) and Michael Uhl and Tod Ensign, *G.I. Guinea Pigs* (New York: Wideview Books 1980) pp. 30–43.

10. Howard L. Rosenberg, *Atomic Soldiers* (Boston: Beacon Press, 1980) p. 131.

11. Ibid.

12. Atomic Energy Commission, press release, December 1, 1947; National Association of Atomic Veterans, "Story of the Eniwetok Cleanup," *NAAV Newsletter* (November/December 1979) p. 14; Giff Johnson, "Paradise Lost," *Bulletin of the Atomic Scientists* 34 (December 1980) pp. 24–29; Uhl and Ensign, pp. 46–53.

13. The Soviets actually exploded their first atomic bomb on August 29, 1949, in Siberia. Although U.S. planes detected the fallout almost immediately, President Truman did not publicly announce the detonation until September 23, 1949. See: Herbert York, *The Advisors: Oppenheimer, Teller, and the Superbomb* (San Francisco: W. N. Freeman, 1976) pp. 33–35.

14. The Atomic Energy Commission was created by Congress with the passage of the Atomic Energy Act of 1946 (P.L. 585, 79th Congress, 60 stat 755). This act created a five member civilian commission, appointed by the President with the Senate's approval, which held a monopoly over

nuclear technology at all levels. The Atomic Energy Commission was charged with certain objectives in the original legislation: . . . "subject at all times to the paramount objective of assuring the common defense and security, the development and utilization of atomic energy shall, so far as practical, be directed toward improving the public welfare, increasing the standard of living, strengthening free competition in private enterprise, and promoting world peace." See: Richard G. Hewlett and Oscar E. Anderson, *The New World, 1939–46: A History of the United States Atomic Energy Commission* (University Park, Pennsylvania: Penn State University Press, 1962.)

15. Aaron Smith, "Nuclear Weapons Testing in Nevada: History and Possible Health Effects," *Nevada Public Affairs Review* 1 (1982) pp. 5–11.

16. Rosenberg, pp. 25–31.

17. Los Alamos Scientific Laboratory, University of California, "Operation Ranger: Operational Program Reports," Vol. V (January–February, 1951).

18. Rosenberg, pp. 32–35.

19. Ibid., p. 37.

20. See: Ibid.; Uhl and Ensign, pp. 58–108; Thomas H. Saffer and Orville E. Kelly, *Countdown Zero* (New York: G. P. Putnam's Sons, 1982); George Washington University, Human Resources Research Office (HumRRO), "Desert Rock I, A Psychological Study of Troop Reaction to an Atomic Explosion," Technical Report No. 1 (February 1951); HumRRO, "Desert Rock IV: Reactions of an Armored Infantry Battalion to an Atomic Bomb Maneuver," Technical Report No. 2 (August 1953); HumRRO, "Desert Rock V: Reactions of Troop Participants and Forward Volunteer Officer Groups to Atomic Exercises," Information Report (August 1953); Johns Hopkins University Operations Research Office, "Troop Performance on a Training Maneuver Involving the Use of Atomic Weapons," (March 15 1952); and United States Army, *Exercise Desert Rock Information and Guide* (1951), available from the Fallout Records Centralization Project, Las Vegas, Nevada.

21. United States Department of Energy, "DOE's Nevada Operations Office: What It Does and Why" (July 1983) p. 1, United States Department of Energy, Las Vegas.

22. Ibid.; and United States Atomic Energy Commission, "Nevada Test Site" in *Nevada, The Silver State* (Carson City: Western States Historical Publishers, 1970) pp. 719–722, and United States Department of Energy, "Announced United States Nuclear Tests, July 1945–December 1982" (January 1983).

23. James H. McBride, *The Test Ban Treaty: Military, Technological and Political Implications* (Chicago: Henry Regnery Company, 1967).

24. Harry S. Truman, *Years of Trial and Hope* (Garden City: Doubleday and Company, 1955) Volume II of *Memoirs*, pp. 312–315.

25. In 1948 communists staged a coup in Czechoslovakia which replaced the existing government with one subservient to Moscow; that same year the Russians attempted to force Western Allies out of Berlin by blockading all land transportation routes into the city. In early 1949 forces led by Mao Tse-tung captured Peking and soon after established the People's Republic of China. And in June 1950 armed conflict broke out between North and South Korea which involved American participation against communist forces.

26. President Truman initiated an employee loyalty program in 1947; the practice was later intensified when President Eisenhower signed an executive order in April 1953 launching an unprecedented, far-reaching investigation into the loyalty of federal employees.

27. William F. Buckley, *The Committee and its Critics* (New York: Putnam, 1962); Robert K. Carr, *The House Committee on Un-American Activities, 1945–1950* (Ithaca: Cornell University Press, 1952); Athan G. Theokaris, *Seeds of Repression: Harry S. Truman and the Origins of McCarthyism* (Chicago: Quadrangle Books, 1971); Dalton Trumbo, *The Time of the Toad: A Study of Inquisition in America* (New York: Harper and Row, 1972).

28. Solomon A. Fineberg, *The Rosenberg Case* (New York: Oceana Publications, 1953); Louis Nizer, *The Implosion Conspiracy* (Garden City: Doubleday, 1973); and Jonathon Root, *The Betrayers; the Rosenberg Case—a Reappraisal of an American Crisis* (New York: Coward-McCann, 1963).

29. Regularly-scheduled air raid drills were held and public meetings were called to teach self-defense against nuclear attack through such measures as assuming correct physical positions during impact and washing off the radioactive fallout afterward. Dozens of how-to films were distributed; their names alone tell the story: "Pattern for Survival" (1950), "You Can Beat the A-Bomb" (1950), "Duck and Cover" (1951), and "Survival Under Atomic Attack " (1951).

30. Rosenberg; Uhl and Ensign; and Saffer and Kelly.

31. Typical of these was a widely-distributed, January 1951 Atomic Energy Commission statement which claimed that "Health and safety authorities have determined that no danger from or as a result of AEC activities may be expected. . . . All necessary precautions will be undertaken to insure that safety conditions are maintained." Similarly, in testimony before Congress in the spring of 1953, an AEC official reported that fallout from atmospheric testing was no more dangerous than medical x-rays. In a *U.S. News and World Report* article (March 25, 1955, pp. 21–26) AEC Commissioner Willard Libby cited evidence from AEC research which indicated that bomb fallout "would not likely be at all dangerous." And Edward Teller, arguing for continued testing in *Life Magazine* (February 10, 1958, pp. 64–66) claimed that radiation from fallout "might be slightly beneficial or have no effect at all."

32. United States Atomic Energy Commission, "Atomic Test Effects in the Nevada Test Site Region" (January 1955), Nevada Historical Society, Las Vegas.

33. Ibid., p. 23.

34. The Iron County sheepherders carried their case to the Supreme Court in 1955 (*Bullock v. U.S.* 145 F. Supp. 827) but their claims were denied based on expert testimony presented by the government which "proved" that radiation had not caused the animal deaths and deformities. The case was recently ordered reopened on August 4, 1982, however, by Judge Sherman Christenson on grounds that the government had been "intentionally false and deceptive. "

35. Nineteen of the twenty-one children of the island of Rongelap who were under twelve at the time of exposure subsequently developed thyroid tumors, forcing the government to pass the Bikini Compensation Act of 1964, which appropriated $950,000 to be distributed among the victims. This act was amended on October 15, 1977, when Congress passed P.L. 95–134 to include the inhabitants of nearby Uterik, who were also exposed to the "Bravo" cloud and suffered radiation-related illnesses.

36. Ralph E. Lapp, *The Voyage of the Lucky Dragon* (New York: Harper and Brothers Publishers, 1957); and Stephen Salaff, "The Lucky Dragon," *Bulletin of the Atomic Scientists* 34 (May 1978) pp. 21–23.

37. *New York Times* (April 1, 1954) p. 20.

38. Only two months after dropping the bombs on Japan, President Truman told a joint session of Congress that "the hope of civilization lies in . . . renunciation of the use and development of the atomic bomb." He urged all nations to join the United States in developing atomic energy solely for peaceful purposes. Uhl and Ensign, p. 32.

39. Atomic Energy Commission press release, December 22, 1947, National Archives, Washington, D.C.

40. Edwin B. Eckel, *Nevada Test Site*, Geological Society of America, Inc., Memoir 110 (1968) p. 2.

41. Albin J. Dahl, *Nevada's Southern Economy*, Research Report No. 8 (Carson City: University of Nevada, College of Business Administration. March 1969), pp. 23–30.

42. A. Costandina Titus, "Back to Ground Zero: Old Footage Through New Lenses," *Journal of Popular Film and Television* 11 (Spring 1983) pp. 2–11.

43. By 1970 about 15,000 scouts had qualified for this merit badge, according to the *Annual Report of Congress of the Atomic Energy Commission for 1969* (January 1970) p. 211.

44. Hilgartner, Bell, and O'Connor, pp. 74–78.

45. For example, in 1953 when Robert Oppenheimer, former director of the Manhattan Project, publicly opposed the development of the H-bomb, he was charged with maintaining communist associations and acting in a way designed to promote the best interests of the Russians, his security clearance was cancelled and his long-term government service was ended. See: Phillip M. Stern, *The Oppenheimer Case: Security on Trial* (New York: Harper and Row, 1969); and York. And in 1957 when Linus Pauling, Nobel prizewinner in chemistry, led a petition drive by scientists in opposition to atmospheric testing, President Eisenhower, in a press conference, implied that the petition was the work of an "organization" which did not have the best interests of the nation in mind. Pauling was also called before the House Un-American Activities Committee which further investigated his anti-nuclear connections. See: Linus Pauling, *No More War* (New York: Dodd, Mead, 1958) pp. 160–172.

46. Harvey Wasserman and Norman Solomon, *Killing Our Own* (New York: Dell Publishing Company, 1982) pp. 92–101.

47. The final vote was 56,049 for Eisenhower and 40,640 for Stevenson. *Political History of Nevada, 1979* (Carson City: State Printing Office), p. 226.

48. Douglas T. Miller and Marion Nowak, *The Fifties: The Way We Really Were* (New York: Doubleday, 1977) p. 413.

49. Ibid., p. 63.

50. Ibid., p. 80. In 1958 four pacifists in a thirty-foot ketch, the *Golden Rule*, tried to sail from Hawaii to Eniwetok; they were detained and arrested by the United States Coast Guard.

51. There were a few instances during the early days of atmospheric testing in which certain individuals expressed opposition to the program. Windows were shattered and some horses were burned by radioactive fallout. However, the Atomic Energy Commission was quick to reimburse local citizens for these property losses, and thus keep complaints to a minimum. One especially dissatisfied resident was Dan Sheahan, owner of the Groom Mine located some thirty-eight miles north of the Nevada Test Site; Sheahan complained that he had to shut down operations during test blasts and this was a great inconvenience and expense for his business. Such protests were the exception, however, not the rule.

52. In response to the needs of the new NTS, some 3000 jobs were created between 1951 and 1958, when the voluntary moratorium went into effect; by 1968, this labor force had increased to 10,187, representing a gross annual payroll of $122.2 million. During the same decade and a half, government investments in the program totaled over $178.8 million. In 1980 the physical plant was valued in excess of $300 million and the operating budget for that year alone was $345 million. See: Dahl, pp. 36–38; Russell R. Elliott, *History of Nevada* (Lincoln, University of Nebraska Press, 1973) pp. 339–341; Joseph A. Fry, "The History of Defense Spending in Nevada:

Preview of the MX," in Francis X. Hartigan, editor, *MX in Nevada: A Humanistic Perspective* (Reno: Nevada Humanities Committee, 1980) pp. 37–43; and Mary Ellen Glass, *Nevada's Turbulent Fifties* (Reno: University of Nevada Press, 1981) pp. 43–46

53. Jerome E. Edwards, *Pat McCarran: Political Boss of Nevada* (Reno: University of Nevada Press, 1982).

54. Rosenberg, p. 32.

55. Sister Margaret P. McCarran, "Patrick Anthony McCarran: 1876–1954," Part II, *Nevada Historical Society Quarterly* 12 (Spring 1969) p. 50; *Las Vegas Review Journal* (May 26, 1953) p. 1.

56. Danial Lang, "Our Far Flung Correspondents: Blackjack and Flashes," *New Yorker* 8 (September 20, 1952) p. 97.

63. *Las Vegas Sun* (March 13, 1955) p. 1.

64. *Las Vegas Review-Journal* (March 11, 1955) p.1.

65. Ibid. (March 22, 1955) p. 1.

66. Ibid. (January 15, 1951) p. 1.

67. *Las Vegas Sun* (January 30, 1951) p. 1.

68. *Las Vegas Review-Journal* (May 24, 1953) p. 4.

69. Uhl and Ensign pp. 76–77, 82–83.

70. "Operation 'Doom Town'," *Nevada Highways and Parks* 13 (June–December 1952) pp. 1–17.

71. *Las Vegas Review-Journal* (May 6, 1955) p. 1.

72. Ibid. (October 18, 1955) p. 4.

73. Lang, p. 91.

74. Georgia Lewis, "'Atomized' Las Vegas Danced 'Atomic Boogie'," *Las Vegas Review-Journal*, "The Nevadan" (January 23, 1983) pp. 6L–7L, 13L.

75. Uhl and Ensign, p. 77.

76. Lang, pp. 95–96.

77. "Operation 'Doom Town'," p. 1.

78. Rosenberg, p. 82.

79. Lang, p. 90.

80. While the problem of radioactivity seemed to be solved, some feared that underground testing could cause earthquakes. Dr. Alan Ryall, a University of Nevada geologist, stated that "effects due to the continued firing of large underground tests would be cumulative, possibly eventually resulting in a sizable earthquake." See Elliott, p. 339.

81. Donald L. Barlett and James B. Steele, *Empire: The Life, Legend, and Madness of Howard Hughes* (New York: W. W. Norton and Company, 1979) pp. 340–347.

82. Ibid., p. 341.

83. Paul Duckworth, *Baneberry: A Nuclear Disaster* (Las Vegas: Harris Printers, Inc., 1976).

86. Ibid.; *Las Vegas Review-Journal* (December 19–21, 1970) p. 1; and *Las Vegas Sun* (December 19–21, 1970) p. 1.

85. *Las Vegas Review-Journal* (December 20, 1970) p. 1.

86. "Smoky and Leukemia: High Rate Confirmed," *Science News* (October 3, 1980) p. 118; Glyn G. Caldwell, et al., "Leukemia Among Participants in Military Maneuvers at a Nuclear Bomb Test," *Journal of American Medical Association* 244 (October 1980) pp. 1575–1578; Joseph L. Lyon, et al., "Childhood Leukemias Associated With Fallout from Nuclear Testing," *New England Journal of Medicine* 300 (February 1979) pp. 39–402; and Edward S. Weiss, et al., "Thyroid Modularity in Southwestern Utah School Children Exposed to Fallout Radiation," *American Journal of Public Health* 61 (1971).

87. U.S. Congress, House Committee on Health and the Environment, Hearings, 95th Congress, 2nd Session (January 1978); U.S. Congress, Senate Committee on Veterans' Affairs, Hearings, 96th Congress, 1st Session (June 1979); U.S. Congress, House Committee on Interstate and Foreign Commerce, Subcommittee on Oversight and Investigations, Hearings, 96th Congress, 2nd Session (August 1980).

88. The Interagency Task Force on the Health Effects of Ionizing Radiation was headed by Peter Libassi; its report, issued to the public in July 1979, concluded that radiation may cause irreparable change in cells, resulting in cancer, developmental abnormalities, and genetic damage.

89. Efforts were made to identify all the soldiers who had participated in atomic test maneuvers, and toll free telephone lines were installed so that "atomic veterans" could check in from anywhere in the country to get information on their dosage levels, etc. See: Saffer and Kelly, pp. 177–179; and Uhl and Ensign, p. 91.

90. A class action suit was filed in Salt Lake City on August 30, 1979, by 1200 "downwind residents" charging the government with negligence: *Allen v. U.S.* (CA No. C-79–515). The widows of two test site workers filed suit following the Baneberry incident: *Dorothy Roberts v. U.S.* (Civil LV. 1766 RDF) and *Louise Nunamaker v. U.S.* (Civil LV. 76–259 RDF). Several cases have also been filed by "atomic veterans": *Jaffee v. U.S.* (79–1543, February 20, 1980) and *Broudy v. U.S.* (79–3829, June 18, 180). To date, not one of these cases has been decided in favor of the plaintiff.

91. Recent radiation compensation bills include H.R. 4766 introduced by Representative Gunn McKay on July 12, 1979; S. 1865 by Senator Edward Kennedy on October 4, 1979; H.R. 872 by Representative Henry Gonzales on January 16, 1981; H.R. 1564 by Representative Norman Mineta on Feb-

ruary 5, 1981; H.R. 2229 by Representative Tony Coelho on March 2, 1981; H.R. 4012 by Representative Robert Davis on June 25, 1981; S. 1483 by Senator Orrin Hatch on July 14, 1981; and H.R. 6052 by Representative Dan Marriott on April 1, 1982. These bills all died in committee. Currently pending in the Senate is S. 921 introduced on March 21, 1983, by Senator Hatch (R) of Utah this bill calls for pro-rated payments of awards up to $500,000 to people who suffer from radiation-related illness as a result of exposure to fallout from atmospheric testing. See A. Costandina Titus, "Governmental Responsibility for Victims of Atomic Testing: A Chronicle of the Politics of Compensation," *Journal of Health Politics, Policy and Law* 8 (Summer 1983) pp. 277–292.

92. The Clark County Commissioners kept the question off the ballot with a vote of 4 against, 1 in favor.

93. *Las Vegas Review Journal* (January 28, 1983) p. 1B.

94. The author wishes to thank Ms. Vera Thompson, Mr. David Millman, and the class of POS 408b (Summer Session II, 1983) for their research assistance.

Will History Repeat Itself? Nevada's Economy After the Crash

1. Nevada History, http://nevada-history.org/charts.html.

2. E. M. Mack, *Nevada: A History of the State from the Earliest Times Through the Civil War* (Glendale, CA: The Arthur H. Clark Company, 1936).

3. R. DePolo and M. Pingle, "Nevada Gaming: Revenues and Taxes (1945–95)," *Journal of Gambling Studies* 13:1 (1997): 49–67.

4. Bureau of Labor Statistics, U.S. Department of Labor, http://www.bls.gov/lau/.

5. The literature on this is large, but for a start consider M. Fleming, "External Economies and the Doctrine of Balanced Growth," *The Economic Journal*: 65:258 (1955): 241–56, and P. Krugman, "Increasing Returns and Economic Geography," "Increasing Returns and Economic Geography," *The Journal of Political Economy* 99:3 (1991): 483–99.

6. D. Bartholet, "Historical Overview of Nevada's Economy and Fiscal Policy: Statehood to 2010," http://unrbusinessresearch.org/wp-content/uploads/2009/06/Historical-Overview-of-Nevadas-Economy-and-Fiscal-Policy.pdf.

7. G. Rocha, "Myth 144: One Unsound State," Nevada State Library and Archives: http://nsla.nevadaculture.org.

8. J. Poot, "A synthesis of empirical research on the impact of government on long-run growth," *Growth and Change* 2000 31:4 (2000): 516–46.

9. R. J. Barro, "Government spending in a simple model of endogenous growth," *Journal of Political Economy* 98:5 (1990): S103–25.

10. P. Krugman, "Fifty Herbert Hoovers," *New York Times*, Dec. 28, 2008.

11. Census Bureau, U.S. Department of Commerce, *Statistical Abstract of the United States*, http://www.census.gov/compendia/statab/.